KEEPERS OF THE COVENANT

RELIGION IN AMERICA SERIES

Harry S. Stout, General Editor

A PERFECT BABEL OF CONFUSION
*Dutch Religion and English Culture in
the Middle Colonies*
Randall Balmer

THE PRESBYTERIAN CONTROVERSY
*Fundamentalists, Modernists, and
Moderates*
Bradley J. Longfield

MORMONS AND THE BIBLE
*The Place of the Latter-day Saints in
American Religion*
Philip L. Barlow

THE RUDE HAND OF INNOVATION
*Religion and Social Order in Albany,
New York 1652–1836*
David G. Hackett

SEASONS OF GRACE
*Colonial New England's Revival
Tradition in Its British Context*
Michael J. Crawford

THE MUSLIMS OF AMERICA
Edited by Yvonne Yazbeck Haddad

THE PRISM OF PIETY
*Catholick Congregational Clergy at
the Beginning of the Enlightenment*
John Corrigan

FEMALE PIETY IN PURITAN NEW
ENGLAND
The Emergence of Religious Humanism
Amanda Porterfield

THE SECULARIZATION OF
THE ACADEMY
Edited by George M. Marsden and Bradley
J. Longfield

EPISCOPAL WOMEN
*Gender, Spirituality, and Commitment in
an American Mainline Denomination*
Edited by Catherine Prelinger

SUBMITTING TO FREEDOM
The Religious Vision of William James
Bennett Ramsey

OLD SHIP OF ZION
*The Afro-Baptist Ritual in
the African Diaspora*
Walter F. Pitts

AMERICAN
TRANSCENDENTALISM
AND ASIAN RELIGIONS
Arthur Versluis

CHURCH PEOPLE IN
THE STRUGGLE
*The National Council of Churches
and the Black Freedom Movement,
1950–1970*
James F. Findlay, Jr.

EVANGELICALISM
*Comparative Studies of Popular
Protestantism in North America, the
British Isles, and Beyond 1700–1990*
Edited by Mark A. Noll,
David W. Bebbington
and George A. Rawlyk

FORSAKEN BY GOD
*Religious Melancholy and Protestant
Experience in America*
Julius H. Rubin

CONJURING CULTURE
Biblical Formations in Black America
Theophus Smith

REIMAGINING
DENOMINATIONALISM
Interpretive Essays
Edited by Robert Bruce Mullin
and Russell E. Richey

STANDING AGAINST
THE WHIRLWIND
*Evangelical Episcopalians in
Nineteenth-Century America*
Diana Hochstedt Butler

KEEPERS OF THE COVENANT
*Frontier Missions and the Decline
of Congregationalism, 1774–1818*
James R. Rohrer

KEEPERS OF
THE COVENANT

*Frontier Missions and
the Decline of Congregationalism
1774–1818*

JAMES R. ROHRER

New York   Oxford
OXFORD UNIVERSITY PRESS
1995

Oxford University Press

Oxford   New York
Athens   Auckland   Bangkok   Bombay
Calcutta   Cape Town   Dar es Salaam   Delhi
Florence   Hong Kong   Istanbul   Karachi
Kuala Lampur   Madras   Madrid   Melbourne
Mexico City   Nairobi   Paris   Singapore
Taipei   Tokyo   Toronto

and associated companies in
Berlin   Ibadan

Copyright © 1995 by James R. Rohrer

Published by Oxford University Press, Inc.,
200 Madison Avenue, New York, New York 10016

Oxford is a registered trademark of Oxford University Press, Inc.

Library of Congress Cataloging-in-Publication Data
Rohrer, James R. (James Russell), 1960–
Keepers of the covenant : frontier missions and the decline
of Congregationalism, 1774–1818 / James R. Rohrer.
p.   cm.—(Religion in America series)
Includes bibliographical references and index.
ISBN 0–19–509166–3
1. Missions—Northeastern States.
2. Congregational churches—Northeastern States—History—18th century.
3. Congregational churches—Northeastern States—History—19th century.
4. Missionary Society of Connecticut—History.
5. Northeastern States—Church history—18th century.
6. Northeastern States—Church history—19th century.
I. Title.
II. Series: Religion in America series
(Oxford University Press)
BV2791.R64   1995   285.8′73′09033—dc20
94–22305

2 4 6 8 9 7 5 3 1

Printed in the United States of America
on acid-free paper

To my parents,

William and Doris Rohrer

Preface

This book began ten years ago while I was writing a master's thesis on revivalism and temperance in nineteenth century America. One day my adviser, Merton Dillon, suggested that there might be information about temperance activity in the microfilm missionary records which the university library had recently acquired. I spent the rest of the day straining my eyes, intently examining seemingly endless journals and letters penned by Congregationalist missionaries in the early republic. I found disappointingly little about temperance, but discovered a cornucopia of information about revivals, evangelism, and religious competition in the northern frontier. From that day I was "hooked" by the Connecticut Missionary Society (CMS).

I soon realized that the evangelists laboring in the new settlements under CMS commissions did not fit the image of the New England clergy which I had formed from reading secondary literature on American religion. It was also apparent that the standard portrait of post-revolutionary Congregationalism was based primarily upon a relatively small number of pastor/theologians in Massachusetts and Connecticut, men like Timothy Dwight, Jedediah Morse, and Lyman Beecher. The hundreds of Congregational ministers who joined the New England exodus to the frontier, the individuals most responsible for the fate of New England orthodoxy, had been all but forgotten by history.

I have written this book in an effort to fill this large hole in our historical consciousness. It is the first published monograph devoted exclusively to the home missionary efforts of the post-revolutionary Congregational clergy. During the past decade I have read all of the early publications of the CMS, as well as the thousands of letters and journals written by the 148 men who received CMS commissions between 1798 and 1818. Wherever possible I have augmented this material with letters, diaries, sermons, and church records in other collections. My account of early republican Congregationalism is based primarily upon these manuscript sources, many of them previously unused.

This study challenges the standard thesis that Congregationalist leaders failed to adapt to the democratic impulses unleashed by the American Revolution. Instead, I argue that New England missionaries clearly recognized the need for change, and that they successfully adjusted themselves to the demands of frontier ministry. Far from being a marginal group of genteel theologians, this book presents them as aggressive evangelists who were fully capable of competing successfully with the Methodists, Baptists, and other emergent evangelical groups spawned during the early republic.

These findings necessarily raise the thorny problem of Congregationalist declension. If the Congregational clergy successfully adapted to change, why then did Congregationalism so quickly lose numerical dominance after the Revolution? Why were the champions of New England orthodoxy apparently—and decisively—bested by the Methodist and Baptist preachers?

This question has grown increasingly important during the last several years. Many scholars and church leaders, in an effort to understand the current declension of the Protestant "mainline," have turned to history for clues. Roger Finke and Rodney Stark, for example, in their recent book *The Churching of America*, point to the post-revolutionary Congregational clergy as Exhibit A in defense of their thesis that religious movements decline when they become too secular. In this study, I take sharp issue with the explanation for Congregationalist declension offered by Finke and Stark. In my conclusion, I attempt to offer an alternative way of looking at the problem.

This book is certainly not the final word on Congregationalism in the early republic. There is much more that needs to be done. I hope, however, that it succeeds in making readers more aware of the complexity of post-revolutionary Congregationalism, and of the historical importance of the missionaries who labored in the new settlements. I hope, too, that it contributes to the current, sometimes painful, debate about religious declension in America. Most of all, I hope that it encourages further research into an important and strangely neglected chapter of American history.

Taiwan   J. R. R.
July 1994

Acknowledgments

I would like to thank Merton Dillon, Richard Shiels, and Paul Bowers, of The Ohio State University, who read and challenged the original draft of this manuscript when it was a Ph.D. dissertation. I owe a special debt of gratitude to Dick, who has nurtured my interest in the history of American evangelicalism, and who has assisted me in more ways than I can count as an adviser, a colleague, and a friend. I also wish to thank Curtis D. Johnson, Bradley Longfield, and E. Brooks Holifield, who read the entire manuscript and gave me encouragement as well as many suggestions for revision.

I am grateful to the Department of History and to the Graduate School at The Ohio State University for travel grants. Ken and Lori Minkema graciously opened their home to me during my trips to Hartford; their marvelous generosity made work a pleasure. I am also indebted to the many competent librarians and archivists at the following institutions, who assisted me during my research trips and who responded promptly to my countless interlibrary loan requests: the American History Research Center, Kent State University; Beinecke Library, Yale University; the Connecticut Historical Society; the Connecticut State Library; Congregational House in Hartford, Connecticut; the Hartford Seminary Library; the Ohio Historical Society; and the Western Reserve Historical Society.

Several individuals rendered especially vital support and encouragement to me during the long process of researching, writing, and revising this book. Without them, it would still be unfinished: Lawrence Greenfield, Russ Crabtree, Gene and Kay Cahall, Mike and Bobbi Jo Rayo, and Carol Ann Park. I thank them for everything. I also wish to thank the many brothers and sisters in Christ at Boulevard Presbyterian Church to whom I dedicated my dissertation. I cannot name you all, but I thank God for your love, prayers, and wisdom.

My colleagues at the Presbyterian Bible College in Hsinchu, Taiwan, have provided me with office space as well as a most congenial environment in which to revise the final manuscript. I am especially grateful to Lo Ming-Chen, who has been more than a colleague and friend. Her English name, Grace, seems especially appropriate, for she has truly been a vessel of God's grace.

Finally, I must thank my parents, William H. and Doris J. Rohrer, who have always been my biggest supporters. Long ago they instilled in me a love for learning, as well as a commitment to service. With inexpressible appreciation, I dedicate this book to them.

Contents

1. Historians and Congregational Evangelism, 3

2. The Missionary Impulse, 15

3. The Committee on Missions, 1792–1797, 31

4. The Connecticut Missionary Society, 53

5. CMS Missionaries and Revivalism, 71

6. The CMS and the Republican Frontier, 103

7. The CMS and Republican Religion, 115

8. Congregational Declension Reconsidered, 143

Notes, 153

Bibliography, 181

Index, 195

KEEPERS OF THE COVENANT

CHAPTER One

Historians and Congregational Evangelism

The American Revolution initiated a fundamental reorientation of Christianity in the United States. The egalitarian ideals of the revolutionary movement promoted dissatisfaction with traditional clerical authority and prompted Americans to seek greater freedom within their churches. "Let us be republicans indeed," evangelist Elias Smith proclaimed to his followers in the early nineteenth century. "Venture to be as independent in things of religion," Smith urged, "as those which respect the government in which you live."[1] The separation of church and state and the triumph of religious voluntarism was perhaps the clearest manifestation of this independent spirit. Republican citizens bristled at coercion of any kind—spiritual as well as political—and were quick to assert their "rights of conscience" against anyone who would restrict them. In such an environment heterodox beliefs and movements flourished, new sects enjoyed the freedom to proselytize and expand, and long-dominant communions struggled to retain the loyalty of their increasingly independent flocks. In Robert Wiebe's words, the young republic experienced a "revolution in choices" in the religious as well as the secular realm, presenting clergymen of the established colonial churches with an unpleasant alternative: compete for popular favor or perish.[2]

In the antiauthoritarian climate of post-revolutionary America, "sectarian innovators" appeared to be more effective evangelists than ministers of the old religious establishments. Preachers of every denomination, Martin Marty has written, engaged in "a Soul Rush that soon outpaced the Gold Rush." The race to harvest souls, Marty observes, was "a textbook example of free enterprise in the marketplace of religion, a competition in which the fittest survived." If we measure success solely in terms of converts, the Methodists and Baptists clearly proved to be the "fittest" churches in the young republic. On the eve of the Revolution the Methodists, only recently established in North America, could claim barely ten thousand adherents. But after the war Wesleyan circuit riders demonstrated a remarkable ability to win Americans to their standard, and by 1840 Methodists outnumbered all other denominations in the United States. Baptist numbers also swelled during the early nineteenth century, particularly in the northern frontier of New England and in western settlements, where (like the Methodists) they sometimes consti- tuted the only significant Christian communion. Presbyterians, in con- trast, enjoyed only modest growth, while Episcopal and Congregational- ist leaders proved unable to capture popular favor.[3]

The relatively rapid decline of New England Congregationalism repre- sents a watershed in the history of American evangelicalism, and presents us with a paradox. At the outbreak of the Revolution the Congregational- ists claimed more communicants than any other denomination in the colonies. Unlike their Anglican counterparts, New England's orthodox clergy typically saw the revolutionary struggle as a redemptive battle against evil, and gave overwhelming support to the patriot cause. After the war evangelical Congregationalists energetically engaged in evange- lism, and many participated enthusiastically in the revivals which swept across New England and the northern frontier repeatedly during the 1790s and early decades of the nineteenth century. Yet orthodox clergy- men were unable to attract new communicants in significant numbers, and by 1840 the Congregationalists stood only fourth in overall member- ship. In the New England states they continued to be the largest commu- nion, although they now shared social and political influence with mem- bers of other denominations. But outside of New England they trailed the Presbyterians and Baptists and lagged far behind the Methodists. Even among the New England migrants who settled the "burned-over district" stretching from Vermont to Connecticut's Western Reserve in northern Ohio, Congregationalists waged a losing battle against "sec- tarian" proselytizers. During the early republic tens of thousands of migrating Congregationalists abandoned the church of their fathers and embraced "innovation."[4]

Why did Congregational influence decline so rapidly after the Ameri- can Revolution, while Methodist and Baptist numbers soared? Although various answers have been proposed, all underline the inability of Con- gregational clergymen to understand the social, political, and cultural changes triggered by the rebellion against British authority. The Congre- gational churches, it is generally agreed, could not or would not adjust to life in a democratizing society.

During the mid-nineteenth century Methodist publications delighted in contrasting the rustic simplicity of early Wesleyan circuit riders with the aristocratic pretensions of Congregational ministers. Popular auto-biographies of pioneer Methodists like Peter Cartwright and James B. Finley portrayed orthodox Yankee missionaries as genteel snobs who were totally unsuited for work among the common people. Most Americans, Peter Cartwright observed, wanted preachers who could "mount a stump, a block, or old log, or stand in the bed of a wagon, and without note or manuscript, quote, expound, and apply the word of God to the hearts and consciences of the people." In short, they wanted simple, spirit-filled Methodist exhorters.[5]

Congregational evangelists, the Methodists insisted, had been spoiled by genteel surroundings and too much formal schooling. They could endlessly dispute points of doctrine but could not bring perishing souls to Christ. "They would come with a tolerable education," Cartwright observed, "and a smattering knowledge of the old Calvinistic system of theology." Well-stocked with "old manuscript sermons, that had been preached, or written, perhaps a hundred years before," the "very forward and officious" New England evangelists headed for the frontier, longing for a chance to display their "superior tact and talent." Likening the Congregational system of ministerial training to a greenhouse, Cartwright dismissed these "hot house" parsons as "profoundly ignorant" of the needs of the American people, and altogether ineffective. He wished that the people "down East . . . might keep their home-manufactured clergy at home, or give them some honorable employ better suited to their genius, than that of reading old musty and worm-eaten sermons."[6]

Scholarly assessments of Congregational evangelism have supported Cartwright's acerbic observations. According to Methodist historian William Warren Sweet, the Congregationalists typically possessed a "smug provincialism which led directly to a decided superiority complex." Their leaders often were "more or less indifferent as to whether or not Congregationalism was planted west of the Hudson River." While acknowledging that Congregationalists did attempt to evangelize the West, Martin Marty claims that they could not compete with Methodists or Baptists because they "were too half-hearted in their adjustments to the rough frontier." A "spirit of phlegmatic complacency," Clifton Olmstead observed, "unfitted" Congregationalists for evangelism beyond settled New England. Unable to appreciate the unique challenges posed by a burgeoning society, "the Congregationalists sentenced themselves to remain essentially a sectional body during the formative stage of the country's history and to play a relatively minor role in the building of the West."[7]

The alliance between Congregationalism and Federalism is often cited as the Congregational clergy's greatest liability. According to Sweet, the Federalist sentiments of most orthodox Congregational ministers "tended to alienate the rural sections and played into the hands of the Baptists, Free Baptists, and Methodists particularly." Even Congregational missionaries sent to the frontier, J. F. Thorning observed, were more concerned "with promoting party interests than in furthering the gospel." In his classic analysis of American denominationalism, H. Richard Niebuhr observed that after the Revolution the "provincial New England denomination" appealed only to the "middle classes of established communities" and "remained aloof from the religious movements of the West." The Congregational clergy, Niebuhr argued, "allied politically with the Federalism against which the West revolted", and in the process seriously jeopardized their standing in society. In the early republic "political and religious conservatism combined to do battle with political and religious radicalism," and inevitably the radical "Western Methodists and Baptists" gained the victory.[8]

Several historians have cited the decentralized Congregational polity as a further obstacle to the denomination's expansion. Unlike the highly organized Methodists, it is suggested, Congregationalists lacked any centralized authority that might effectively coordinate missionary efforts. More than a century ago the Congregationalist author William W. Patton noted that "our system, as bequeathed to us by the early fathers of New England, was poorly equipped for anything beyond parish-work." Following this line of reasoning William Warren Sweet thought it was significant that the most aggressive Congregational missionary efforts were launched in Connecticut, where the Saybrook platform had created a more centralized polity which closely resembled Presbyterianism. Connecticut Congregationalism, however, was no match for the organizational genius of the Methodists, whose ever-expanding network of classes, circuits, and conferences, Donald Mathews has observed, became a model for nineteenth century social movements of all types.[9]

Recently numerous scholars have stressed the limited appeal of Calvinist theology. "Structurally," Robert Wiebe maintains, Congregationalists "were geared for expansion; doctrinally they were not." During the half-century after the Revolution, as Americans experienced what Gordon S. Wood aptly calls a "democratization of mind," common people felt drawn toward churches which articulated a populist theology. In Nathan Hatch's words, "the new republic witnessed a revolt of substantial proportions against Calvinism" as Americans sought to reconcile their Christian faith with the egalitarian ideals of their revolution. The God of the Puritans, whose seemingly arbitrary and immutable eternal

decrees held an entire universe in absolute subjugation, held little appeal
for a society that defined itself in terms of opposition to tyranny. Many
Americans found it easier to believe in a deity who left the human will
free to choose salvation, and who benignly invited all his people without
distinction to approach the throne of grace.[10]

Hatch and others also find evidence of a grass roots reaction against
the clericalism of the Congregational clergy. After the Revolution Americans preferred churches which conferred spiritual authority upon all
believers, regardless of their social or educational attainments. Despite
their theological differences the most successful communions in the early
republic all "endowed common people with dignity and responsibility."
Methodists, Freewill Baptists, Universalists, Christians, and many other
post-revolutionary sects relied heavily upon untutored preachers and lay
exhorters, who drew upon the natural idiom of the common people to
proclaim the word of God. These growing communions affirmed the
ability of common folk to accurately discover for themselves the meaning
of scripture without the guidance of man-made creeds, abstract theologies, or college-trained clergy. "People," Hatch writes, "gladly accepted a theology that addressed them without condescension, balked at
vested interests, and reinforced ideas of volitional allegiance and self-
reliance."[11]

Orthodox Congregational ministers, the standard interpretation maintains, failed to appreciate the power of the egalitarian impulse among the
people. As well-born community leaders they expected a degree of deference that their society could no longer give them. Clinging to the out-
moded belief that a gentlemanly elite ought to govern both church and
state, they vainly set themselves against the "ignorant demagogues" and
"sectarian dividers" who delighted the average citizen. In their desperate
effort to breathe life into a dying tradition the Congregationalists only
succeeded in further distancing themselves from the American people.

In short, the standard characterization of Congregational evangelists
presents them as arch-conservatives—even reactionaries—in a society
which gladly embraced radical change. Their relationship to republican
culture is nearly always described in terms of opposition. Faced with the
constitutional separation of church and state the Congregational clergy
upheld New England's standing orders. In a society becoming inexorably
democratic they denounced democracy. In an era that exalted simplicity
and the commonplace, they affirmed gentility and "high culture." They
maintained a dogmatic tradition when the people rejected rigorous theology. They clung to the communal ideals of New England's past while
Americans elevated individualism to a sacred principle.

Even the revivals which quickened dozens of Congregational churches in the 1790s and early 1800s have been interpreted as reactionary events. With a few notable exceptions historians of the Second Great Awakening place the New England revivals within the context of a battle between Calvinist orthodoxy and democracy. The Congregational clergy, led by such redoubtable conservatives as Timothy Dwight and Lyman Beecher, supposedly instigated the revivals in an effort to revitalize their besieged followers and inspire them to greater exertions against the forces of secularism and democracy. William McLoughlin describes post-revolutionary Congregational revivalists as "nativists" who attempted "to call America back to the old-time religion and traditional way of life that were inevitably fading." The distinction between the "conservative New England phase" of the Awakening and the "democratic" southern phase is sharply drawn: Methodist and Baptist revivals constituted mass popular movements *in favor* of change, while Congregationalist revivals were feeble reactions *against* change.[12]

The standard portrayal of Congregational evangelists in the early republic can perhaps best be described as a caricature. Like all caricatures it resembles reality up to a point, but is far from being a realistic representation. It is the essence of caricature to exaggerate selected features of reality while softening or ignoring other aspects. Thus the caricature suggests something truthful while distorting the truth. In the case at hand, the standard portrayal of the Congregational clergy captures unmistakable aspects of reality: these were conservative men who felt deeply uneasy about the direction their society was going, and, to be sure, most of them could accurately be described as members of an educated elite by the standards of their age. But the one-dimensional "genteel parson" lampooned by Peter Cartwright and dismissed by historians is a straw man that had very few actual historical counterparts.

This study is an extended essay about Congregational evangelism in the early republic. It argues that the Congregationalists clearly recognized the changes occurring in their society, and saw the need to adjust their ministry in order to survive and to respond to the needs of their people. As we shall see, they were neither complacent nor half-hearted in their efforts to expand beyond New England, nor too arrogant to learn from the successes of others. Despite their social and theological conservatism, Congregational missionaries proved resourceful and innovative in their response to the challenges of "the rough frontier." In their efforts to adjust their ministry to a rapidly changing society, they were being molded by the same revolutionary forces that transformed other Americans. Indeed, to the extent that they openly embraced change, they were as much a part of the revolution in American Christianity as the Methodists and other more democratic evangelical groups.

II

New England's Congregational establishment had always been Janus-faced; it confronted the future while staring into the past. The core of Puritan belief, "the New England Soul" as Harry S. Stout has called it, was an unshakable conviction that New Englanders were a special covenanted people who occupied a vital position at the center of redemptive history. Although events challenged this conviction many times between the 1630s and the Revolution, at the birth of the American republic most Congregational ministers continued to see New Englanders as God's chosen people. They were certain that God would never forsake them nor revoke their liberties so long as they remained loyal to the faith of their fathers.[13]

The belief that they were a special people placed a unique burden upon Congregational evangelists after the Revolution. Along with members of other denominations, they confronted a dilemma which has challenged Christians for nearly two millennia: how can the church's teachings be kept relevant and effective as society changes? What traditions must be jettisoned, what compromises can safely be made, and what fundamental values cannot be compromised without abandoning the faith itself? The problem, never an easy one to resolve, becomes most pressing when societies undergo revolutionary change. In the wake of the American rebellion no communion could avoid confronting the dilemma, although some denominations resolved it more easily than others. Emerging churches like the Methodists adjusted to revolutionary change most readily, while long-established communions such as the Anglican wrestled under the weight of their cherished colonial traditions. The dilemma proved especially painful for orthodox Congregational ministers, who viewed themselves as the guardians of a sacred covenant that did not rest upon the shoulders of Anglican priests or sectarian exhorters. As they attempted to adjust to a radically changed society, they could never forget their obligation to keep faith with their hallowed forefathers.[14]

The sense that they were the keepers of the covenant—chosen guardians of everything that was best in the Reformed tradition—limited the Congregational clergy's openness to change even as it compelled ministers to innovate. No orthodox clergyman, surveying the stream of migrating New Englanders and the growth of dissenting communions, could fail to recognize that a new age had dawned. If they were to preserve the faith of their fathers they would have to learn new ways of relating to parishioners and forge new weapons to combat error and uphold truth. But unlike their more democratic countrymen, orthodox clergymen could never feel exhilarated by breaking with colonial traditions. Their commitment to keeping the covenant at once dictated that they must change and that they must not change too much.

The line between necessary change and fatal compromise was never self-evident; each minister had to draw it for himself in the discharge of his daily pastoral responsibilities. In baptizing babies and catechizing youth, preaching sermons and counseling sinners, organizing churches and mediating disputes, each Congregational evangelist wrestled with the tension between republican cultural expectations and cherished orthodox traditions. Some ministers found it easy to amend traditional ministerial roles and to adopt new modes of preaching and shepherding. Others were less willing or able to innovate. Their openness to new social and political values, especially changing attitudes toward authority, varied considerably. But to some degree most Congregational evangelists attempted to reconcile their inherited traditions with the increasingly egalitarian and individualistic ethos of the people. Given the depth of their commitment to preserving a covenanted society, the most impressive fact about orthodox evangelists is not their conservative bias, but rather the degree of creative adaptation they were capable of achieving.

Nothing tested the adaptability of the orthodox clergy more than the rapidly expanding northern frontier. Beginning in the 1760s a stream of Yankees had left their homes in southern New England to settle lands in the "new settlements" of Vermont and western New York. Another stream of New Englanders had settled the Susquehanna Company lands in the Wyoming Valley, a region claimed by both Pennsylvania and Connecticut. After the Revolution this stream of emigration became a torrent. Between 1790 and 1830 more than eight hundred thousand Yankees moved to frontier regions in the West, stamping an indelible New England mindset upon hundreds of communities between the Hudson River and the Mississippi. The preservation of Congregationalism as something more than a provincial denomination depended largely upon the ability of the orthodox clergy to provide an adequate ministry for this uprooted populace.[15]

Once they had left the land of their fathers behind, New England migrants encountered strong pressures to abandon or compromise their religious traditions. The new settlements of the northern frontier lacked the standing orders which had regulated New England life for generations. In western states the absence of even a weak religious establishment promoted an often virulent proselytism among members of every denomination. As we shall see, Congregational migrants often had to wait several years or more before they could organize churches or settle an orthodox pastor, leaving them vulnerable to the appeals of sectarian neighbors. The demographics of the frontier also encouraged a softening of religious loyalties. Settlers often found themselves living alongside families who hailed from towns—or even states—far removed from their own home villages. The process of building frontier communities required settlers to forge bonds with strangers who did not necessarily value the same traditions or share the same social assumptions.

In the half-century after the Revolution several hundred Congregational ministers took up the task of ministering to the settlers in the new settlements. Many were sent forth by the dozens of state and local missionary societies organized by orthodox New Englanders in the 1790s and early nineteenth century. Others evangelized as they journeyed back and forth between their homes and the new settlements, visiting family members or former parishioners who had joined the exodus from New England. Newly licensed candidates for the ministry sometimes received their first taste of the pastor's life in vacant frontier congregations, where they "preached supply" while waiting for calls to settle permanently closer to home. As frontier communities grew more prosperous and could afford full-time ministers, increasing numbers of young candidates looked to the West for permanent places to locate. Those who accepted calls from frontier congregations often spent much of their time and energy evangelizing nearby towns that had no settled orthodox pastor. Some ministers left the pulpit to become farmers in the West, only to be pressed back into service by the appeals of urgent neighbors. A few preached under the auspices of land companies or wealthy proprietors who wished to provide orthodox moral guidance to the families who had purchased their land.

For these Congregational ministers, accustomed as they were to homogeneous congregations closely knitted together by generations of marital, political, and economic relationships, the shock of the "disorganized" frontier could be overwhelming. In the new settlements congregations frequently consisted of people who held widely divergent theological perspectives. New Light and Old Light Congregationalists often stood shoulder to shoulder with skeptics, Baptists, Presbyterians, and Arminians of various stripes. Settlers divided by deep theological differences now found themselves confronted with the task of establishing towns together. Although sectarian discord often disrupted frontier settlements, the pressure to accommodate divergent viewpoints constantly threatened to subvert Congregationalist efforts to establish thriving, pure churches and covenanted communities among New England's emigrating offspring.[16]

The Connecticut Missionary Society (CMS), the principal focus of this book, was the largest and most influential orthodox missionary agency.

During the two decades following its creation in 1798, the CMS employed 148 missionaries to itinerate in Vermont, New York, Pennsylvania, and the territory northwest of the Ohio River. The ministers supported by the Society occupied the front line in the orthodox struggle against the Methodists, Baptists, and other "sectarian" proselytizers. They grappled day in and day out with the challenges posed by frontier existence and republican culture. The first four chapters of this study will trace the evolution of the CMS, and assess the organization's place in early republican society. Chapters 5 through 7 will examine in greater detail the men who served as missionaries and their response to selected aspects of frontier culture. I will pay particular attention to their efforts to accommodate changing circumstances and assess the limits of their adjustment. Finally, I will suggest a reinterpretation of Congregational "declension" in the early republic.

This study focuses upon Connecticut and the Connecticut Missionary Society because of the rich manuscript source material left by home missionaries from that state. Congregationalists created dozens of smaller state and local missionary organizations during the early republic, but the documentary evidence for these agencies is much more fragmentary than the voluminous CMS papers. In order to keep this study within manageable limits, I examined only those missionaries who received appointment prior to the close of 1818, the year in which Connecticut formally disestablished the Congregational churches. According to standard interpretations, the Connecticut clergy in this era struggled desperately to stave off religious voluntarism; some scholars have regarded the CMS as an expression of this anti-democratic impulse. Hence, the papers left by orthodox Connecticut evangelists from this period offer an excellent opportunity to test the validity of existing scholarship on Congregationalism in the early republic.

Since this book focuses upon evangelism, the theological controversies that divided eighteenth- and nineteenth- century Congregationalists will receive only marginal attention. The fragmentation of New England churches during the Great Awakening, the doctrinal feuding between the various orthodox factions, and the gradual liberalization of Calvinism are all relevant to this study, but as these themes have been thoroughly discussed by many other scholars they do not need to be treated at length here.[17] From time to time, however, I will consider theological developments insofar as they influenced the missionary efforts of the Congregationalist clergy.

Before proceeding further, it will be helpful to clarify a few essential terms. For the purpose of this study, the word "orthodox" refers to all trinitarian Congregationalists who adhered to the major tenets of Calvinism, regardless of their precise stance on specific controversies such as admission to communion, baptism, the nature of benevolence, and other doctrinal questions. Old Lights and New Lights, New Divinity "consistent Calvinists" and Old Calvinists have all been defined as orthodox. It should be kept in mind, however, that the men who dominated the Congregationalist missionary movement were overwhelmingly Edwardseans who typically regarded the other clerical factions as insufficiently orthodox. Hence, whenever they used the term "orthodoxy" it generally meant Edwardseanism.

The definition of "Congregational" has proven far more troublesome. Under the Saybrook Platform of 1708 Connecticut Congregationalism closely resembled Presbyterianism, and by the late eighteenth century Connecticut people often used the terms interchangeably. In 1801 the General Association of Connecticut and the Presbyterian General Assembly ratified a Plan of Union that until the 1820s virtually erased all distinctions between the two denominations in many western regions. Under the Plan, Congregationalist and Presbyterian settlers could form united churches and call pastors of either denomination. The Presbyterians agreed to recognize Congregationalist pastors in their frontier presbyteries and synods, while Congregational ministerial associations in the West recognized Presbyterian pastors. The Plan, which constituted a significant accommodation to changing circumstances, makes it difficult to impose a tidy scheme of classification upon the sources. In most northern frontier presbyteries many communicants considered themselves to be Congregationalists and a majority of ministers were New Englanders employed by Congregational missionary organizations. In other instances ordained Presbyterian ministers supplied pulpits in Congregational churches, and sometimes received calls to settle. I have chosen to include such "Presbygational" clergymen in my study whenever they received financial assistance from the CMS.[18]

A thorough examination of Congregationalist evangelism in republican America is long overdue. Scholars, enamored with the Puritans of the seventeenth century, have produced an astonishing volume of research on virtually every aspect of life in early New England. They have been far less kind to the Puritans' post-revolutionary descendants. The presupposition that Congregational clergymen stood implacably opposed to all forms of democratic change—a stereotype first articulated in the eighteenth and nineteenth centuries by Jeffersonian critics of New England's standing orders—has powerfully shaped the historiography of American evangelicalism. Repeated endlessly with little critical reflection by generations of historians, it has served to obscure important features of early national religion by discouraging careful analysis of the orthodox response to republican culture. While scholars have produced a wealth of published research on the "democratic" evangelicalism best exemplified by the Methodists and Baptists, to date there is not a single monograph devoted to the extensive missionary efforts of New England's ecclesiastical establishments. As a result, there is virtually no detailed evidence to substantiate the standard generalization that Congregationalism was an insignificant force on the frontier, or that orthodox evangelists uniformly represented a perishing genteel religious culture.[19]

Although Methodists and Baptists capitalized most successfully on the post-revolutionary changes in American society, Congregationalist missionaries were an integral part of the frontier experience in New England, New York, Pennsylvania, and throughout the Midwest. They contributed significantly to the development of hundreds of American communities, and in many places the fruit of their labor is still evident today. During the past several years, as I have traveled throughout the area that was once America's northern frontier, I have repeatedly come across churches established by Abner Benedict, Giles Cowles, Seth Williston, and the many other obscure evangelists whose efforts are assessed in the following pages. Every Sunday morning, in urban centers like Cleveland, Ohio, and in rural settings like Cortland County, New York, tens of thousands of Americans gather in hundreds of such places to worship God and seek direction for their lives. The names of the missionaries who first organized these churches have been all but forgotten, but after more than a century and a half the congregations still gather, and they continue to affect the lives of countless people. As one who has worshiped with some of these congregations I have been forcibly struck by a reality that membership statistics alone cannot reveal: for them, as for generations of worshipers before them, these living communities lie at the heart of the American experience.

CHAPTER

TWO

The Missionary Impulse

Evangelism did not come naturally to most Congregational ministers during the late eighteenth century. Although R. Pierce Beaver has called New England "the well-spring of American missionary concern and action,"[1] orthodox pastors in the colonial era displayed remarkably little interest in evangelism beyond their own parishes. In theory, of course, Puritans possessed a strong motivation for missionary endeavor. According to Calvinist doctrine Christian magistrates were obliged to seek the conversion of heathen subjects, and the royal charters of both Massachusetts and Plymouth imposed this responsibility upon the founders of New England. The "principall Ende" of settlement, the Massachusetts charter asserted, was to "Wynn and incite the Natives . . . [to] the onlie true God and Saviour of Mankinde," an objective underscored by the colony's General Court when it adopted a Great Seal depicting an Indian, bow and arrow in hand, pleading with Englishmen to "come over and help us." But during the next century and a half only a relative handful of Puritan ministers actually undertook missions to New England's native inhabitants, and no effort was made to preach the gospel to unchurched whites in other colonies. In 1797, surveying the history of recent Christian missions, the Connecticut General Association frankly observed that New England's contribution was paltry compared to the efforts made by evangelicals in England and on the Continent. Reflecting upon the "myriads" of Americans languishing "in darkness and the shadow of death," the ministers sadly confessed that "we must see our labors in a very diminutive point of view."[2]

Various factors restricted Congregational evangelism during the colonial era. The early settlement of North America took place against the

15

(1) backdrop of almost constant religious strife in Europe. The Reformation settlements of the early seventeenth century, which gave to each dominant church a geographic area of spiritual control, greatly reduced proselytism among competing sects, and ushered in an era of relative toleration and peace. This European trend powerfully influenced the outlook of religious leaders in the American colonies. Until the mid-eighteenth century ministers of the established colonial denominations generally respected the communicants of other churches and rarely proselytized among them. The missionary impulse was further weakened by financial

(2) realities. As Lois Banner has observed, long-term missionary ventures were expensive, while American churches typically were poor. Colonial churchmen had many competing claims upon their material resources, and ministerial salaries, the construction and expansion of meetinghouses, and routine maintenance costs all took priority over evangelism.[3]

(3) Beyond these factors, which affected all colonial communions, the theological convictions of orthodox New Englanders served to limit Congregational missionary efforts. The Puritans, as many scholars have observed, did not come to America to convert sinners but to establish pure churches and covenanted communities governed by regenerate saints. Possessing strong ecclesiastical sensibilities, they could not conceive of individual Christians apart from a confessing community of faith. The "duties of Christian love," the church at Dedham, Massachusetts, typically declared in 1637, required the saints "to exhort, admonish, privately comfort" and "relieve the wants of each other etc." Christians were to seek close "union and communion" by attending upon "all the ordinances of Christ's instituted worship," since the spiritual condition of every believer was "such as stands in need of all instituted ordinances for the repair of the spirit and edification of the body of Christ."[4] In the minds of most orthodox New Englanders this communal dimension of Christian life was always paramount. For them the church was not primarily an evangelistic enterprise; it was an organic body that nurtured, admonished, and sustained those saints whom God converted and called together into sacred fellowship.

Nonetheless, Puritan leaders could not altogether ignore the obligations laid upon them by Christ's mandate to preach the gospel to all the world. Throughout the seventeenth and eighteenth centuries New England magistrates upheld the conversion of the pagan Indians as an important objective of colonization, and often expressed embarrassment that so little was being done to accomplish that goal. "It is a scandale to our Religion," Governor John Winthrop lamented in the 1640s, "that we shewe not as much zeal in seekinge the conversion of the heathen, as the Papists doe." Although the lament was echoed by many other Puritan leaders during the following century, there was little that could be done to remove the "scandale." The ecclesiastical system New Englanders established made each congregation virtually autonomous, and vested most governing authority in the laity. Clergymen received ordination only after receiving a call from a congregation, and once ordained were bound by sacred covenant to serve the saints who called them. The Puritan minister could not preach beyond his own parish without the consent of his flock, and as most would-be missionaries discovered, congregations rarely wished to grant their shepherd permission to leave on mission.[5]

These traditional barriers to effective evangelism did not altogether vanish with the Revolution. But during the final quarter of the eighteenth century orthodox New Englanders for the first time displayed a strong commitment to missionary action, and ministerial associations in both Connecticut and Massachusetts began to develop systematic plans to send "gospel preaching" into other regions. This sudden departure from colonial precedent undoubtedly stemmed in part from the pressure of sectarian competition, as Donald Mathews has suggested. But other factors affected the changing priorities of the Congregational clergy as well, including new theological currents and the gradual deterioration of New England communities due to religious strife, economic problems, and mass migration. Even before the Revolution, when sectarian competition had not yet become a major threat to the orthodox establishment, the normally inward-looking Congregationalists had begun to display a heightened sense of responsibility for the welfare of the Indians and white settlers beyond their own parishes.

The revivals that broke out in New England churches during the 1730s and 1740s proved to be important agents of change. The Great Awakening provided a strong new impetus to colonial missionary efforts, although the effect upon Congregational evangelism was not immediate. The evangelical fervor unleashed by the revival helped to spark the Methodist movement in America, and inspired Anglican, Presbyterian, and Baptist missionaries who itinerated from town to town preaching the message of new birth. Only a handful of Congregational ministers itinerated, however, and most orthodox leaders strongly disapproved of the practice. Itinerancy jeopardized the normal interdependent relationship that existed between congregations and pastors, and also threatened to further fragment New England's religious establishment, which the Awakening had divided into pro- and anti-revival factions. Doctrinal feuding split dozens of congregations into rival camps and left many others in danger of schism. Preoccupied with intramural strife, few ministers felt a strong inclination to engage in evangelism beyond their own parishes, and those New Lights who did wish to itinerate could not request leave without alienating influential parishioners.

Nonetheless, the Awakening inspired fresh thinking about eschatology and Christian ethics that in the long run powerfully influenced American and European missions. Perhaps most important, the revivals fueled New Light hopes for the speedy commencement of the millennium and triggered an outpouring of eschatological writings that helped to define the self-understanding of later orthodox missionaries. Jonathan Edwards, aptly described by Perry Miller as the "greatest artist of the apocalypse," played an especially important role. Edwards articulated a millennial interpretation of revivalism that American missionary literature continued to draw upon well into the nineteenth century. In *Some Thoughts Concerning the Present Revival of Religion in New England* (1742), this greatest of New Light theologians optimistically asserted that the Awakening was probably "the dawning, or at least a prelude of that glorious work of God, so often foretold in Scripture, which in the progress and issue of it shall renew the world of mankind."[6]

As developed in this and several later works, Edwards's eschatological thinking was distinctly postmillennial. Rejecting the notion that Christ would return bodily to rule the earth for a thousand years, he asserted that the millennium would commence with the pouring out of the "seventh vial" referred to in Revelation, the act which signified the final destruction of Antichrist. A golden age would follow, during which Christ would be spiritually present in a unique way, the gospel would spread triumphantly throughout the world, and Christians would grow increasingly more Christlike. In this gradually developed millennial kingdom Christ would rule the earth through his people until, at the close of the age, he would return bodily to establish a new heaven and a new earth. Edwards fervently believed that the world was already living under the sixth vial, and that with the aid of further outpourings of God's grace, Antichrist soon would fall and the long awaited millennial age would dawn.[7]

Most, though not all, New Light ministers shared Edwards's postmillennial vision, with its explicit emphasis upon missionary action. As good Calvinists they rejected any notion that humans could establish the millennial kingdom through their own efforts. Still, their theological system assigned an important role to human agency. God, they believed, would act through his church to spread the gospel and establish his reign throughout the earth. Edwards and many of his followers assumed that the church in America would play an especially large role in this drama of redemption. Evangelistic outreach on the part of New England's churches, therefore, would be an essential element of the final chapter of human history.

New Light writings on social ethics also helped to promote a growing commitment to mission, particularly the large body of literature on benevolence inspired by the posthumous publication of Edwards's *Dissertation on the Nature of True Virtue* (1765). "True virtue," Edwards asserted, "most essentially consists in benevolence to Being in general." This love of "Being in general," he believed, was the primary alteration produced by regeneration. While purely natural principles governed the wills of all unconverted persons, regeneration implanted in the hearts of converted Christians a supernatural benevolent affection which motivated them to love Being in general.

In an effort to reconcile traditional Puritan teaching on human depravity with the popular natural moral philosophy of the eighteenth century, Edwards also acknowledged the existence of a secondary, inferior order of virtue. While true virtue could be attained only through supernatural grace, the unregenerate could rationally attain a high level of enlightened social morality due to humanity's innate natural virtues. Agreeing with such natural philosophers as the Earl of Shaftesbury, Edwards asserted that the natural human inclination to seek happiness and avoid misery contributed to the public good by checking selfish social behavior. Because personal happiness was self-evidently bound up with the good of others, self-love inclined humans to promote justice and benevolence. Edwards stressed that such natural virtue possessed no saving merit, because it left the sinful heart's disposition toward selfishness unaltered. Nonetheless he accepted it as necessary to the preservation of social harmony in a fallen world.[8]

Many of Edwards's leading students grappled with the implications of the *Dissertation* for orthodox theology and sought to reformulate some of their mentor's most controversial ideas. Samuel Hopkins, especially, dedicated himself to improving Edwards's treatise, and in the process helped to define one of the major components of later orthodox missionary thinking. Hopkins agreed with Edwards that regeneration filled the converted heart with supernatural benevolence, and that this mystical love was the primary evidence of salvation. But he regarded Edwards's "Being in general" as an unnecessarily amorphous term, and redefined it as love toward "God and our neighbors." This amendment helped to clarify the ethical obligations of Christian life.[9]

More fundamentally, Hopkins rejected Edwards' distinction between "true" and "secondary" virtue as a dangerous concession to theological heresy. Completely rejecting the claims of the natural moral philosophers, he argued that virtue is altogether disinterested, and can only be attained as an unmerited gift from a gracious God whose primary attribute is disinterested love for his creatures. Hopkins recognized no middle ground between the total selfishness of the natural man and the completely "disinterested benevolence" of the regenerate saint. For him, there was no proper place in God's universe for human self-love.

Hopkins's concept of disinterested benevolence lay at the core of the "New Divinity" which during the last quarter of the eighteenth century captured most of the pulpits in northwestern Connecticut and western Massachusetts. Led by Hopkins and two other Edwards students, Joseph Bellamy and Nathaniel Emmons, the New Divinity men decried the rationalist leanings of liberal Congregationalists such as Charles Chauncy and Jonathan Mayhew, as well as the lack of evangelical zeal displayed by Old Light Calvinists. Their own theological system simultaneously emphasized human inability and human agency. On the one hand they strenuously proclaimed the absolute sovereignty of God, the total depravity of man, and the moral inability of humans to will anything but sin. Thus, they averred, salvation depends totally upon unmerited grace. On the other hand they regarded evangelism as the greatest manifestation of that disinterested benevolence which God implants in the hearts of regenerate saints, and missionary outreach as a distinguishing characteristic of the coming millennial age.[10]

Their emphasis upon disinterested benevolence helped to humanize the orthodox rationale for missionary endeavor. Traditionally Puritan theology taught that God's chief attribute was his absolute sovereignty rather than his love. While God certainly desired human happiness, Jonathan Edwards reasoned, his "goodness and love to created beings is derived from, and subordinate to His love of himself." Puritan evangelists like John Eliot always stressed *gloria Dei* as the proper goal of missionary labor. "Behold, ye *Indians,*" Cotton Mather characteristically exclaimed, ". . . it is God that has caused us to desire his *Glory* in your salvation."[11]

Edwards's New Divinity followers continued to emphasize *gloria Dei* as a missionary motive, but they stressed that God's glory was manifested most completely in disinterested efforts to attain human happiness. In their view missionaries glorified God by pouring themselves out for the well-being of their fellow sinners. Charles Backus, New Divinity pastor of Somers, Connecticut, and an early supporter of the Congregational missionary movement, struck a common note in 1798 when he argued that evangelism was inspired both by "the desire to glorify God" and by the "love of mankind." Disinterested benevolence, Backus declared, impelled the Church "to desire the salvation of sinners" since God was glorified in the redemption of fallen humanity, and true Christians "make the divine glory the ultimate end of their lives."[12]

Thus the Awakening in New England gave rise to a school of New Light theology predisposed to missionary action. Not surprisingly, New Divinity ministers played leading roles in the Congregational missionary associations created during the 1790s and early nineteenth century. As we shall see in a later chapter, the formation of the Connecticut Missionary Society in 1798 was clearly tied to the millennial expectations of Edwardsean clergymen, and throughout its early history the organization was dominated by proponents of the New Divinity. Indeed, despite official efforts to be noncontroversial, CMS employees and publications were so thoroughly imbued with the New Divinity viewpoint that theological rivals sometimes attacked the society as an engine for the propagation of "Hopkinsianism."

In the last quarter of the eighteenth century the New Divinity was the fastest growing clerical faction in both Connecticut and Massachusetts, a fact which helps to explain the growing commitment to missions after the War. Prior to the Revolution Edwardsean clergymen occupied only a few dozen New England pulpits, primarily in the rural backcountry of the Berkshires. More liberal Calvinists dismissed them as uncultured ranters, whose evangelical zeal and seemingly anachronistic theological views rightly offended sensible Christians. But by the 1790s adherents of the New Divinity filled most of the pulpits in northern Connecticut and western Massachusetts, and had become an influential force even in the larger cities and centers of learning. In 1792 Yale President Ezra Stiles, an Old Calvinist critic of the Edwardseans, complained that most students preparing for the ministry embraced New Divinity principles and that congregations had difficulty finding candidates with other viewpoints.[13]

The spread of Edwardsean theology testifies to the conservative mood of Congregationalists in the Revolutionary Era. New Divinity ideals appealed to New Englanders, Joseph Conforti suggests, because they were profoundly countercultural. During the second half of the eighteenth century the economic and demographic expansion of New England threatened to sweep away traditional communal values. At a time when growth was promoting individualistic materialism and the atomization of society, Conforti writes, Edwardseans reaffirmed the inherited Puritan ethic that stressed "corporate obligation, personal restraint, and communal harmony and simplicity."[14] New Divinity men contemptuously denounced self-interest of any kind, adhered dogmatically to a seemingly old-fashioned Calvinist understanding of redemption, and embraced without apology the pure church ideals of New England's founders. In calling such men to be pastors, congregations symbolically reaffirmed their connection with the past and their commitment to communal values which social and economic changes threatened to subvert.

In this regard the rise of the New Divinity paralleled the conservative impulse within New England's revolutionary movement. Robert Gross, among other historians, has documented this dimension of the struggle in his landmark study of Concord, Massachusetts. For the townspeople of Concord, Gross observes, the Revolution offered an opportunity to put aside village divisions and close ranks in defense of New England's ancient customs. In 1775, he writes, Concord's "economy was stagnant, the land was worn out, the town was losing its young." Confronted with this crisis, feuding leaders "blamed each other for violating ancestral ideals" and joined together in the name of their fathers "to defy the assault on New England's sacred heritage."[15]

Throughout the Revolution New England religious leaders exhibited the same desire to preserve traditional values. For the Congregational clergy in general, Harry S. Stout has observed, the rebellion against British authority constituted a reaffirmation of the people's dedication to the covenant bequeathed by the founders. New England communities, the ministers prophesied, had fallen upon hard times because the people had turned to kingship, learned to imitate corrupt English manners, and embraced Anglican moral philosophy. But resistance to tyranny demonstrated that God's elect had not abandoned the covenant. Eventually peace and harmony would return, and all the world would know, in the words of William Emerson, "that there is a God in New England."[16]

The emergence of an orthodox missionary movement during the revolutionary generation reflected the same conservative tendencies. Nothing symbolized more powerfully the growing discontinuity between past and present than the steady migration of New Englanders that began in the 1760s. This movement, which was only the start of a century-long exodus from New England, produced social strains as traumatic as those caused by the war itself. Emigration weakened key social institutions, dividing families, severing friendships, and splitting congregations. At a time when revolutionary change was sweeping across America, migration undermined human relationships that were essential to the stability of New England communities. Missionary action was a logical response to this threat. When churches in Connecticut and Massachusetts decided to send missionaries to their "destitute children and neighbors" in the new settlements, they reaffirmed in the strongest possible way their continued dedication to the corporate values passed down by the generations before them.

II

In June 1774 the Connecticut General Association gathered at the Congregational meetinghouse in Mansfield to deliberate upon the pressing concerns of the colony's orthodox churches. During the preceding decade many of the clergymen had watched friends and parishioners depart for cheaper, more fertile land in the new settlements. Sometimes these migrants severed all ties with Connecticut, but often they kept in contact—if only sporadically—with the kinsmen they had left behind. In brief visits or more commonly in letters, many settlers spoke of loneliness 5∟ and isolation, of homesickness and the "moral desolation" of their new surroundings. Concerned for the spiritual welfare of these uprooted folk, the ministers at Mansfield resolved to send missionaries to "ye settlements . . . forming in the Wilderness to the Westward & Northwestward." In making this commitment, the clergy began a new chapter in the history of American Congregationalism.[17]

The Association probably did not fully realize the historical significance of the action. In some ways, the proposal to send missionaries to the frontier was a simple extension of long recognized pastoral responsibilities. Unlike orthodox clergymen of the seventeenth century, who exercised spiritual authority only within their own parishes, eighteenth century ministers could preach and administer the sacraments in neighboring parishes when circumstances warranted. In 1693 a group of ministers published *A Pastor's Power,* which asserted the right of churches without settled ministers to call upon neighboring pastors for baptism and communion. Throughout the eighteenth century Connecticut ministerial associations assumed responsibility for the care of all vacant congregations within their bounds, and routinely appointed ministers to serve in neighboring parishes for brief periods of time.[18]

The proposal to send missionaries to "the scattered back settlements" reflected the same sense of responsibility, but extended the principle far beyond its customary limits. Recognizing that effective missionary action would require some degree of centralized administration and considerable financial support, the clergymen recommended that each orthodox church in Connecticut contribute to a missionary fund to be controlled by an *ad hoc* subcommittee of the General Association. Anticipating a favorable response, the Association selected three ministers to spend five or six months each on missionary tours in the spring of 1775. Never before had Connecticut clergymen envisioned evangelism on such a large scale. The plan represented a sharp departure from the Association's historic hostility toward itinerant preaching.

While the rising revolutionary fervor undoubtedly heightened the

General Association's sense of corporate responsibility, the actual arrival of hostilities created unfavorable conditions for a fledgling missionary campaign. In early 1775 the *rage militaire* overshadowed all other public concerns. In the western district of Fairfield County, for example, the ministerial association voted in the autumn of 1774 to raise the recommended subscription, but by the following summer only a handful of Fairfield people had answered the call. The results were the same in parishes throughout Connecticut. When the General Association convened in June at Norwich, virtually nothing had been accomplished. The three missionaries appointed in the autumn had never embarked upon their tours, and without any mission fund there was no point in selecting replacements. "The perplexed & melancholy state of public affaires," the General Association sadly concluded, "has been a Discouragement to this Design, & a Reason why the Collections have not been brought in, as was expected."[19]

Nonetheless, during the course of the war the Association received occasional donations for the missionary cause, and by 1780, with the fighting in New England for the most part over, the ministers were prepared to try again. That year the Association appointed two missionaries to preach in the new settlements. During the following decade several more Connecticut ministers were sent forth as itinerant evangelists, some commissioned by the General Association and some by their own county associations. Virtually all of these early home missionaries served in western Vermont, a region notorious for "profanity and irreligion."[20] Vermont, more than any other frontier of the Revolutionary Era, symbolized to Connecticut clergymen the danger to orthodoxy posed by the new settlements.

Prior to the 1790s, when central New York was opened to settlement, most Connecticut migrants took up land within the infamous "New Hampshire Grants" between the Connecticut River and Lake Champlain. Between 1749 and 1764 New Hampshire Governor Bennington Wentworth granted three million acres of the future state of Vermont to speculators and settlers, and by 1776 seventy-four new towns had been established in the region. The fertile lands of the Connecticut River Valley attracted the most attention, and quickly filled up with relatively prosperous migrants from the older, established communities of Connecticut. Settlements in the Valley were often laid out to resemble the towns that migrants left behind, and typically they displayed a remarkable degree of social and religious homogeneity. Most settlers in the area felt a strong attachment to the Congregational church, and retained the traditional orthodox vision of tightly-knit covenanted communities. As a result the Connecticut Valley would never be an important mission field;

all but three churches organized in the region prior to 1780 had permanent pastors within two years of their organization.[21]

A different state of affairs prevailed in the hill country of northern Vermont and the townships on the west side of the Green Mountains. These less fertile areas filled up much more slowly, and the settlers tended to be less prosperous than Valley folk. "West siders" from Connecticut generally hailed from the hill towns of Litchfield County. Other west siders came from the Berkshires in western Massachusetts and northern New York, as well as from New Hampshire and Rhode Island. Given their diverse origins and relative poverty, settlers in northern and western Vermont generally displayed less commitment to establishing churches or building covenanted communities. The individual pursuit of wealth was more likely to take precedence over corporate interests. The migrants, one early observer noted, "do not fix near their neighbors and go on regularly, but take spots that please them best, though twenty or thirty miles beyond any others."[22]

As a result western Vermonters tended to suffer more from the effects of displacement and isolation. Most settlements lacked the means to support a permanent orthodox pastor. According to one study of Vermont Congregationalism, the average west side township still had no orthodox church five years after settlement, and lacked regular orthodox preaching for many more years.[23] In such an environment Congregational settlers faced a difficult challenge. They either could look to sectarian preachers for guidance, provide for their own religious observances, or stop attending corporate worship altogether.

Not all Connecticut migrants lamented this situation. Western Vermont attracted many dissenters from New England's Congregational establishments, and well into the nineteenth century missionaries in the region complained of opposition from skeptics, Freewill Baptists, Methodists, Universalists, Episcopalians, and deists. Nathan Perkins, one of the earliest Connecticut missionaries to tour the area, passed through Pownal in 1789 and found "no religion, Rhode Island haters of religion—baptists, quakers, & some presbyterians—no meetinghouse." Perkins, the New Divinity pastor of the church in West Hartford, estimated that roughly one-tenth of the people he encountered on his tour were "quakers and anabaptists—Episcopalians, and universalists." Perhaps another quarter were deists who "would chuse to have no Sabbath no ministers—no religion—no heaven—no hell." Perkins was hardly an objective observer, and he almost certainly exaggerated the numerical strength of the dissenters at that time. Still, his observations underscore the alien quality of the society that was emerging west of the Green Mountains.[24]

Dissenters notwithstanding, many western Vermonters missed the spiritual and emotional support provided by the church, and longed for regular corporate worship and orthodox preaching. Sometimes settlers wrote to their former pastors or to the Connecticut General Association, pleading for assistance. In 1793 a committee of settlers in Monkton, Vermont, sent a typical letter to the Association, urging the clergymen to send more missionaries to the region. They appealed not only on their own behalf, but for all of the "vacant churches . . . scattered up and down in the Northern wilds of Vermont who have . . . been as sheep without a shepherd except temporary supplies which we have occasionally enjoyed."[25] Such letters testify to the unbroken sense of kinship binding emigrants to the relations they left behind, particularly the continued respect and affection many migrants felt for their pastors in Connecticut.

Despite the growth of lay anticlericalism in the eighteenth century, as J. William Youngs, Jr. has observed the bond between the Congregational minister and his flock generally remained a close one. The covenant between the minister and his people was intended, like marriage, to be permanent. To guard against mismatches, pastoral candidates served on probation for months or even years before receiving a call to settle. During this period the candidate and the congregation carefully scrutinized each other; if either felt uncomfortable with the match, ordination did not occur. Generally congregations looked for men who shared their theological and social predilections, and favored candidates who had grown up in the same geographical region. Often prospective ministers had already developed close personal ties with leading townspeople before accepting a call to serve as their shepherd. Once settled, the average clergyman remained with the same flock for more than twenty-five years; many served for half a century.[26] During these years the orthodox minister figured prominently in virtually every significant community event, and shared with his parishioners their most joyous and painful experiences. The affection between the pastor and his people, fostered by this long and intimate familiarity, did not die when migration forced their separation.

For at least some Connecticut emigrants the loss of their shepherd was among the most painful aspects of migration. One woman, on the eve of her departure from North Haven, confessed to her pastor, Benjamin Trumbull, that "it seems hard for me to leave my kind neighbors in general; but more especially to leave so good a minister, whose counsels I have every Sunday." Grateful for his pastoral visits when she was "sick and in distress," the woman bade Trumbull a tearful farewell, praying that "the omnipotent arm of Divine Providence may protect you while in this world . . . and if we should meet no more in this world, may we meet in the world of glory."[27]

Such migrants often experienced terrible alienation once they reached the new settlements. One frontier woman wrote poignantly to a Connecticut minister of her continued affection for the church she had left behind. "I make it my practice to walk alone into a little grove of oakes, and especially on the Sabbath, at the hour I think you are going to the house of God." There, the woman mused, "I think I feel somewhat as the children of Israel did when they hanged their harps on the willows and exclaimed 'If I forget thee, O Jerusalem, let my right hand forget her cunning. If I do not remember thee, let my tongue cleave to the roof of my mouth.'"[28]

Pious settlers could reduce the sense of alienation by meeting together on Sundays for informal worship, and some fortunate villages succeeded in securing the occasional services of licentiates from Connecticut. Licentiates, or ministerial candidates, were essentially apprentice pastors. After completing a brief course of theological training under an ordained minister, young men who felt called to become orthodox clergymen applied to a county ministerial association for a license to preach. Once licensed the licentiate was considered to be a candidate for ordination, and as such was authorized to preach and make family visits. Given the chronic shortage of ministers in eighteenth century America, licentiates generally preached only briefly before receiving a call to settle permanently as pastors.

Some candidates, however, experienced such strong doubts about their calling to the ministry that they wished to postpone ordination. Others were so poorly gifted for the office of pastor that no congregation would call them. Others received calls from congregations that did not suit them. For such men the new settlements offered a perfect opportunity to gain experience and earn a subsistence by "preaching supply" for destitute settlers. As "supply" preachers they could test their aptitude and skills without the risk of permanent commitment. Vermont alone offered dozens of settlements in need of ministers, and many candidates sojourned there at least briefly. A few remained so long that they were virtually professional licentiates. In 1789, near Burlington, Vermont, Nathan Perkins encountered one such case, "an old college acquaintance, a candidate who had preached to 90 vacancies & been a candidate for 18 years."[29]

Migrants sometimes harbored prejudices against licentiates. Most candidates were young men, only a year or so out of college, and they often lacked self-confidence and social maturity. Generally they were unknown to frontier settlers, and not surprisingly they sometimes had difficulty gaining the trust of older church members who might still feel close personal bonds to their own pastors in Connecticut. Nonetheless, candidates could perform invaluable service in the new settlements. Thomas Robbins, one of the earliest missionaries in the Western Reserve of Ohio, began his preaching career as a candidate in western Vermont during the 1790s. Robbins experienced terrible doubts about his call to the ministry, and constantly battled feelings of inadequacy. He found separation from his family and friends almost unbearable, and questioned whether he was providing genuine comfort to the people he visited. But despite his inexperience Robbins developed a close relationship with many Middlebury residents, who continued to seek his spiritual guidance after he returned to Connecticut. "The townspeople," one Vermont friend sadly observed after his departure, no longer assembled together "with that solemnity which attended our meetings when you was with us." Another correspondent, begging Robbins to come back to Middlebury, lamented "the want of what we enjoyed in the summer."[30]

While ministerial candidates like Robbins would always be an essential component of Congregational missionary efforts, they could not adequately meet the spiritual needs of uprooted immigrants. They could not baptize the children of the faithful nor administer the sacrament of communion. Nor could they examine the faith of converts or gather orthodox settlers together into a church. These ecclesiastical rituals, central to the faith and experience of New England Congregationalism, could be performed only by ordained clergymen. Unless more ordained pastors could be sent to the frontier, or unless the regulations governing ordination were altered, few Congregational churches could be planted in the new settlements and many orthodox migrants sooner or later would be forced to abandon the faith of their fathers.

This reality defined to a great extent the objectives of Congregational evangelists in the eighteenth and early nineteenth centuries. Unlike Methodist circuit riders, who concerned themselves primarily with the conversion of souls, the Congregational missionary was passionately dedicated to the preservation and extension of his inherited religious values. Nathan Perkins, for example, hoped to be an instrument for bringing the unregenerate to salvation, but he spent much of his 1789 mission nurturing the faith of those already converted and shepherding them into organized fellowships. The emotional high point of his "Evangelical tour" occurred near Essex, Vermont, where he "gathered & incorporated a church, & admitted a member, and drew ye form of Covenant." The importance of upholding correct doctrines and fostering faithful observance of covenant obligations could not be exaggerated. "I have zealously & uniformly endeavored to hold up ye truth plainly,"

Perkins noted, ". . . & done all I could, in conversation, as well as Sermons, to give ye nature of true Religion;—to impress its duties; to guard from errors;—from superstition & enthusiasm."[31]

Repeatedly during the next two decades Congregational missionary literature stressed the necessity of keeping covenant with kinsmen in the new settlements, upholding the faith of the fathers, and building up the corporate body of Christ. Missions were vital, the Connecticut General Association asserted in 1794, because many frontier folk were "from this state, our neighbors and fellow christians; nay, our sons and daughters." Missionaries would help "to prevent their falling into error, a state of dissipation and forgetfulness of God," as well as to encourage "their good feelings and habits" and to "instruct and animate them, till they shall be able to settle churches and a regular ministry" among themselves.[32] The fear that the children of the twice-born might be robbed of their sacred heritage in the wilds of the frontier constituted the primary motive for the earliest orthodox home missionaries. Congregational evangelists preached the gospel to all who would listen, and earnestly prayed for the salvation of souls, but their most urgent task was to plant new orthodox churches and to sustain the faith of New England migrants in the frontier.

CHAPTER

THREE

The Committee on Missions, 1792–1797

Connecticut pastors had legitimate reasons to worry about the welfare of their townspeople in the new settlements. The isolation and loneliness experienced by many migrants was traumatic, and few licentiates or ordained clergymen were available to minister to their needs. During the 1780s the pressing demand for orthodox preachers in Vermont alone far exceeded the supply of missionaries. When central and western New York opened to settlement in the early 1790s the shortage of Congregational ministers quickly reached crisis proportions. By 1795, the Connecticut General Association estimated that there were already more than two hundred settlements in Vermont, New York, and Pennsylvania where Congregational migrants resided without any orthodox shepherd.[1] Over the next several years, as emigration from New England accelerated, the number of vacant settlements dramatically increased.

The flow of immigrants into New York from Connecticut and Massachusetts was extraordinary. Speculators lured Yankees westward with the promise of rich farmland and easy credit. At a time when farmers in southern New England could expect to pay between fourteen to fifty dollars per acre for even average land, prime New York farm sites could be purchased for as little as two dollars per acre. New York speculators facilitated access to their land by the hasty construction of wagon roads across the state. As early as 1792 the Catskill Turnpike connected Hartford with Wattle's Ferry on the Susquehanna River. From here Connecticut migrants could follow the northern branch of the Susquehanna into the fertile region south of the Finger Lakes, or turn southward into the hills of northern Pennsylvania.[2]

Another important route, the Mohawk Turnpike, gave New England migrants easy access to the Mohawk Valley. Completed between Albany and Utica as early as 1793, the highway was soon extended as far west as Avon and renamed the Great Genesee Road. By 1797 "Genesee Fever" had swept Connecticut and Massachusetts, and one traveler counted almost five hundred wagons a day passing through Albany heading for the promised land in the West.[3]

Congregational leaders struggled to devise a missionary system that could keep pace with this surge of emigration. As they did so they encountered a host of obstacles. Both in Connecticut and in the new settlements they found their efforts challenged by the emergent anti-authoritarian mood of the society, and by the insurgent religious and political groups that post-revolutionary American culture fostered. These challenges forced missionary leaders to plan their actions with an eye toward public opinion, and to revise in subtle ways traditional orthodox assumptions about the ministry and its relationship to the laity and the state.

Recognizing the need for an expanded missionary effort, in 1792 the Connecticut General Association decided to seek state support. In June a committee of ministers petitioned the General Assembly for "a general contribution thro'out the state" to support evangelists in the new settlements. In October of that year Connecticut legislators granted the petition, setting aside the first Sabbath in May for an annual collection "in the several Religious societies and Congregations in this State." The General Assembly instructed the minister or clerk of each Connecticut church to "pay over such contributions to the Reverend Ezra Stiles, Nathan Williams, and Jonathan Edwards," who would appropriate the funds to support "such missionaries as the General Association . . . shall from time to time employ."[4]

Connecticut's dissenting churches were quick to protest the Assembly's action. Critics of the standing order denounced the measure as an assault upon republican liberty, and a shameful example of aristocratic privilege. The Baptist Church in New London, under the leadership of Elder Zadock Darrow, openly defied the state's magistrates. Meeting on April 18, 1793 to consider possible courses of action, the New London Baptists voted unanimously "after considerable conversation" to boycott missionaries appointed by the General Association. While acknowledging that evangelists were desperately needed in the new settlements, the Baptist dissenters insisted that they be selected "in an equal and impartial manner, consistent with the just rights and privileges of mankind."[5]

In a statement published in the *Connecticut Gazette* the New London Baptists proclaimed that they had no choice but to defy the General Assembly. "We cannot, consistently with our principles," they asserted, contribute to support missionaries who "build according to the Saybrook Platform." Denying that civil governors could exercise ecclesiastical authority, Darrow's congregation declared that "our Hon. General Assembly have no right to direct what we shall do, as a religious society; their power extending only to us individually as members of civil society." Expressing a willingness to participate joyfully in any "just" plan to support missionaries, the Baptist group closed with a prayer that Connecticut magistrates might soon "as much regard the distinction between civil and ecclesiastical power, as the greater part of the states in the Union appear to do."

Most of Connecticut's dissenting congregations joined the New London Baptists in their protest. Of the 165 religious societies that donated money for missions in 1793, all but three were Congregational churches. Two dissenting congregations—the Baptist Church in Greenwich and the Episcopal Church in Chelsea—numbered among the smallest contributors in the state. The New London Baptists took up a collection as directed, but voted to retain the funds until "an equal method of appointing . . . missionaries is *recommended* by the authority of this State." All told, Connecticut dissenters contributed barely £1 of the more than £380 raised for the missionary cause.[6]

Opposition to the missionary collection foreshadowed greater challenges to come. In October 1793, the General Assembly passed the controversial Appropriation Act, assigning receipts from the sale of Connecticut's Western Reserve to a perpetual fund. The income generated by this fund was to be appropriated by "the several Ecclesiastical Societies, Churches, or Congregations," to be used for the support primarily of ministers and secondarily of schools. Since the established churches would be the primary beneficiaries of the Appropriation Act, religious dissenters vociferously demanded repeal of the law.[7]

Between 1793 and 1795 an anticlerical coalition of dissenters and disaffected Congregationalists mounted a continuous assault upon the state legislature, and upon the perceived political clout of the orthodox clergy. By May 1795, opposition to the Appropriation Act was so intense that both the Assembly and the more aristocratic Council of Assistants acquiesced in killing the 1793 legislation. In its place they substituted a law earmarking the entire fund for public schools, which had been severed from ecclesiastical control in 1794. If two-thirds of the voters in a school district wished to allocate funds to support the ministry they could petition the legislature for permission to do so. But such funds would be divided among all of the different churches in the district in proportion to their respective memberships.

As James Beasley has noted, the Appropriation Act crystallized the formal organization of an anticlerical faction that would eventually evolve into a strong Republican party. Opposition to the Act united Connecticut dissenters and many insurgent Congregationalists, who disapproved of their clergymen "deviating from their proper line of duty, and assuming that which belongs to the province of others." In the General Assembly the movement for repeal was led by Congregational representatives like Charles Phelps of Stonington, who believed that ministers ought to devote themselves fully to the spiritual needs of their parishioners and leave politics to the peoples' elected representatives. Phelps urged the legislature to "guard against putting power or wealth into the hands of the clergy." This, the anticlericals feared, could only lead to the creation of an independent ministry. Once ministers found themselves "enriched by the funds which . . . were provided for their support," Phelps argued, they would become "negligent, and instead of minding the proper duties of their office," they would be "taken up with useless controversies and altercations." Representative William Judd, a member of Farmington First Congregational Church, agreed with Phelps that the Act would inevitably lead to "ecclesiastical tyranny."[8]

In such a charged political atmosphere state support proved to be a mixed blessing for Congregationalist missionary leaders. On the one hand, legislative backing insured a steady flow of funds for orthodox evangelism through 1795, when the Act mandating annual missionary collections expired. During this period the General Association's Committee on Missions received nearly one thousand dollars in donations from Connecticut churches, and was able to send out more than a dozen evangelists to Vermont, New York and Pennsylvania.[9] On the other hand, missionary leaders opened themselves up to anticlerical assaults upon their motives and goals. Enemies of the standing order construed obligatory missionary collections as proof of an unholy alliance between state lawmakers and the "ecclesiastical tyrants" seeking to create an "independent ministry."

Problems in the political arena were matched by multiplying signs of restiveness closer to home. Even in their own congregations many orthodox clergymen had to contend with growing pockets of anticlerical sentiment. Within the history of New England Congregationalism there had always been a long, honorable tradition of "loyal opposition" to clerical power, and this tendency was increasingly evident during the 1790s.

As Sidney Mead has observed, American churches of every denomination had been characterized from the first by a remarkable degree of lay power. In all of the colonies there had been few ministers during the early years of settlement, and congregations were widely scattered. Only gradually did it become possible for clergymen to organize themselves into conferences, presbyteries, conventions, or county associations. Whatever their polity colonial congregations initially had acted as autonomous bodies, and ministers necessarily had to share governing authority with lay leaders. This reality became a permanent hallmark of colonial religion. In ecclesiastical matters, as in social and political affairs, Americans traditionally exhibited a fierce localism and resisted any attempts to divorce clerical authority from congregational consent.[10]

Colonial Congregational pastors had enjoyed tremendous influence in Connecticut towns, but were nonetheless bound to their people by a sacred covenant which demanded mutual subordination. During the early eighteenth century New England's orthodox clergy briefly acquired a measure of autonomy and began to assume the characteristics of a separate clerical estate. The right to preach the gospel was conferred by ministerial associations, candidates for ordination were examined and recommended by the same bodies, and the ordination ceremony itself came to be performed by the clergy. In many churches the office of ruling elder disappeared, and some ministers pressed for the power to veto decisions reached by congregational meetings. This centralizing tendency, as J. William Youngs, Jr., has noted, was arrested by the Great Awakening, which triggered a dramatic reassertion of lay power and forever undermined any courtly pretensions that the clergy may have harbored.[11]

Thus, even before the Revolution, New England churches were held together by the laity's willingness to freely support their shepherd. Congregational ministers had to rely upon political sagacity and carefully conform to the "peculiar provincialisms" of their parishes in order to maintain their influence. The antiauthoritarianism unleashed by the Revolution only made this task more difficult. Instead of uniting New Englanders around their "sacred heritage," as the clergy had prophesied, the rebellion triggered a widespread revulsion against all traditional sources of authority. As a consequence Congregational pastors found themselves confronted by unprecedented challenges to their leadership during the 1780s and 1790s.

Lay insurgency expressed itself in various ways. Perhaps the most troublesome was the significant increase in clerical dismissals during the years following the war, often for causes that would have seemed trivial or insufficient in colonial America. Although the covenant between a pastor and his people theoretically was as binding and permanent as marriage, congregations in the early republic evinced a new willingness to sever readily their ties with ministers who challenged lay leaders too stridently. Even popular pastors found themselves increasingly at odds with townspeople over financial support, or frustrated by uncompromising opposition from lay leaders. Whenever this occurred ministers generally had only two options: leave town or surrender to their opponents.[12]

Ammi Robbins, one of the first orthodox Connecticut missionaries, was among the many Congregational pastors who confronted this dilemma. In 1793, shortly after returning from a missionary trip through New York, Robbins asked the people of his Norfolk parish to increase his salary. Although he had preached in Norfolk without dissension for thirty-two years and had a large family barely able to live comfortably, "to his great mortification they would not do it." Determined "to carry the matter to the last extremity," Robbins called for a second town meeting to state his case, but after "long debate and great opposition" his request was again denied. The unwillingness of his people to provide "a just recompense" stunned the aging clergyman, who had always enjoyed warm relations with his flock. Nonetheless he acquiesced rather than sever his pastoral relationship with them.[13]

The growth of dissenting communions constituted the single most dramatic expression of grass-roots populism. Although the Congregational churches remained dominant during the 1790s, Baptist numbers increased steadily and Methodist circuit riders routinely invaded the state. The strongly populist message of these denominations appealed to the less affluent segments of Connecticut society and increased the defensiveness of orthodox leaders. The Methodists, who were particularly despised by the Congregational clergy, at first converted relatively few people to their standard, but they frequently addressed large gatherings and may well have exerted a strong influence upon popular religious attitudes. Young people, perhaps, found the Methodist rejection of Calvinism and orthodox tradition especially appealing. Passing through Thompson, Connecticut, in 1795, Francis Asbury noted that "the ancient people are stirred up by the Baptists, and the young ones by the Methodists." Given the antiauthoritarian mood of the times, orthodox ministers like Moses Welch of Mansfield had good reason to fear the influence of "Methodistical stragglers" upon their parishioners. Unless prompt action was taken to meet the threat, Welch feared, the Methodists might gain a secure foothold among "the ignorant—the disaffected—the irreligious, and such as are under chh. censure."[14]

Antiestablishment antagonisms hampered the effectiveness of orthodox missionary efforts. Much of the burden fell upon the shoulders of the six men who served on the General Association's Committee on Missions between 1793 and 1797: Yale President Ezra Stiles; James Dana of New Haven First Church; Jonathan Edwards, Jr. of New Haven North Church; Thomas Wells Bray of North Guilford; Benjamin Trumbull of North Haven; and Nathan Williams of Tolland. All the committee members except Williams ministered in the New Haven vicinity and could conveniently gather together to conduct missionary business between meetings of the General Association. The committee was authorized to collect and disburse missionary funds and to select replacements for ministers who declined missionary appointments. They were also responsible for corresponding with evangelists and responding to petitions for assistance. Most important, however, the committee was to prepare an annual report to the General Assembly and the public, accounting for all expenditures and publicizing the providential blessings that God worked through the Association's missionaries. Thus, in addition to discharging their own pastoral responsibilities, committee members had the task of supervising efficiently the missionary efforts in the new settlements and justifying legislative support in the face of anticlerical criticism. From the outset the committee experienced frustration at every turn.[15]

The General Association determined in June 1793 that missionaries ought to be ordained pastors settled over some Congregational church. While ministerial candidates could preach the gospel they could not gather new churches, "administer the seals of the covenant," or assist with the ordination or installation of ministers. Candidates also lacked the status and prestige associated with the ministerial office, and therefore could not "with so good a grace" impress upon migrants "a sense of the importance of the stated . . . preaching of the gospel and other means of grace," or persuade settlers "to exert themselves to this end."[16]

But to the dismay of the Committee on Missions, more than half of the ministers commissioned by the General Association between 1793 and 1795 declined appointment, and several of those who accepted missions completed only part of their tours. A few ministers cited purely personal reasons for declining missions. Jeremiah Day of New Preston, fifty-six years old and in poor health, feared that the "extremity of winter" would be "too great to encounter at the present stage of my life." Day declined an appointment in 1793, and in 1794 agreed to an abbreviated tour that would not be too "fatiguing." Cyprian Strong of Chatham, also in his fifties, cited the "dependent circumstances" of his family as well as "the ill effect journeying has on me" as grounds for refusal. William Robinson, pastor of the church in Southington, believed that the association's plan violated the biblical principle that evangelists ought to "go out *two* & *two,*" and expressed a willingness to accept a mission only if he could travel with "Mr. Strong of Chatham." Theodore Hinsdale of North Windsor considered the call to preach "to those who sit in comparative darkness" an important matter, but concluded that the proposed compensation of 4.5 dollars per week was insufficient.[17]

In many cases, however, ministers declined appointment because they faced opposition from their own parishioners. Often they feared that their absence would strengthen the hand of schismatics or promote the growth of sectarianism. Moses Welch wanted to undertake a mission but encountered "general opposition" from his people. "For a year or two past," Welch explained to the younger Jonathan Edwards, Methodist troublemakers had been "hovering round one quarter of the Parish; and are at this time making great exertions to gather a chh." The "most judicious" men in his Mansfield parish agreed that Welch could more effectively "prevent the inroad of the enemy" than could a temporary pulpit supply.[18]

Azel Backus, a young New Divinity preacher serving his second year as pastor of the Bethlehem Church, was "determined to enter on the business" but soon found a "small portion of my own people extremely bitter against my complying." Backus's predecessor, the famous New Divinity leader Joseph Bellamy, had alienated some parishioners by his frequent absences to preach in other churches, as well as his passionate attachment to strict pure church principles. The force of Bellamy's charismatic personality and his tremendous prestige helped to preserve an uneasy unity within the Bethlehem church during his lifetime, but with his death in 1789 his opponents seized the opportunity to assert themselves. Young Backus, inexperienced and unable to command the respect accorded to Bellamy, was poorly equipped to wage battle for control of his congregation. The insurgents talked "loud of the itineration of my predecessor at parish expense," the young clergyman sadly informed Edwards, "and seem disposed to make it a point of conscience to hinder my going." While the leading church members strongly supported their new shepherd, "matters being thus . . . I think it my duty to give a positive denial."[19]

Noah Merwin of Washington and Samuel Nott of Franklin also wished to go on missions, but they found their way blocked by opposition at home. Nott's church and society "were both unanimously opposed" to his leaving, and he concluded that he was "not called in providence to go." Three-fourths of Merwin's people "manifested a willingness that I should go the proposed tour," but the remainder were hostile to the plan. Merwin feared that "the uneasiness would be such if I went, that it is not advisable for me to go."[20]

New Light ministers like Backus, Merwin, and Nott were torn between conflicting commitments. On the one hand the "destitution" of the new settlements and their own evangelical convictions strongly pulled them toward missionary action. On the other hand they wished to remain faithful to the New England Way, with its ideal of a permanent, settled ministry. Between their obligation to be faithful shepherds and their desire to keep covenant with emigrants, where did the path of duty run? Virtually all Connecticut pastors had friends and relatives in the new settlements who longed for assistance from home. Yet at the same time parishes throughout the state seemed to be racked with dissension and threatened by subversion. Never before had it seemed more essential for pastors to remain close to their people at home. In their replies to the Committee on Missions, Connecticut's orthodox clergymen repeatedly registered their confusion: which calling ought they to heed? What did God expect them to do?

William Lyman, the young pastor of the Millington Society in East Haddam, poignantly expressed their dilemma. Lyman earnestly wished to enter upon "the glorious undertaking," and informed Edwards that nothing in his domestic situation stood in his way. Many of his closest friends believed that he was morally obligated to go to the new settlements, and urged him to accept a mission. But still, he confessed, he "puzzled much over his duty." The Millington congregation had recently enjoyed unusual "seriousness," and several members insisted that "they in a peculiar manner need my counsel & assistance & more than ever look to me for instruction." Although Lyman considered this to be a "groundless" objection, he feared "an alienation . . . of the people's affections from their minister" should he leave against their wishes. "Ought I or any minister for the sake of going abroad four months," Lyman asked Edwards, "run the hazard of this among the people with whom I am connected for life, when the prospect is threatening?"[21]

Most ministers, when confronted with this dilemma, chose to decline the call to mission. Their refusal left the committee in a difficult position. What was to be done with the money donated to the General Association for missionary work? One possibility was to employ licentiates, who could at least preach the gospel and visit lonely settlers. Nathan Williams believed that the committee "should send candidates, provided a sufficient number of gentlemen already appointed cannot be obtained." In a letter to Benjamin Trumbull, Williams noted that several influential members of the General Association concurred with his opinion. But clearly most clergymen opposed the use of candidates, not wishing to spend their limited resources on evangelists who could not fulfill the Association's primary mission objectives.[22]

Another alternative was to employ ordained ministers who had recently been dismissed from their pastoral charges. But in the 1790s, despite their increasing numbers, such men still had difficulty overcoming the stigma attached to clerical dismissal. Settled pastors often regarded dismissed men suspiciously, even when they came properly recommended by a ministerial association or presbytery. Although dismissed ministers were available to serve as General Association missionaries, none were appointed by the Committee on Missions.

The committee's ambivalence toward dismissed ministers was clearly reflected by Edwards in a 1796 letter to Trumbull. The Reverend Nathan Strong of Hartford urged the committee to appoint "Mr. Daggett from Long Island," a Presbyterian preacher who recently had been dismissed from his congregation. Edwards, himself recently dismissed from his own New Haven parish, confessed to Trumbull that he "knew of no objection against his appointment, but that he's a dismissed minister." Considering the crisis, Edwards reflected, the committee should probably utilize men like Daggett: "When the alternative is put, shall we send a dismissed minister of good credentials or let the service go unperformed, I have no hesitation which to prefer." Nonetheless, the clergyman feared that reliance upon dismissed pastors would likely lower the overall "character" of the missionaries, and he left the appointment of Daggett to the discretion of Trumbull and the other members. Significantly, the committee gave no further consideration to Strong's recommendation.[23]

The shortage of acceptable missionaries created numerous difficulties for the committee. Most obviously, it meant that many petitions for assistance went unanswered and that the cause of orthodox Congregationalism suffered in the new settlements. Orthodox migrants, who often received visits from unlearned, "irregular" preachers, must have lost at least some of their attachment to their inherited religious traditions when their urgent appeals to the Connecticut General Association appeared to fall upon deaf ears.

But the shortage of missionaries also exacerbated the committee's public relations problem at home. Each year between 1793 and 1797 Connecticut citizens donated to the General Association far more money than the committee was able to spend. This embarrassing chronic surplus of funds made it more difficult to justify continued legislative support for missions, and added fuel to anticlerical charges. Although the annual committee reports detailed the causes for the surplus, such assurances did not altogether allay popular concerns about the creation of a financially independent ministry.

Missionary leaders paid attention to anticlerical agitation. By early 1795, half a decade before the full-blown development of the Jeffersonian Party, the Committee on Missions already doubted the reliability of political support for orthodox evangelism. Believing that their request for additional legislative assistance would be rejected by the General Assembly, the committee drafted an address to frontier settlers, warning them that in the future they would have to "see to their own spiritual needs more or less." Responding to attacks upon their motives, the committee assured migrants that Congregational missionary efforts were "strictly benevolent," and lamented the anticipated withdrawal of state support. As a consequence, the clergymen advised, the laity in the new settlements would have to take upon themselves the task of religious leadership. "Strictly observe the Sabbath," the address urged, "constantly assemble yourselves on that holy day . . . and unite in prayer and praises, in reading the scriptures and the best sermons you can obtain." Wherever they traveled in 1795, the Connecticut missionaries sadly informed settlers that aid from home would soon cease.[24]

Anxiety about the loss of state support proved to be premature. Despite the animosity triggered by the Appropriation Act controversy, the General Assembly voted to extend legislative aid for an additional three years. State-mandated missionary collections continued to be raised each year in Connecticut until 1825, long after disestablishment of the Congregational churches had at last become a constitutional fact. Nonetheless, public opinion in the 1790s was already sufficiently divided to make the state assembly an unpredictable friend. In the wake of the repeal of the Appropriation Act, legislative backing could never be taken for granted, and orthodox leaders could not ignore the possibility that public opinion might swing against them.

By the late 1790s missionary leaders knew that "the people" were a force to be reckoned with. Several months after the Assembly voted to renew state backing, Jonathan Edwards, Jr. reflected upon the need to soothe antiestablishment resentment. Despite the difficulties in securing missionaries, he warned Benjamin Trumbull, the committee had to find some way "to get the service done." Missionary leaders, Edwards observed, had at their disposal more than £450 in public donations. "If this large sum be dead in the hands of the committee or they enjoy the interest, the public will justly clamour."[25]

In 1798 missionary leaders sought to bypass the more democratic Assembly in their bid for state support, and quickly learned that the public could not be ignored. Seeking a charter for a newly created state missionary society, the General Association petitioned the more aristocratic Council of Assistants alone. To Benjamin Trumbull's "great mortification" the request was "totally rejected." Although every Council member supported the proposal, they correctly recognized that for "them to grant the petition without the other house of Assembly would occasion disgust in the members of that house, and tend to disaffect the people in general."[26]

Such experiences underscored the changing political climate of New England. The Congregational clergy could no longer assume political support for their plans, even among magistrates who were over-whelmingly orthodox in faith. Missionary leaders were beginning to learn the importance of public relations. In republican America, Nathan Hatch has noted, leaders could not claim automatic authority based upon education, status, or ordination. Influence increasingly depended upon the ability to inspire and maintain popular confidence.[27]

II

The post-revolutionary crisis in public authority was even more apparent to the men who served as missionaries in the new settlements. As holders of a dignified office they were accustomed to receiving respectful treatment; yet in the wilderness to the north and west they often found themselves scorned and held up to public ridicule. Although most settlers welcomed them warmly, they found everywhere anticlerical critics who opposed their efforts. They also discovered a shocking ignorance of orthodox doctrines and a perverse apathy toward covenant obligations among many New England migrants. Moreover, the missionaries experienced at first hand what could only be an abstraction to the committee back in New Haven: the frontier was vast and the vacant settlements seemingly numberless. Perhaps most ominously, to whatever mission field they were sent, they found the ground already occupied by zealous sectarian preachers who were energetically turning settlers away from the faith of their fathers.

The men who confronted these dismal circumstances seem to have been predisposed to evangelistic work by their education and theological orientation. The available biographical information on the thirteen missionaries employed by the General Association between 1793 and 1795 suggests that all of them were New Lights. All thirteen pastored "pure churches" which demanded evidence of regeneration of those seeking admission to communion. At least four had been students of Joseph Bellamy. Most remarkably, seven belonged to a tight-knit circle of Edwardsean pastors from Litchfield County, a region notorious for its New Divinity proclivities. The remaining six missionaries came from six different counties, and were the sole representatives from their respective associations to accept appointment.[28]

The predominance of Litchfield pastors in the early missionary movement was not by design. Neither the General Association nor the Committee on Missions appears to have adhered to any theological litmus test in making mission appointments. None of the committee members came from Litchfield County. Although Edwards, Trumbull, and Williams all embraced Edwardsean theology, Ezra Stiles, who played an active role on the committee until his death in 1795, was hostile to the New Divinity. James Dana, an Old Light who served on the committee throughout its existence, was a sometimes bitter adversary of the younger Edwards and the state's New Divinity preachers, who charged him with Arminianism and other doctrinal errors.[29]

It seems likely, therefore, that a process of self-selection accounts for the unusual support that these Litchfield pastors gave to the cause. It is reasonable to suppose that their evangelical convictions inclined the Litchfield circle to accept missionary appointments, and that the close personal bond between them reinforced their commitment to the cause and made it easier for them to secure temporary supply preaching while they were away from home. Perhaps, too, Litchfield congregations, which were being heavily depleted by the migration to Vermont and New York, were unusually eager to send their ministers to visit kinfolk in the new settlements. William Lyman observed in 1803 that congregations in northwestern Connecticut were less "monopolizing" of their ministers than churches in the south and east, and much more likely to be "reconciled to the temporary absence of their Pastors . . . for missionary purposes."[30]

Despite their enthusiasm for the cause, the missionaries employed by the General Association quickly became frustrated by their inability to effectively complete the duties assigned to them. The committee expected each missionary to perform the full range of pastoral responsibilities incumbent upon settled Congregational pastors. Their written instructions directed them to "gather churches, catechize children, ordain ministers, administer sacraments and discharge all ministerial duties as occasion might require." In addition they were also to gather detailed information about each settlement they visited, so that the committee could plan future missions more effectively. Since the General Association lacked any clear idea of the number or location of the various new settlements, each missionary was assigned a broad geographical region and vaguely directed to minister in whatever settlements he encountered.[31]

The mission field assigned to each missionary was far too large to cover thoroughly in the four months allotted for each tour. Samuel Ells, for example, was directed to visit the "various towns north and south of the Mohawk River" and all towns "northwestward towards Lake Ontario as far as there are any." Aaron Kinne's tour from "Whitestown through all the Genesee Country as far as Tioga Point" involved a round trip of more than thirteen hundred miles. All the missionaries soon discovered, as

Kinne informed the committee, that the new settlements were far "more numerous than had been suspected."[32]

Faced with this reality each missionary had to make a difficult decision. They could proceed slowly, concentrating upon the most important settlements, and linger long enough in each place to visit families, catechize children, comfort the ill or dying, attempt to gather a church and perform "all ministerial duties." Alternatively, they could move more quickly, visiting as many settlements as possible, and focus their energy upon preaching the gospel and gathering information for the Committee on Missions.

Most of the missionaries chose to follow faithfully their instructions to gather churches and shepherd settlers, a decision that limited the number of towns they could reach. Most of them also chose to divide their four month mission into two shorter tours, an arrangement that further reduced the time they had to itinerate on mission ground.[33] As a consequence towns that showed the brightest prospects for supporting a church received the most attention from the missionaries, while many other settlements received only a single brief visit or were bypassed altogether.

The earliest Congregational missionaries and their Methodist competitors clearly had differing priorities. Methodist preachers typically moved quickly from settlement to settlement, preaching the gospel wherever they found an audience. Wherever enough converts existed they would organize a Methodist class, and then leave it to the local class leaders to manage the day-to-day affairs of the church.

Congregational evangelists instead concentrated upon the myriad pastoral duties of their office. Unlike the Methodists, they seldom preached daily. Ammi Robbins, for example, visited sick people on his Mohawk Valley tour, administered communion, attended the ordination of a minister at Clinton and delivered the ordination sermon. He visited schools, "catechized children at six times and places," and "attended numerous religious conferences," but preached only "eighteen or twenty times."[34]

Samuel Ells also made it a point to visit families, baptize babies, and administer communion during his tour of upstate New York. He spent nearly a week at Whitestown gathering a church, and upon the invitation of the Indians at New Stockbridge took time to arbitrate a schism between the followers of white missionary John Sergeant and a rival faction who looked to the leadership of the native preacher John Occam. After "careful investigation & council," Ells instructed the members of each congregation to publicly ask forgiveness of God and each other. Then, having examined privately each church member "on points of faith and doctrine," he "constituted them one church." Before leaving New Stockbridge, Ells drafted Articles of Faith for the newly unified church and led the people "to a new choice of Mr. Sergeant as their minister."[35]

Such pastoral commitments consumed most of the missionaries' limited time. David Huntington, pastor of the Congregational church in Marlborough, Connecticut, devoted so much energy to these various ministerial responsibilities that in four months he covered only as much territory as some missionaries managed to visit in half the time. Touring the settlements along the Susquehanna River in New York and Pennsylvania, he visited the sick and dying, attended many funerals, performed fifty baptisms, and examined nearly eighty candidates for communion.[36] In Walton, New York, where he lingered long enough to gather a forty-two member church, many townspeople became deeply attached to him. A letter from a Walton committee assured the General Association that Huntington had diligently followed his written instructions. With "the greatest plainness and . . . tenderness and love to the souls of men," the settlers reported, the missionary "preached the Gospel of salvation publicly and from house to house." He privately examined "professors" of religion, organized a church, administered the Lord's Supper, "and gave advice and direction to the Flock." He "did also catechize and instruct the youth in this place," the committee wrote, "and endeavor to teach them the right way of life." Grateful for his attention, the people of Walton considered Huntington "in some sense as an Apostle to them, and are willing to own him tho' not their immediate Bishop."[37]

Examples

Huntington successfully established a strong Congregational church in Walton, but his approach left him with time to visit only a few other principal settlements. Aaron Kinne, pastor of the church in Groton, favored a different tactic. Kinne, believing that he had been called "to encourage the religious people wherever they might be and reach as many as possible," thought it best to dispense with time-consuming pastoral responsibilities. Because roads were poor in western New York, and horses scarce, many settlers were not able to travel far to hear missionary sermons. Kinne attempted as much as possible to carry the gospel to the people, a decision that required him to concentrate upon preaching and to move quickly. Unlike Huntington, who traveled less than eight hundred miles and preached less than fifty sermons in four months, Kinne logged more than thirteen hundred miles and delivered well over one hundred sermons during his tour.[38]

David Higgins of Lyme also preferred to travel quickly on his tour of northern Vermont, but would linger longer in settlements where the people strongly entreated him to stay. "I made it my general practice to go to a place & give information who I was & upon what business I came," he reported, "& leave it with the people to proceed according to their own feelings." On the one hand Higgins wished to avoid "the appearance of forcing my services upon the people contrary to their wishes." On the other hand he did not want to be "so hasty in my rout as not to . . . serve them as much as was thought expedient." Higgins believed that "the gospel is of sufficient value to recommend itself," and that it was therefore wrong "to tarry in a place longer than a day and give one lecture unless I was particularly requested by the people." Settlers who did not welcome missionary preaching when it was offered to them freely, Higgens observed to Benjamin Trumbull, "were unworthy of it." Under this system the young missionary preached as many as seven or eight times in some towns, but in many other places he preached only once.[39]

Under the circumstances no approach proved to be fully satisfactory. Regardless of how they proceeded the missionaries alienated some settlers. If they moved slowly they could cultivate personal relationships with migrants, answer objections or doubts about orthodox doctrines raised by sectarian preachers, and more easily establish stable Congregational churches in the settlements they visited. At the same time, however, they engendered disappointment among the inhabitants of the neighboring towns that they bypassed, and left many Congregational settlers without spiritual support from ministers of their own order. If they proceeded quickly they could provide at least a modicum of encouragement to a much larger number of orthodox settlers, but could not as effectively lay the foundation for the introduction of a settled Congregational clergy. Only properly covenanted churches could call a pastor, but congregations could not covenant together without the assistance of an ordained minister. Even under ideal conditions the gathering of a new orthodox church sometimes involved a slow, cumbersome process. In the new settlements, where conditions were far from ideal, missionaries generally could not accomplish the task in the course of a brief visit.

Indeed, as Ammi Robbins discovered, it was sometimes impossible to organize new churches even when extensive time and energy were devoted to the effort. Passing through Whitesburg, New York, in July 1793, Robbins preached a sermon and baptized the children of those settlers who had previously "owned the covenant" in some orthodox church. Many townspeople, including a large number who were not "professors" of religion, urged Robbins to organize a church so "that they may be prepared for settling a minister." Robbins agreed, but faithful to his pure church principles, he "was determined not to gather a ch. if not visibly clean." Following a process established by his New England forefathers, he convened a meeting of all the professors and "examined them one by one." Satisfied with the orthodoxy and apparent piety of the twenty-eight settlers who submitted themselves for examination, Robbins presented them with an appropriate covenant and confession of faith, "to which they mostly consented." The missionary then exhorted them "to become acquainted with one another," and if after several days they still expressed a united desire to be joined together as one body, "a day would be appointed to form a chh."[40]

The process followed by Robbins, as well as the other Congregational missionaries, clearly reflected the persistence of such traditional Puritan values as unity, consensus, and harmony. In frontier regions of the republic, however, it was difficult to establish churches based upon such values. The settlers of Whitesburg, like the settlers of many western communities, had migrated from different towns and states, and were still relative strangers when Robbins visited them. Not surprisingly, those who professed faith scrutinized each other carefully and proceeded with great caution in covenanting together.

To Robbins's great disappointment, discord quickly appeared as the Whitesburg professors became acquainted with each other. Three days after he drafted the covenant he again "visited from house to house," encouraging the people to openly share their sentiments. At a conference held later that night disturbing rumors surfaced and Robbins began to doubt the propriety of gathering a church in the town. Over the following week he convened several more conferences, but at each one the professors "appeared much divided," and "objections were raised respecting the moral conduct of some." After nearly two weeks of discouragement Robbins at last gave up the attempt, and exhorted "them to labor to have all difficulties removed as speedily as possible" so that a church might be gathered at some "better prepared time."[41]

The failure of Robbins and the orthodox professors to form a church greatly disappointed many Whitesburg inhabitants. Throughout his stay Robbins received a stream of visitors—many of them unchurched—who were "all anxious about the ch."[42] Surely these citizens, determined to obtain regular stated preaching in Whitesburg, must have grown impatient with the slow, methodical process required to gather a "pure church," and were probably highly susceptible to the message of the "sectarian" preachers Robbins encountered on his tour.

All of the missionaries agreed that the absence of Congregational churches left New England migrants more open to new doctrines and modes of worship. Wherever they went the missionaries found preachers of other denominations energetically proselytizing Congregational settlers. Samuel Ells lamented that in the Mohawk Valley between Schenectady and Fort Stanwick, the only ministers were "laymen under the profession of Baptists, Separates, & Methodists." These "illiterate

preachers," Ells warned, "were busy and using every art" to pull orthodox settlers away from their attachment to Congregationalism, "and in
some places they did so more than others." Ells hoped that the appearance of orthodox ministers would "save those settlements from the bad
effects of such doctrines & practices which these men especially the
Methodists had advanced."[43]

Aaron Kinne reported that in the Genesee country most professors
appeared to be orthodox, but the Baptists clearly were increasing rapidly.
Jeremiah Day, who itinerated along the Susquehanna and Delaware
rivers in southern New York and Pennsylvania, also found most of the
settlers to be "Presbyterians according to the New England and Kirk
forms." But orthodox migrants often united in worship with settlers who
were "Baptists, or Methodists, or Universalists," as well as those who
followed "the Hierarchy of Holland." Day, like Ells, was distressed that
Congregationalists in the region had no settled orthodox ministers to
guide them, while "Illiterate Baptist preachers are pretty plenty" and
"itinerant and circular" Methodists made frequent visits to settlements
throughout the region.[44]

In their assessment of sectarian gains, the missionaries consistently
employed what might be called a "supply-side" analysis. Baptists and
Methodists made inroads, they believed, simply because they had more
ministers in the new settlements and could therefore reach more people.
Their outlook has at least some support from the findings of recent
studies on the Second Great Awakening. Terry Bilhartz, in a study of
early national Baltimore, concludes that the Methodists prospered primarily because they evangelized more aggressively than other denominations. "Religious change," Bilhartz rightly observes, "was as related to
the dynamics of the transmitters of evangelical religion as to the psyches
of the receivers."[45]

This assessment conflicts with the "demand-side" interpretation offered by historians like Nathan Hatch, who find evidence of a mass
popular movement against Calvinism and the genteel orthodox clergy.
Where Hatch regards early republican culture as fundamentally incom-
patible with orthodoxy, Connecticut missionaries were confident that the
crisis confronting them was organizational rather than theological in
nature. "A considerable proportion of the people" adhered to the Baptists, Jeremiah Day reported, "because they rarely can have any other
preaching." Day claimed to have conversed with Baptist converts who
thought that "the children of believers had a right to baptism," but who
nonetheless "joined themselves to that sect because there was no other
religious community to which they could unite." As for the Methodists,
Day was certain that most people were "captivated more by their appar-

ent zeal, and address to the passions, than from an attachment to their peculiar sentiments." If the "people of various sects enjoy settled orthodox ministers, who were friendly to experimental religion," Day informed Jonathan Edwards, Jr., "I believe they would . . . prefer them to their present establishments."[46]

Day's assessment, although perhaps overly optimistic, nonetheless accurately reflected a reality of frontier religion that is too often overlooked by modern scholarship: denominational attachments were often determined as much by necessity or circumstance as by theological considerations. Until frontier communities grew large and wealthy enough to support multiple rival churches, settlers generally attended whatever religious services were available to them. In most cases they cordially welcomed any evangelists who would visit them, and listened attentively to preachers of all doctrinal positions. This attitude of openness often frustrated orthodox missionaries like David Higgins, who in 1795 complained ruefully that Vermonters would listen to whatever "wretched characters" came among them, "even strangers . . . not properly recommended."[47] But the same openness could prove just as threatening to Baptist and Methodist leaders, who sometimes voiced similar worries when Congregational shepherds appeared among the people. As we shall see in a later chapter, orthodox ministers could also be adept at winning popular favor, and were able to proselytize successfully among settlers who had attached themselves to the more "democratic" sects.

Even so, Congregational preachers encountered strong opposition in some settlements. The missionaries typically identified their detractors as "infidels and deists" or as "skeptics." Some critics, however, were undoubtedly anticlerical Christians, motivated by an intense hatred of New England's religious establishment and the supposedly "aristocratic" orthodox clergy. Missionaries in New York apparently encountered such opposition only in a handful of towns, such as Catskill and Tioga Point, where large numbers of poor Universalists were concentrated. But Asahel Hooker and Cotton Mather Smith, who toured northern and western Vermont, felt the sting of anticlerical hecklers repeatedly, and even found themselves vilified in local newspapers. So venomous were the attacks upon Hooker and Smith that loyal Congregationalists in several Vermont towns sent apologies to the Connecticut General Association, expressing their "mortification" that anything should have been done or said to discourage orthodox missionaries in the region.[48]

Some of the most stinging attacks upon Hooker and Smith were launched by John C. Ogden, a combative Episcopal missionary who possessed a virtually boundless hatred for the Congregational clergy. Described by a biographer as "a pillar of nascent Republicanism,"

Ogden did much to establish the Jeffersonian myth of the orthodox priest-politician. Throughout the 1790s he assailed the supposedly hidden designs of the Connecticut missionaries in Vermont, who were motivated, he charged, solely by the desire to extend the power and wealth of the Connecticut standing order. In 1798 the irascible cleric secured a national audience for his crusade against Connecticut orthodoxy when Jeffersonian editor William Duane published several Ogden diatribes in the Anti-Federalist Philadelphia *Aurora*. It was Ogden who first identified "Pope Timothy Dwight" of Yale as the leader of the conspiratorial "New England Illuminati," a charge destined to become a permanent feature of republican folklore.[49]

Ogden relished direct confrontation with his foes, and missed few opportunities to antagonize them. When Ezra Stiles died in 1795, the Episcopal gadfly penned a gleeful letter of "condolence" to Benjamin Trumbull, expressing his hope that the Yale Presidency might now fall to a "man of candor, whose bigotry will not violate the laws of his country & the duties of Christian charity." Ogden also took aim at Jonathan Edwards, Jr., suggesting that his dismissal from his pastoral charge had undoubtedly been providential. The unemployed divine, he observed, might now go "as an Apostle or Patriarch" to establish a "colony of Hopkintonians" in the Connecticut Western Reserve. There, the Episcopalian gibed, his pure church principles would "as usual increase deists and anabaptists," and provide an ideal opening for Episcopal missionary efforts in the region. The bigoted Dr. Edwards, Ogden concluded, "has been so excellent a recruiting officer for the church in New Haven, that Episcopalians must wish him prosperity."[50]

Shortly after his arrival in Vermont, Asahel Hooker received a visit from Ogden, who had recently blasted Congregational missionaries in a Bennington newspaper article under the pseudonym "Vermonters." Ogden suggested to Hooker that he would gladly accept a commission from the Connecticut General Association to itinerate in Vermont. Given his familiarity with the people and his presence on the ground, he asserted, he would make an ideal recipient for the funds donated by Connecticut citizens for the missionary cause. When the dumbfounded Hooker accused him of hypocrisy, Ogden erupted in fury. Leaping from his chair, "and standing on his tip-toes, with hands extended and head . . . falling a little backwards," he ordered Hooker to "inform the Genl. Assoc. *that he was ready to meet them on any ground.*"[51]

Hooker mistakenly dismissed Ogden as a "prodigy of pomposity, self-importance, and bigoted attachment to his own denomination." Few Vermonters, he assured the committee in New Haven, paid any attention to Ogden's accusations against Connecticut missionaries.[52] Yet the repeated insults hurled at Congregational itinerants in Vermont suggested otherwise. Although John C. Ogden may well have been as bigoted as any orthodox divine, as Asahel Hooker observed, he was also an immensely popular Jeffersonian polemicist. There were undoubtedly many settlers who regarded him as an earnest champion of republican liberty.

In 1794, while touring Connecticut, Francis Asbury read "a most severe letter from a citizen of Vermont . . . striking at the foundation and principle of the hierarchy, and the policy of Yale College, and the Independent Order." It is very possible that Asbury had come upon one of Ogden's pieces. Whatever the authorship, the Methodist apostle found the essay enormously inspiring. "It was," he noted in his diary, "expressive of the determination of the Vermonters to continue free from ecclesiastical fetters, to follow the Bible, and give liberty, equal liberty, to all denominations of professing Christians." If such was indeed the case, Asbury reflected, "why may not the Methodists (who have been repeatedly solicited) visit these people also?"[53]

That many rational citizens could share the views of John C. Ogden, a man whom Benjamin Trumbull regarded as self-evidently "wicked and foolish," was cause for concern.[54] Connecticut missionary leaders could hardly ignore mounting public hostility toward the standing order at home and the multiplication of populist sectarian preachers in the new settlements. Clearly, an increasingly vocal segment of the American populace was determined to revolutionize both church and state.

Nonetheless, orthodox leaders remained optimistic. They were confident that a more effective system of evangelism could successfully establish a strong orthodox presence in America's "desert places," and that most New England migrants would continue to support the faith of their fathers if given the opportunity. In order to provide settlers with that opportunity, however, it would be necessary to increase the supply of ordained ministers, a task which demanded some alteration in the traditional orthodox understanding of polity. Also, it would be essential to find alternative ways to fund Congregational evangelism, freeing missionary leaders from dependence upon unpredictable political supporters. In 1797 and 1798, filled with an urgent determination to spread the kingdom of Christ, Connecticut Edwardseans overhauled the state's missionary apparatus, and launched a new phase of the Congregational missionary movement.

CHAPTER

FOUR

The Connecticut Missionary Society

When the General Association of Connecticut convened at the Congregational meetinghouse in Windham in June 1797, an atmosphere of expectancy pervaded the gathering. For several years evangelicals in both England and America had been praying fervently for a general revival of God's people. Now, many New Light ministers believed, an awakening was at hand. From across the ocean came stirring news of wondrous missionary advances in Africa and the South Seas, while at home unusual "seriousness" seemed evident among many congregations throughout the state. New Divinity stalwart Charles Backus of Somers reported the commencement of "a great work" among his people, triggered, he believed, by a series of "sermons upon the inspiration of the scriptures." In April word arrived of a "considerable awakening" in New York City, followed within weeks by missionary Seth Williston's report of a marvelous outpouring of God's Spirit in the Chenango settlements. These developments fired the imagination of New Lights and fueled millennial hopes that transformed the budding missionary movement.[1]

Millennial expectancy led Congregational missionary leaders to view their task in a broader global context. Prior to 1797 the annual *Narratives* published by the Committee on Missions concentrated solely upon the need to provide orthodox guidance to uprooted New England migrants. Then, in 1797, the committee introduced a strongly millennial rationale for missions, noting the "remarkable union of different denominations in England and Scotland for the propagation of the gospel among the heathen." Such examples, the committee observed, should inspire Connecticut churches to work for the "extension of Christianity" so that "the Redeemer's Kingdom may come."[2]

Connecticut New Lights had always been sensitive to religious developments in Britain. Eighteenth-century Calvinist evangelicals on both sides of the Atlantic, Susan O'Brien has observed, "were highly conscious of one another's activities." During the Great Awakening of the mid-eighteenth century, New England ministers shared revival news with correspondents in Britain, and received in return reports of the powerful evangelical revivals in England, Wales, and Scotland. Through the exchange of ideas and information Calvinist clergymen forged a "transatlantic community of saints" that powerfully influenced the development of American missions.[3]

The establishment of a United Concert for Prayer was perhaps the single most important fruit of this transatlantic network. Prior to the 1740s it was commonplace for British and American clergymen to set aside fast days for the revival of religion, but these observances were not coordinated and each congregation acted independently. During the early 1740s evangelical ministers in Scotland began to coordinate their fast days, and in October 1744 they invited American and English clergymen to join them in an international United Concert for Prayer. The Scottish proposal called upon congregations and individuals to commit themselves to monthly and quarterly times in which to pray for a universal revival of religion. The plan proved popular both in Britain and America, where New Light clergymen gave it enthusiastic support. Jonathan Edwards, for example, boosted the Concert in 1747 in his *Humble Attempt to Promote Explicit Agreement and Visible Union of God's People in Extraordinary Prayers,* a widely read tract that inspired evangelicals in both England and America throughout the eighteenth century.[4]

The United Concert for Prayer helped to create an international evangelical movement. When believers gathered together to pray for revivals, they did so with a heightened awareness that they were part of a global body. Pastors typically reinforced this sensibility by reading foreign correspondence or published revival narratives during Concert meetings, so that people could focus their prayers upon concrete events hundreds or even thousands of miles away. The Concert created a mass transatlantic audience for religious information, and fostered the impression that a remarkable global outpouring of the Holy Spirit was at hand. Revivals in even remote villages soon entered the consciousness of evangelicals throughout the Anglo-American world, and became the common concern of all praying believers. Through their earnest petitions, it seemed, Christians everywhere could personally contribute to the great awakening of religion.[5]

During the 1760s and 1770s interest in the United Concert temporarily waned, but in 1784 a group of Northamptonshire English Baptists revived the movement after reading Edwards's *Humble Attempt*. Unlike the original Concert, which appeared on the heels of powerful revivals in Britain and America, the call for a renewed concert for prayer preceded any notable revivals, and was in fact one of the chief signals to Anglo-American Calvinists that a second "awakening" was at hand. The resuscitation of the concert once again created a transatlantic network of evangelicals committed to praying and working for an awakening of God's people, and generated an international demand for news of revival or portents of revival.[6]

The "prayer call of 1784" had a great impact upon the development of Anglo-American missionary work. William Carey, the English Baptist evangelist, claimed the United Concert as his inspiration when in 1792 he organized the Baptist Missionary Society to carry the gospel to Africa and Asia. The London Missionary Society, created in 1795 by a coalition of evangelical Independents, Episcopalians and Presbyterians, also drew inspiration from the Prayer Call and the millennial expectancy generated by the Concert.[7]

New England Calvinists followed these developments closely. Although it is unclear precisely where or when the monthly concert was first revived in the United States, by the close of 1794 New Lights in at least some Connecticut towns had adopted the observance. On October 8, 1794 the North Hartford Association recommended that churches throughout the state unite in a "general concert . . . for a revival of religion."[8] The prayer concert initiated in North Hartford probably contributed to the brief revival of religion that broke out in Hartford's two Congregational churches in that month, an event that stirred the millennial hopes of the state's Edwardsean clergy. "Have you heard of the remarkable seriousness & attention at Hartford—very extraordinary," Ammi Robbins wrote to his son Thomas. "O, that a secure stupid land might be aroused—Tis easy for God to open the Eyes of men tho' even so fast closed."[9]

Robbins, confident that the Hartford revival had been sparked by the Concert for Prayer, eagerly commenced monthly prayer conferences in his own Norfolk parish. "Antecedent to a revival of religion & the spread . . . of the Kingdom of the Redeemer," he explained to his flock on December 21, 1794, there must be a discernable "growth of prayer" and a "united supplication" for Christ's reign. The scriptural prophecies concerning the universal spread of Christianity remained unfulfilled, he declared, but the recent developments in Britain and Hartford were "hopeful tokens" that a glorious new age was dawning. The time had come for "all serious people" to unite in prayer for revivals, Robbins prophesied, and "who knows what God will do?"[10]

Other New Light ministers shared the same hope. On January 1, 1795, Benjamin Trumbull's North Haven congregation voted to observe the concert for prayer. Later that year the Connecticut General Association urged all orthodox churches to unite in "extraordinary prayer for the revival of religion and the advancement of Christ's Kingdom upon the earth," a call that was taken up by faithful evangelicals in many towns.[11]

The United Concert did much to publicize the operations of the British missionary organizations. The transatlantic communication network kept corresponding American clergymen abreast of the exciting developments in England, and they in turn passed the news on to their parishioners and to other ministers. As had been true four decades earlier, pastors commonly read foreign correspondence at prayer concerts, a practice that gave their expectant people a sense of participation in the great cosmic drama of redemption. The progress of the missionary movement in Europe not only inspired orthodox New Englanders with the hope that another awakening was at hand; it also underscored the inadequacy of the existing Congregational missionary efforts in America and the need for a new approach to mission.

The news of the first LMS mission to Tahiti, for example, convinced at least some Congregational leaders that New Englanders needed to commit themselves more ardently to Christ's great commission. "We in this land have been too long unmindful of that great object," the Reverend Chandler Robbins of Plymouth, Massachusetts, observed to his nephew Thomas, while "they are doing great things in this way in England." In early 1797 Chandler received from an English correspondent, the Reverend Robert Little, a lengthy account of the expedition to the South Seas which fired his imagination and filled him with anticipation of the universal spread of the gospel. "All the promises & prophecies are in our favor," Little reminded Robbins. "You will, I doubt not, unite your prayers with 1000s in this land for a blessing on this important undertaking."[12]

At the next prayer concert in Plymouth Robbins obligingly read Little's narrative to his spellbound congregation. He considered the mission news to be so important that he copied the lengthy account and sent it to his kinsman Thomas, then boarding at the home of the Reverend Stephen West in Stockbridge, Massachusetts. Chandler suggested that Thomas pass the account on to West and other ministers, so that they might have more "particular" information about the English expedition.[13]

From Stockbridge the news probably went out to various towns further west and north. West's home was a common resting place for ministers heading to and from the new settlements, and thus functioned as an important link in the transatlantic information network. Several months earlier, when missionary Seth Williston had stopped at West's house on his way to the Chenango country, West showed him an "animating" account of the "missionary society in England." Throughout his tour in New York Williston continued to receive periodic news from Stockbridge about missions and revivals in other parts of the world, information which the young evangelist passed on to the migrants in the Chenango settlements.[14]

Through such informal chains of communication New England evangelicals in the 1790s gradually became convinced that God was again pouring out his Spirit throughout the world. Long before the dramatic Connecticut revivals of 1798, the date sometimes cited by scholars as the beginning of the "Second Great Awakening" in New England, at least some New Light ministers were already certain that God was doing a great work among them. The increased interest in missions and the prayer concert were regarded as signs that the Holy Spirit was arousing evangelical Christians from the spiritual lassitude that had supposedly prevailed since the great revivals of the mid-eighteenth century.[15]

It is important, therefore, not to equate the "Second Awakening" with the powerful revivals that broke out in New England at the close of the decade. When eighteenth century Calvinist evangelicals spoke of an "awakening" they meant an inner spiritual event initiated by God's sovereign will. Increased "seriousness" among God's people was an outward manifestation of this inner awakening. The United Concert and missionary efforts were concrete acts of obedience which awakened Christians took in response to God's prompting, and were among the visible means that God employed to convert the unregenerate and to expand his earthly Kingdom. Revivals, or "holy showers," were the final stage—in a sense the ultimate goal—of the spiritual process of "awakening." If we wish to understand the awakening from the perspective of contemporary participants, we must never separate revivals from the "spiritual means" that God supposedly used to execute his will. Connecticut New Lights regarded prayer concerts, missions, and revivals as interrelated parts of a single spiritual phenomenon. From this perspective we might reasonably mark the beginning of the "Second Great Awakening" at the renewal of the United Concert for Prayer in the early 1790s.[16]

The years immediately preceding the creation of the Connecticut Missionary Society, then, witnessed a steady increase in millennial expectancy as "awakened" Anglo-American evangelicals prayed and worked for a universal revival. This hope was the source of the tremendous optimism exhibited by Congregational missionary leaders during the 1790s. Despite anticlerical criticism, sectarian competition, and the difficulties confronting Congregationalism in the new settlements, most orthodox leaders were confident that God would soon sweep away all errors and opposition, and would crown their efforts with success. Although many historians have shared the assumption, clearly articulated by William McLoughlin, that the Second Awakening in New England was staged by anxious orthodox clergymen who wished to revitalize "the old time religion that was inevitably fading,"[17] the writings of Congregational evangelists in the mid-1790s instead reflected a growing expectation that a revival of "experimental religion" was imminent.

The journal of Seth Williston is revealing. Williston was a young licentiate in 1796 when he received a commission from the General Association to visit the Chenango settlements in central New York. Williston was a zealous Edwardsean who faithfully observed the United Concert for Prayer and who eagerly looked for the dawning of the glorious millennial age. He hoped that God might do something wondrous through his mission, a desire that was fueled by periodic reports of awakenings in England and America. He longed, he wrote near the start of his journey, to see "these western settlements . . . built up by the pouring out of the Spirit," and he prayed constantly that God would use him as an instrument of revival.[18]

Millennial visions often filled Williston's imagination. "The world is in an uproar," he noted one day after reading some newspapers, "it is travailing in pain to bring forth the millennium." During his tour Williston digested various books which nurtured his millennial expectancy and led him to carefully take note of the signs of the times. Among these was Jonathan Edwards's *History of the Work of Redemption,* the great theologian's most thorough treatment of eschatology. Once, finding it difficult to pray freely in a public house, Williston meditated in his journal that "it will not be so in the millennium." Each day he looked for evidence that "the Lord is at work," and every encounter with an "apparently thoughtful" settler kindled his hope that he might "see a work of God here yet."[19]

By the end of his four-month mission Williston had become convinced that God was indeed arousing the people in the Chenango settlements. Unwilling to return to Connecticut when many settlers appeared to be wonderfully "serious" and perhaps a dozen seemed suddenly to be "in a new world," he decided to remain in the West to preach for whatever compensation the settlers could provide. At Chokonut, New York, on

November 10, 1796, the young evangelist for the first time publicly announced his belief that "a work of God was actually begun among us," a message that caused "some melting in the assembly." During the next several months a steady stream of settlers appeared to come "under conviction," and Williston's hopes soared. "The Lord has really come down among us," he observed in his diary, "Glory to grace! Grace triumphs!"[20]

Certain that an awakening had commenced, Williston took steps to publicize the event and to fan the religious excitement into a revival. He wrote an account of "the religious attention" for *The Theological Magazine,* a short-lived Calvinist paper published in New York City.[21] He also reported the awakening to Nathan Strong, the New Divinity pastor of Hartford First Church. Convinced that the Holy Spirit was doing something marvelous among the settlers, Williston proposed to Strong a remarkable measure: might the North Hartford Association ordain him to serve as an evangelist at large? This would enable him to continue full-time missionary work in the Chenango settlements, to organize awakened settlers into new churches, and to admit converted sinners into full communion.[22]

Williston's request had few if any precedents in the history of New England Congregationalism. Ordination normally took place only after a candidate had received a formal call from a congregation, and it was regarded as the start of a lifelong covenant with that people. To request ordination without first passing through the process of call, and to claim ministerial authority without accountability to any gathered church, departed from the Puritan ideal of a permanent settled ministry.

Unfortunately we do not know the inspiration behind the office of "evangelist at large." Perhaps the idea came directly from the scriptures, which obviously provide clear examples of itinerant Apostles. Perhaps Williston's model was George Whitefield or the itinerants of the Great Awakening. Perhaps, too, contact with Methodist circuit riders suggested the proposal.[23] At any rate, the idea struck a responsive chord in Hartford, and in February 1797, Williston received from Strong instructions to return to Connecticut to receive ordination from the North Hartford clergy.[24]

The ordination of Seth Williston on June 6, 1797 clearly reflects the dawning of a new evangelical conception of ministry as a religious profession rather than a sacred office.[25] Williston's authority as an "evangelist at large" was not dependent upon his relationship with a congregation; it was conferred by clergymen interested in nourishing the awakening and promoting revival. The desire to pursue a more instrumental approach to revivalism required orthodox leaders to create a new kind of specialized clerical office that was defined not relationally but functionally. In essence the evangelist at large was a professional missionary.

That Williston's ministry was a new, specialized calling quite distinct from the traditional Congregational pastorate was very apparent to the young evangelist. He had a deep sense of being set apart by God for the particular purpose of itineration, and he clearly anticipated that other men would soon receive the same special call. Not long after his ordination he was led to meditate upon "the importance of the evangelical office." His heart "was drawn out to pray that God would raise up and qualify men for the work of evangelists, for the service of the new settlements in particular." Indeed, Williston had already targeted a student at Williams College who seemed to possess the requisite gifts, and he prayed that the young man "might be reserved for this special service."[26]

The ordination of Williston to serve as a professional missionary was a product of the perceived "awakening." So, too, was the concurrent move to establish a new missionary organization to replace the Committee on Missions. Inspired by the belief that God was waking his people, the South Hartford Association met on June 6, 1797, the same day that Williston received ordination, to consider more effectual means "for raising funds to support missionaries." A week earlier the West Fairfield Association, noting the missionary advances in England, recommended that the upcoming General Association organize a society "for the purpose of enlarging the Redeemer's Kingdom and propagating the gospel among the heathen." The New London Association, considering it "highly important" that missions to the new settlements be continued and "extended to the natives of our country," also urged the General Association to adopt a new system of evangelism.[27]

When the General Association convened at Windham, then, many delegates had already received a mandate to work for a new missionary agency. For models they looked to the recently established London Missionary Society and to the Baptist Missionary Society. The Association appointed James Dana and Benjamin Trumbull of the Committee on Missions, as well as Yale President Timothy Dwight, to correspond with leaders of the British organizations. At the same time they appointed Levi Hart of Griswold, Joseph Strong of Norwich, and Samuel Miller, a delegate from the Presbyterian General Assembly, "to draft an address to the several associations" on the formation of a Connecticut Missionary Society similar to the British agencies. Each district association was directed to consider the proposal and to be prepared to recommend specific measures at the General Association's next meeting in June 1798.[28]

The proposed Connecticut Missionary Society received enthusiastic support from British evangelical leaders. John Love, Secretary of the London Missionary Society, rejoiced that his organization had inspired imitation in New England and had served to strengthen the faith of American Christians "in divine promises." The Trustees of the LMS, Love informed Dana, Trumbull, and Dwight, were especially pleased that the Connecticut General Association planned to broaden its missionary efforts to embrace the pagan natives of North America. Soon, Love predicted, "the whole American wilderness" would be transformed by a "host of *Elliots* and *Brainards*."[29]

Connecticut New Lights strongly endorsed the proposal. The staunchly Edwardsean North Hartford Association eagerly hoped for the expansion of the missionary effort so that "as the wilderness literally buds and blossoms as a rose, it may also become vocal with the praises of the CREATOR and REDEEMER." Indeed, several months before the CMS was organized, the North Hartford ministers launched their own missionary society as "a temporary expedient." Having ordained Williston as an evangelist, the Association employed him to continue his work in the awakened Chenango settlements. By the end of the summer of 1797 it was apparent that they could not provide him with an adequate income unless they raised special funds to support his mission. Hence, on October 4, 1797 the North Hartford clergy met in Farmington at the home of the Reverend Joseph Washburn to resolve themselves "into a missionary society for the purpose of collecting funds from the pious and benevolently disposed." This temporary measure, they asserted, was prompted by the "present aspect of Providence in Zion," and they stood "ready to coalesce with a more general society for missions, whenever any shall be formed in this state."[30]

Although the North Hartford Missionary Society (NHMS) existed for only a year before it merged with the newly created CMS, it had a lasting impact upon Congregational evangelism in America. The Connecticut Missionary Society formed around the nucleus of the Hartford organization, and was modeled upon it. Because the North Hartford Association planned to appeal directly to the public for donations, it vested governing authority over the NHMS in a Board of Trustees composed of equal numbers of clergymen and prestigious laymen. This same structure was adopted six months later by the CMS, perhaps due to the influence of Nathan Strong, who helped to draft the constitutions of both agencies. There was also a marked continuity in the leadership of the two organizations. Five of the eight Trustees of the NHMS later served as directors of the Connecticut Missionary Society, including the three most influential officers of the state association.[31] Connecticut Lieutenant-Governor Jonathan Treadwell, President of the CMS from 1798 to 1822, was a

Trustee of the North Hartford society. So, too, were Strong and Abel Flint, Hartford's two orthodox pastors, who served the state society as Secretary and Corresponding Secretary respectively, and who controlled the daily operations of the CMS during the first decade and a half of its existence.

The General Association formally organized the Connecticut Missionary Society on June 21, 1798, at the Congregational meetinghouse in Hebron. Although in theory the entire General Association constituted the new state society, in practice the CMS functioned from the first as an independent voluntary organization. The constitution gave the Board of Trustees full authority to govern the society, and the Trustees in turn delegated most administrative responsibilities to Strong and Flint. Unlike the old Committee on Missions, which adhered to no single theological perspective, the new organization was controlled firmly by Edwardsean clergymen who believed, as the Association declared, that "God is awakening his people." The three men who drafted the Constitution of the CMS—Strong, Levi Hart, and the younger Jonathan Edwards—were all New Divinity pastors. All six of the clergymen appointed to serve as Trustees were well-known Edwardseans, as was Lieutenant-Governor Treadwell, who presided over the meetings of the Board.[32]

The CMS was founded upon the postmillennial expectation that "the time is near in which God will spread his truth through the earth." Like the defunct Committee on Missions the new society intended "to support and promote Christian Knowledge in the new settlements," but like the LMS it also planned to carry the gospel to "heathen" people who had not yet heard the name of Jesus Christ.[33] However, the society was to launch only one major mission to the native Americans during its entire lengthy history, David Bacon's failed effort to gain a foothold among the Ojibwa of the Northwest Territory from 1800 to 1804.[34] Following this expensive failure the Trustees opted to concentrate principally upon evangelism among white settlers, and to leave the Indians to organizations devoted specifically to natives or foreign missions. Nonetheless, the inclusion of Indians in the original objectives of the CMS underscores the eschatological impulse that motivated the General Association in 1798.

II

The Connecticut Missionary Society soon attracted anticlerical opposition. New England's nascent Jeffersonian Party assaulted the new organization as a tool to promote ecclesiastical tyranny and Federalist political views. A typical attack was published on November 1, 1798 by James Lyon of Fairhaven, Vermont, editor of the Anti-Federalist paper *The Scourge of Aristocracy*. The Connecticut clergy, Lyon asserted, had "formed associations, which are the counterpart of the Illuminati and Propaganda Societies of France," in order to "increase sedition and superstition by projects about . . . missions and the millennium." In return for the clergy's political assistance, the *Scourge* reported, the "Connecticut aristocracy" would give the ministers "public money and property" to advance their designs. This treason would continue so long as the stupefied people of Connecticut continued to "acquiesce without question."[35]

Some scholars have accepted the premise that the CMS was established, at least in part, to advance Federalist political objectives. J. F. Thorning argued in 1931 that orthodox missionaries were more concerned "with promoting party interests than in furthering the gospel." Jack Ericson, editor of the microfilm edition of the CMS Papers, flatly asserts in his introduction to the manuscripts that the General Association "definitely wanted to perpetuate the Standing Order on the frontier." The missionaries, Ericson insists, "had the duty . . . to combat Republicanism . . . as the settled ministers were doing in Connecticut."[36]

The officers of the CMS were undoubtedly staunch Federalists. All twelve of the original Trustees of the organization were prominent members of Connecticut society, and five of the six lay officers—Jonathan Treadwell, Jonathan Brace, Heman Swift, Roger Newberry, and John Davenport, Jr.—were Federalist officeholders. The Trustees valued order and stability in society, and embraced the traditional vision of a covenanted community governed by educated men who had been called to positions of leadership. Benjamin Trumbull probably spoke for all of them when, shortly after the election of 1800, he complained disdainfully of the popular "madness for change and novelty" that was sweeping the nation.[37]

Despite these convictions, however, the Trustees had no intention of using the CMS as an "electioneering machine," as their democratic opponents often claimed, nor of erecting *de facto* standing orders in the wilderness. The inclusion of prominent officeholders on the Board of Trustees was designed to lend to the new organization a greater degree of respectability, a tactic that would be followed by most benevolent agencies established in the United States during the next half-century.[38] In and of itself the arrangement had little political significance. Six months earlier the same structure had been adopted for fund-raising purposes by the NHMS, an organization that clearly had no interest in "electioneering." Certainly Nathan Strong and Abel Flint, who held the most authority within the CMS, were determined that the missionary society would not become involved in political controversies.

Orthodox missionary leaders assumed, of course, that their efforts to promote orthodoxy on the frontier had political implications. They shared the universally held American conviction that religion and morality were indispensable components of republican liberty, and therefore believed that "the civil and political as well as the religious welfare of our brethren in the New Settlements require that the gospel should be preached to them." They also shared the common conservative belief that the "disorganizing principles" unleashed by the Revolution had given rise to "Jacobin absurdity," and that the spread of orthodox religion would help to strengthen respect for traditional New England values. As one Federalist friend remarked to Thomas Robbins, "in this demoralizing age of the world the profession which you have chosen is the great stay and support of order, government and social happiness." The orthodox clergy, New England Federalists generally agreed, provided "[t]he principal barrier against that anarchy and licentiousness which is overspreading the world."[39]

This central component of the Old Federalist creed often appeared in CMS publications. An 1804 tract, entitled *A Summary of Christian Doctrine and Practice: Designed Especially for the Use of People in the New Settlements,* warned migrants about the dangers posed by the disorganizing frontier, and urged them to maintain traditional habits of deference. Society, the tract asserted, required the proper subordination of wives to husbands, children to parents, servants to masters, and of various other "inferiors" to "superiors."[40]

But despite their dislike of the democratic impulses stirring within American society, Connecticut missionary leaders adamantly opposed participation in partisan politics. In part this reflected the strong anti-party sentiment shared by most citizens of the republic, but held with particular fierceness by orthodox New England conservatives. Partisanship weakened the values of harmony and consensus that orthodoxy continued to uphold, and was therefore regarded as a threat to both civil government and Christian morality. Seth Williston, after carefully digesting "seven Albany & New York papers for news," noted sadly in his diary that "there are two parties now in our land denominated Federalists, who are by the opposite party called Aristocrats, and . . . democrats." These factions "have each their newspaper magazines, which they are loading and discharging with great virulence." After reading both sides, Williston reflected, "I declare myself pleased with neither." In a similar frame of mind Thomas Robbins in 1805 prophesied that "the Spirit of party and electioneering which has deluged our country is sinking our national character to speedy contempt, and our free government to certain ruin." Several years later, in one of his first missionary sermons, the Reverend Giles Cowles warned the people of Austinburgh, Ohio, to resist "party spirit, division & contentions," which would ruin their community if not checked.[41]

The strength of this antiparty conviction became apparent after Jeffersonians gained firm control of the national government in 1800, a "gloomy and awful" development which left Ammi Robbins physically ill.[42] Despite their contempt for the new administration the Board of Trustees in May 1801 instructed CMS missionaries to "contribute all that lies in your power toward supporting the government of your country." Calvinist theology dictated that Christians submit to all lawful authority, even to governors they found morally repugnant. Though "times are boisterous and threatening," Ammi Robbins reflected, "there is one who is over all." Son Thomas agreed, and in a sermon delivered at Danbury, Connecticut, shortly after Jefferson's election, he reminded his audience that "the powers that be are ordained of God." Though he feared for the future of his country, he observed that there could be no doubt that the sovereign Lord had ordained the outcome of the election to serve his own inscrutable purposes, and that true Christians must loyally submit to the new administration. "When rulers are placed in their stations in a constitutional manner," he concluded, "they deserve and I trust will ever have our support."[43]

The CMS also had sound organizational reasons for avoiding partisan politics. Although they continued to receive legislative assistance, the Trustees decided at the outset to seek financial autonomy for the new organization. Between 1798 and 1817 a top priority was the building and maintenance of a permanent fund sufficient to finance missionary efforts even if political support should fail. Donations raised by the annual May collection were quickly expended upon missionaries in the field; all other money acquired by the Society was automatically placed in a permanent fund to be invested or loaned upon good security. In 1802 the Trustees successfully lobbied the state legislature for a charter of incorporation, a status which conferred the right to hold up to $100,000.[44]

Capital for the permanent fund came from diverse sources. Missionaries often received small donations from settlers. David Higgins, for example, collected slightly more than sixteen dollars during an 1801 tour of New York, a fairly typical sum.[45] In 1800 the Society established the *Connecticut Evangelical Magazine,* which circulated widely throughout New England and achieved a modest following among readers in other areas of the nation. All subscriptions to the *CEM* went into the permanent fund, "to produce something handsome for our missionary society."[46]

The revivals which spread across New England and the northern frontier between 1798 and 1803 prompted a flood of anonymous contributions to the CMS, including cash, stocks and bonds, real estate, and personal effects. Revivals also fostered the creation of countless local voluntary organizations, such as the female benevolent societies established throughout New England. The CMS was a popular beneficiary of the charitable contributions raised by these associations.[47] Finally, some Connecticut ministers assigned the profit from the sale of their published sermons or books to the CMS.[48] Invested wisely, these myriad sources of income gave the Society impressive financial stability. Between 1798 and 1825 the Permanent Fund generated more than $35,000 in interest for the missionary effort.

Opponents of Connecticut's religious establishment, of course, regarded the wealth of the CMS as proof that Federalist clergymen were using their status to acquire illicit power. The Trustees of the CMS, it was rumored, enriched themselves at the expense of the Society, especially by drawing large sums from the treasury to cover modest travel expenses. It was also rumored that Nathan Strong retained a portion of *CEM* subscriptions for himself. These rumors, which Benjamin Trumbull denounced as a plot "to stab the character of the Trustees . . . and especially to ruin my character," prompted an official rebuttal which was placed in various Connecticut newspapers. Given this acrimonious political climate and the suspicion which the CMS was bound to engender, the Trustees prudently insisted that missionaries strictly avoid involvement in partisan politics.[49]

Strong and Flint, given responsibility for selecting the missionaries, carefully screened every candidate to insure that they were not only doctrinally sound but also discreet in their speech and behavior. Whenever possible Strong personally interviewed potential missionaries at his home in Hartford, and often made confidential inquiries respecting their personal character of trusted mutual acquaintances. Despite the chronic shortage of ministers in the frontier, most candidates were rejected because their discretion was questionable. The CMS wanted only cautious men who could be relied upon to "gather rather than scatter." Thus the Reverend Benjamin Judd of Milton was turned down, despite otherwise impeccable qualifications, because he did "not possess that PRUDENCE which is indispensable in a missionary." "When you think of the observing eye of adversaries," Abel Flint wrote to Thomas Robbins in 1803, "you will be careful . . . that no just occasion of offense may be given to those who are disposed to think and to speak evil of the design on which you are sent."[50]

The missionaries generally appear to have followed their instructions conscientiously. The voluminous reports, journals, and sermons of CMS employees for the years 1798 to 1818 are virtually devoid of political content. Occasionally the records suggest that their opponents deliberately provoked them, perhaps hoping to involve them in political controversy, but with one notable exception the missionaries seem to have resisted the temptation to counterattack. Thomas Robbins, for example, was repeatedly insulted by Jeffersonian partisans, and suspected that democratic hecklers were responsible for the periodic disappearance of his horse. In 1805 he was dismayed that the "principal people" of Canfield, Ohio, were spreading "false and ungenerous reports about me, with regard to an interference in the late election." Nonetheless, he kept his indignation to himself. Indeed, despite his staunch Federalist convictions, Robbins was broad-minded enough to concede that "most of the ministers and serious people in this part, and of all classes, are Democrats."[51]

The single notable exception to the rule perfectly illustrates the determination of the CMS Trustees to avoid controversy. Joseph Badger, the first Congregational missionary in the Western Reserve, faced implacable opposition from influential Democrats in the region. "They called him by hard names & rendered him a suspect character," the Reverend Calvin Chapin of Rocky Hill later reported to the Trustees. "Federalism was extremely unpopular, & Mr. Badger was a federalist. Unprincipled men whom he opposed would declare this." When some of these "unprincipled men" ran for public office in 1805, Badger foolishly attacked them from the pulpit. "He would . . . if any of them were present, single them out as unprincipled men without calling names & would reprove them . . . in terms that all present knew how to apply." Badger's indiscretion played into the hands of his anticlerical enemies, who "defamed the missionary society through him." Gleefully they "propagated the opinion that it was an electioneering institution founded and supported" simply to revive "fallen and hated federalism." Within a few weeks of the election Badger, until then an extremely effective missionary, had "lost much of his popularity & perhaps all of his influence."[52]

On January 22, 1806, the CMS Trustees sent a letter to Badger and the other missionaries in the Reserve, reminding them of their instructions to avoid all unnecessary controversy. Evangelists, the letter asserted, must guard "against the influence of prejudice and party zeal, which, if indulged, will . . . annihilate your usefulness as ministers of the Gospel of Peace." Thomas Robbins probably expressed the sentiments of many other missionaries when he responded in his diary to the Trustees' warning: "I don't know but little, & say less upon the subject. I find it no self-denial." The chastened Badger, his reputation damaged beyond repair, soon resigned his commission.[53]

The CMS not only avoided overt "electioneering," but it also refused to take stands on public issues that might prove controversial. Nathan Strong, the chief editor of the *Connecticut Evangelical Magazine* from 1800 to 1815, was committed to keeping the journal as inoffensive as possible. The CEM endeavored to spread "such sentiments, instruction & intelligence as are calculated to promote true religion," while "no political discussion or innuendos are permitted to slide in." Letters and articles submitted for publication were carefully screened to omit any statements that might be construed as politically partisan. In 1803, for example, the CEM printed a letter from George Burder of the London Missionary Society which praised American revivals and reported upon British missionary work. But Strong deleted a paragraph in which Burder expressed fear of a French invasion and asked God's blessing upon England. Such a sentiment, Strong feared, might offend Jeffersonian Francophiles who detested the British more than Napoleon.[54]

In deliberately backing away from all political controversy, the CMS jettisoned one of the major traditional roles of the Congregational clergy. As Harry Stout has shown, New England pastors had always advised their flocks on political matters, especially in their occasional sermons and weekday lectures. This was their obligation as faithful shepherds. Since no dimension of life was beyond the sovereignty of God and no topic independent of God's word, it followed that orthodox ministers had a duty to address public affairs as well as issues of personal morality and salvation. Thus, when Loyalists complained about patriot preaching during the rebellion against Britain, the Reverend William Gordon of Roxbury, Massachusetts, responded axiomatically that "there are special times and seasons when the minister may treat of politics." During periods of public crisis such as the Revolution, Stout notes, the clergy would have been "remiss if, as God's watchmen, they failed to sound the alarm."[55]

It is hardly surprising that after the Revolution, as democracy threatened to "revolutionize" the New England social order, some orthodox clergy engaged in heated political discourse. The paranoic denunciations of democratic Jacobinism hurled by Timothy Dwight and Jedediah Morse, for example, were altogether normal expressions of orthodox pastoral concern. It is much more significant that many New England ministers said little or nothing about politics, and that Congregational missionary leaders sought to divorce themselves completely from controversial public issues. The sweeping changes wrought by the Revolution made it self-defeating for the clergy to attempt to guide people in their political decisions, a fact that men like Nathan Strong and Abel Flint firmly grasped.

Whatever politicking some settled New England ministers may have engaged in, the evangelists sent to establish orthodox churches in the new settlements quietly accepted the democratic predilections of most frontier folk, and confined their energy to the promotion of "experimental religion." Congregational missionaries accommodated to the reality of republican political life, and in the process unwittingly helped to advance the emergence of the modern secular state. By steering clear of politics CMS employees tacitly abetted the growing compartmentalization of American life into distinctly secular and sacred spheres. While in principle they continued to believe in a covenanted society in which every citizen was required to obey the commandments of God, in practice they abandoned political means to achieve this end.[56]

The Connecticut Missionary Society was established and directed by men who passionately believed that God was awakening the world. They felt an urgent call to plant new churches in the wilderness and to spread the kingdom of the Redeemer. To advance this cause they willingly subordinated their political concerns to the greater task of evangelism. Strong and Flint pursued the narrow institutional objectives of the CMS with single-minded determination. Clearly, they believed, the millennium would come, "not by might nor power, but by the divine Spirit" alone.[57]

CHAPTER

FIVE

CMS *Missionaries and Revivalism*

In August 1798, less than two months after the creation of the Connecticut Missionary Society, the Reverend Samuel J. Mills of Torringford noticed "unusual religious appearances" among his flock. The young people began to meet weekly by themselves for prayer and spiritual exercises, "an event so extraordinary" that it soon "excited a spirit of general inquiry throughout the society." By the autumn it was evident that God was reviving the Church at Torringford. A remarkable "solemnity appeared on the countenances" of the people, Mills wrote in a narrative published in the *Connecticut Evangelical Magazine*. "They found their hearts so much opposed to God, and to his law and to his gospel, as to see that nothing short of divine power could ever subdue them." Filled with a terrible anxiety about their sinful condition, many professors of religion now feared that their previous hopes of salvation had been grounded upon false impressions. For more than a year the "seriousness" and "solemnity" prevailed in Torringford, humbling the proud and hard-hearted, disturbing the lukewarm and the comfortable, and finally reconciling dozens of awakened sinners to the sovereignty of God and "the duties of unconditional submission and disinterested affection." Mills, an earnest Edwardsean who had long prayed for a revival of religion, was amazed by the power of this divine outpouring of grace. "Such a day as this, Sir, we never even dreamt of," he observed to Thomas Robbins in the fall of 1799. "It is the Lord's doings & marvelous in our eyes."[1]

The "divine shower" which stirred Mills's people fell upon many other Congregational churches as well. In the closing two years of the eighteenth century at least twenty Connecticut towns experienced powerful revivals, and many more felt to some degree the influence of the "reviving Spirit." The Reverend Edward Dorr Griffin later recalled, with perhaps a bit of exaggeration, that in 1799 he could stand at his door in New Hartford, Connecticut, "and number fifty or sixty contiguous congregations laid down in one field of divine wonders, and as many more in different parts of New England." The revival extended beyond Connecticut northward as far as the settlements in northern Vermont and New Hampshire, and westward into the Genesee country. The Awakening, some orthodox divines believed, was the mightiest outpouring of divine grace since apostolic times.[2]

The Awakening in New England coincided with the remarkable camp meeting revivals which occurred throughout the Appalachian backcountry between 1797 and 1805. These western meetings, most often associated with Presbyterian sacramental occasions, resembled in many ways earlier revivals which had accompanied Scots-Irish communions during the preceding half-century. But the "season of revival" which swept through virtually the whole of the Trans-Appalachian West at the turn of the nineteenth century far surpassed in range and intensity any previous American religious excitement. The "Great Revival," as it came to be called, was typified by the famous Gasper River and Cane Ridge meetings, in which thousands of participants engaged in extended ecstatic exercises and hundreds of worshipers exhibited extraordinary physical manifestations of the Spirit, such as falling, fainting, and "holy shouts." The Cumberland region of Kentucky and Tennessee, the epicenter of the excitement, witnessed the largest gatherings and the most remarkable "bodily exercises." But emotionally-charged camp meetings were also commonplace during the first few years of the nineteenth century in large sections of Virginia, the Carolinas, and Georgia, as well as the western counties of Pennsylvania.[3]

Calvinist evangelicals in both New England and the western states regarded the revivals as signs of a global outpouring of the Holy Spirit. Western Presbyterians as well as Connecticut New Lights linked the religious excitement to the prayer concert and the missionary movement, and stressed the international dimensions of the Awakening. "In this country revivals of religion and a spirit of missions were preceded by a Concert of prayer in the evangelical churches," the Presbyterian *Western Missionary Magazine* (wmm) explained in 1804. "This is to be regarded as the beginning and the presage of a change for the better." The newspaper, published by the Synod of Pittsburgh, observed that the "news of the missions" in England "seemed to electrify" pious American Christians, and was "instrumental in producing" the revivals. "The effect produced by the tidings of what the London Missionary Society was doing," the WMM recollected, "resembled the effect produced among a people in a state of oppression, by hearing that a deliverer has arisen."[4]

Most modern historians have ignored the international dimension of the Awakening, preferring instead to investigate revivals in specific communities or geographical regions. Social historians typically regard revivals as responses to complex socioeconomic, demographic, and political factors which apparently varied significantly from place to place. Their findings suggest that revivals in different communities appealed to divergent groups of people and had various causes. From this perspective the Awakening seems to lack the unity and coherence which contemporary participants assumed.[5]

Historians who adopt a regional focus also cast doubt upon the existence of a coherent awakening. The "holy showers" in New England and the Trans-Appalachian camp meetings have generally been treated as separate phenomena, coinciding but having little or no significant connection. Indeed, many scholars assume that eastern and western revivals had essentially different natures. The revivalism which swept the West was Arminian, William Warren Sweet has noted, and helped to promote individualism and democracy, while New England revivalism was Calvinistic, and aimed at the perpetuation of an aristocratic social order.[6]

According to a standard paradigm, the well-educated, genteel orthodox clergy of New England promoted revivals in an effort to combat democracy and secularism, to stave off disestablishment, and to bolster their own sagging status. They detested the wild enthusiasm of the more democratic western revivals, and carefully checked the emotions of their own people. To the aristocratic New England Congregationalists, William McLoughlin has written, "the camp meeting revivals of the years 1798–1808 were barbarous emotional outbreaks . . . crude appeals to the animal emotions of illiterate, half-savage men and women who had strayed too far from the institutional order of decent society." The New England revivals bore only a "very slight" resemblance to the dramatic western camp meetings, George Marsden has remarked. "Eastern evangelicals . . . generally took great pains to dissociate themselves from such extremes, fearing that emotional excesses would give a bad name to all revivals." Nathan Hatch offers a similar assessment, noting that "Yankee evangelicals . . . could not be expected to endorse the kind of emotional excess and hostility to institutions that the West had spawned."[7]

The response of orthodox missionaries to revivals in the new settlements suggests a more complicated story. The CMS, itself a product of the Awakening, provided an important link between revivals in New England and the West. Through Congregational evangelists the news of the

Connecticut revivals spread to hundreds of frontier communities. Employees of the CMS worked to expand the scope of the Awakening, and promoted revivals throughout northern New England, New York, western Pennsylvania, and the Old Northwest between 1798 and 1818. In some instances Connecticut missionaries appear to have sparked revivals in the new settlements; in other instances they found revivals already under way and attempted to build upon them.

Those CMS missionaries who labored beyond the Allegheny Mountains in the early years of the nineteenth century experienced firsthand the dramatic camp meetings of the West. Without exception they embraced the western revivals as works of divine grace, participated themselves in camp meeting exercises, and in at least a couple of instances attempted to introduce the camp meeting among Connecticut migrants in the Western Reserve. In western Pennsylvania and the Northwest Territory, settlers shouted and fell not only under the preaching of backwoods exhorters, but also in worship services conducted by the gentlemanly graduates of Yale.

Through the letters of these missionaries, which were often read at prayer conferences back in Connecticut, many orthodox New Englanders received glowing accounts of the remarkable "physical manifestations" in the West. It is likely that these narratives conferred a degree of respectability upon a form of religious experience that orthodox New England clergymen of the 1790s commonly associated with "methodistical enthusiasm." Thus, ironically, CMS missionaries may unwittingly have helped to prepare some Connecticut parishes to listen more sympathetically to the Methodist circuit riders who were invading New England at the time.

II

Ecstatic religious behavior was, of course, a part of the Congregationalist heritage. Connecticut New Lights well knew that emotional trauma and falling had attended the Great Awakening a half-century earlier. Jonathan Edwards recorded that when George Whitefield preached in Northampton in 1740, some awakened sinners lost control of themselves and responded by shouting and falling down. Similar "bodily exercises" appeared elsewhere in New England during the height of the revival, especially in response to the appeals of itinerant evangelists like Gilbert Tennent and Eleazer Wheelock. Wheelock, pastor of the Congregational church in Lebanon, embarked upon a preaching tour of eastern Connecticut, Rhode Island, and southeastern Massachusetts in the fall of 1740, and provoked intense emotional outbursts in many towns. In Taunton, Massachusetts, he noted in his diary, "30 cried out: almost all the negroes in the town. . . . Colonel Leonard's negro in such distress that it took 3 men to hold him. I was forced to break off my Sermon before I had done, the outcry was so great."[8]

Nonetheless, Edwards and his followers had ambivalent feelings about emotional trauma and "physical operations" of the Spirit. On the one hand, shouting and falling undeniably accompanied the Awakening in many towns; that the Holy Spirit could produce such manifestations seemed incontrovertible. On the other hand, New Lights did not consider bodily exercises to be an essential element of revival. Uncontrollable shouting or falling could never be regarded as reliable signs of conversion. Regeneration, Edwards stressed, involved a miraculous change of the sinner's inner disposition, producing an extraordinary degree of love, joy, and understanding. Physical exercises alone could reveal nothing about an individual's inward spiritual condition.

Rationalists and Old Light opponents of the Awakening believed that revivals resulted from delusion and unchecked enthusiasm, a bias that was seemingly confirmed by incidents of shouting and falling. In eighteenth century parlance "enthusiasm" denoted an unbalanced reliance upon the purely subjective, mystical dimension of Christian experience. Without denying the need for a vital personal piety, orthodox New England leaders had always stressed *sola scriptura*. The Bible, rationally interpreted through the assistance of the Holy Spirit, was the only reliable guide for Christian doctrine and practice. The depravity of human nature and the absolute mystery of God rendered all subjective religious experiences far too ambiguous and distorted to be considered trustworthy.[9]

Opponents of revivalism often indiscriminately labeled all apologists for the Awakening as enthusiasts. "Enthusiasm" supposedly made sinners forget the vast chasm between man and God, and invariably led to spiritual pride. Enthusiasts, it was argued, believed without any rational proof or scriptural warrant that their inner dreams, visions, and impulses were direct operations of the Holy Spirit. They foolishly bestowed upon their subjective impressions, critics charged, an authority equal to the Bible. They arrogantly claimed to have received clear communications from God which were not vouchsafed to other Christians, and presumed to possess a familiarity with the divine will which many sincerely pious folk lacked. Some even claimed the ability to differentiate between the elect and the damned, an attribute belonging solely to God. Unless checked, opponents of the Awakening warned, enthusiasm inevitably hardened proud sinners against biblical truth, created discord within Christ's Body, and resulted in ecclesiastical schisms.[10]

It was precisely this accusation which the president and faculty of Harvard College leveled against George Whitefield in 1744. Citing references to prophetic dreams and visions scattered throughout the evangelist's published writings, the *Harvard Testimony* reminded New Englanders that inner voices might "as well be the Suggestions of the evil Spirit" as of God. What good could possibly come to those "who stand ready to be led by a Man that conducts himself according to his Dreams, or some ridiculous and unaccountable Impulses and Impressions on his mind?" Whitefield, the Harvard faculty charged, was "an uncharitable, censorious, and slanderous man," who self-righteously condemned his critics as *"Men of no Religion, unconverted,* and *Opposers of the Spirit of God."* Moreover, the evangelist erroneously taught that true Christians will necessarily be able to feel "the indwelling of the Spirit," an unscriptural assertion that led many deluded sinners to conclude that "their religious Agitations" were *"feeling the Spirit,* in its operations on them." As a natural consequence of these delusions, the College concluded, Whitefield's followers came to "despise their own ministers" and other fellow Christians who did not share their enthusiasm.[11]

Edwardseans, of course, denied that revivals, or even unusual physical exercises, necessarily indicated enthusiasm. They warmly embraced the Awakening as a work of divine grace, stressed the necessity of conversion, and insisted that regeneration involved a transformation which was definitely *experienced* by the elect. At the same time, however, they acknowledged that the danger of enthusiastic delusion existed in every revival. Many supposed conversions later proved to be momentary false impressions, and some "awakened" people undeniably displayed a self-righteous censoriousness toward others. Clearly, too, some unqualified men did take upon themselves the task of evangelism, falsely imagining a divine call to preach the gospel. Most lamentably, the Awakening led to schisms in dozens of New England parishes, as the critics of enthusiasm had prophesied.

Edwards and his followers decried such excesses and labored to distinguish between the pure, holy essence of the revival and those aspects rooted in enthusiasm. In his famous apology for the Awakening, *Some Thoughts Concerning the Present Revival of Religion in New England* (1742), Edwards presented a balanced analysis of "bodily exercises" which strongly influenced evangelical Calvinists well into the nineteenth century. "Extraordinary external effects," the theologian observed, could certainly be produced by the Holy Spirit, but also by the natural human will when influenced by prevailing custom or the influence of others. Distinguishing between the effect of the Spirit and the effect of custom was virtually impossible, Edwards argued, and in many cases both influences were at work. Edwards believed that authentic physical manifestations of the Spirit were truly irresistible, and therefore "it would be very unreasonable . . . to frown upon all these extraordinary external effects." So long as the manifestations were "in no wise disproportioned to the spiritual cause," bodily exercises could safely be regarded as "natural, necessary, and beautiful."[12]

The danger, Edwards asserted, lay in the natural tendency to value external effects *per se*. Enthusiasm resulted whenever preachers encouraged awakened sinners "in going in these things to the utmost length that they feel themselves inclined." To prevent the external manifestations of the Spirit from becoming an end in themselves, Edwards insisted that persons in "extraordinary circumstances" should be urged "not to make more ado than there is need of, but rather to hold a restraint upon their inclinations." Unless pastors gently restrained these awakened sinners, Edwards advised, "extraordinary outward effects will grow upon them . . . without any increase of the internal cause." Then they "will find themselves under a kind of necessity of making a great ado, with less and less affection of soul, until at length almost any slight emotion will set them going." Such poor persons, Edwards concluded, become "more and more violent and boisterous, and will grow louder and louder, until their actions and behavior become indeed very absurd."[13]

Edwards's treatise became standard fare for eighteenth-century New Lights, and helped to condition their response to subsequent revivals. The Congregational missionaries who carried the gospel into the new settlements longed to see an awakening, but were ever vigilant against outbreaks of enthusiasm which might carry deluded sinners into heresy or lead them into a false sense of security. Thus Nathan Perkins devoted himself to combatting "superstition & enthusiasm" during his 1789 "evangelical tour" of Vermont. Several years later, convinced that an awakening had commenced in the Chenango settlements, Seth Williston preached a sermon "to guard awakened sinners against false illuminations & the wiles of the devil."[14]

During the decades following the Great Awakening, New England Congregationalists gradually came to associate emotional trauma and physical exercises with the disciples of John Wesley. From the perspective of orthodox Calvinists, Methodism seemed to be an inherently "enthusiastic" heresy. Wesley taught that all converted Christians could experience perfect holiness through a second work of divine grace called Sanctification. In this second crisis experience the Holy Spirit instantaneously purged the soul of corrupt motives and desires, enabling the sanctified Christian to avoid all volitional sins through a regimen of rigorous self-examination, methodical devotion, and careful avoidance of worldly temptations. For Wesley and his followers, Sanctification was a conscious, empirical experience often characterized by an overpowering sense of ecstasy.[15]

Unlike Edwardsean Congregationalists, Wesleyans frankly encouraged sinners to seek external signs of their inner transformation. The early sanctified Methodists in both Britain and America were notorious for their emotionalism. Physical exercises of various types became commonplace at Methodist gatherings. In 1775, for example, a series of Methodist meetings in Brunswick County, Virginia, produced the kind of physical manifestations that soon became a distinguishing feature of Methodism throughout the nation. "Some would be seized with a trembling," one observer wrote, "and in a few moments drop on the floor as if they were dead; while others were embracing each other with streaming eyes, and all were lost in wonder, love, and praise."[16]

Most Congregationalists assumed that these Methodist exercises constituted enthusiasm rather than authentic operations of the Holy Spirit. By the 1790s Connecticut Edwardseans typically denounced Methodism in terms reminiscent of earlier rationalist attacks upon their own party. Methodists were deluded schismatics. They were filled, a group of orthodox New Yorkers observed to Abel Flint in 1799, with "extraordinary fanatic zeal." Seth Williston found the Methodists to be "selfish," self-righteous, and censorious. "They appear to have a zeal but not according to knowledge," a Vermont correspondent observed to Nathan Strong several years later. Methodist meetings were rank with "the frenzy of enthusiasm."[17]

In light of these considerations it is not surprising that Connecticut New Lights of the 1790s identified "seriousness" and "solemnity" as the primary signs of God's Spirit, and looked upon physical exercises with suspicion. By the close of the eighteenth century the church schisms created by the Great Awakening half a century before were at last healing, and the Edwardseans themselves had emerged as the dominant clerical faction in the state. Although they longed for another awakening, Connecticut New Lights did not wish to reopen old wounds or raise once again the charge of "enthusiasm." Undoubtedly, too, they wished to dissociate themselves from the enthusiastic Methodists, who were energetically proselytizing disaffected people in many Connecticut parishes.

Indeed, when revivals at last broke forth in New England in 1798–1799, the presence of the upstart Methodists threatened the social respectability of the Awakening. Revivals touched Methodist meetings as well as orthodox congregations, and physical manifestations of the Spirit played a conspicuous part in some of these gatherings. Near New London, Connecticut, in early 1799, "the Lord came down in mighty power" at a Methodist quarterly meeting. According to Shadrack Bostwick, a circuit rider who participated in the meeting, "many were struck and fell from their seats prostrate upon the floor, crying in bitter agonies, some for converting, and others for sanctifying grace!" Such a response may have startled some of the new converts from orthodoxy, but Bostwick, soon to become the first Methodist circuit rider in the Connecticut Western Reserve, took the physical exercises in stride. "It happened well," he reflected matter-of-factly, "that brother McCombs and myself had been formerly favored with such scenes in the South, and well knew what to do."[18]

Such physical exercises and disorderly behavior apparently played little or no role in the Congregational revivals. Orthodox ministers consistently described the "marvelous displays of divine power" in their parishes as "solemn." Their people evinced remarkable "seriousness" and received "deep impressions" of their guilt and helplessness. Convicted orthodox sinners experienced dreadful "anxiety" and "distress" over their spiritual condition, but nonetheless remained composed. In Bristol, the Reverend Giles Cowles reported, "the assembly was solemn as the grave." Sinners in Norfolk "were bowed with a sense of the presence of the Lord." Some subjects rejoiced and praised God, while others cried out, "[W]hat must we do?" Yet, Ammi Robbins observed, "they were by no means noisy or boisterous, but, in silent anguish, seemed to be cut to the heart."[19]

Connecticut New Lights, eager to avoid the divisiveness which had accompanied the Great Awakening, pointedly emphasized the orderliness and rationality of the revivals. "At first," Giles Cowles confessed, "it was in some, perhaps an affection of the passions," but this soon subsided. On the whole, Cowles concluded, "It has been remarkably free from all irregularity and enthusiasm. The convictions have been rational, but deep and powerful." The Reverend Jonathan Miller of Burlington made the same point. "Undoubtedly in the beginning of the work numbers were moved with little more than a sympathetic affection, arising from the novelty and seriousness of the impressive scene," he remarked, but this phase quickly gave way to "the most rational conviction of gospel truths." In Norfolk, Ammi Robbins noted, the orthodox revivalists conscientiously labored to guard "young converts" against "errors and intemperate zeal."[20]

These ministers, along with seventeen others, wrote revival narratives for the *Connecticut Evangelical Magazine* as the "divine showers" in Connecticut were beginning to wane. The CMS launched the magazine in

1800 to publicize the revivals and to mold the public's perception of the Awakening. "After the numerous revivals of religion with which the Holy Spirit of God blessed some parts of this state," Thomas Robbins later recalled, New Lights needed a religious publication to communicate "to the Christian public accounts of this great work of grace." The Trustees of the CMS hoped that the revival narratives would help to sustain the spiritual effects of the Awakening, and might also promote revivals in other places. Nathan Strong and Abel Flint, who were "responsible for the respectability of the Magazine," carefully scrutinized the narratives to insure that they did not contain controversial statements or details that could damage the Society.[21]

Unfortunately we cannot know whether or not Strong and Flint significantly edited the revival accounts, since none of the original manuscripts have survived. It is possible that revivals in Congregational parishes were actually more "enthusiastic" than the CEM suggests. Certainly both the editors and the authors themselves wished to present the revivals as supernatural works that could be embraced by even the most enlightened and reasonable citizens. All the narratives included brief descriptions of miraculous conversions, often involving prominent deists or skeptics who had tried to resist the Spirit's actions. Such incidents, presumably, argued against enthusiasm as an explanation for the revivals.

There is strong evidence that the authors of many of the narratives consulted together upon how best to portray the Awakening, and carefully considered the wording with an eye toward public opinion. In May 1800, a group of ministers from Litchfield and Hartford counties who "had been in the work" gathered together in West Simsbury to write an account of the revival for the new missionary magazine. Their purpose, Jonathan Miller informed Nathan Strong, was to "give people an opportunity to determine whether it be all a work of enthusiasm or not," and to "take off the prejudice of candid people against awakenings." Fearing that the editors of the CEM "might alter the impression of the work," the ministers appointed Miller and Giles Cowles to negotiate with Strong and Flint upon any proposed changes in their written account. Apparently the narrative drafted by this group of clergymen was never published; it might well have been a prototype for the series of accounts that later appeared in the magazine. Nonetheless, the incident clearly suggests that CEM material was carefully crafted to deflect anticipated criticism from rationalists and liberal Christians.[22]

Connecticut New Lights during the Second Great Awakening evidently considered skepticism and infidelity to be greater challenges to orthodoxy than the upstart Methodist circuit riders. When news of the extraordinary Kentucky revivals began to appear in Hartford newspapers in late 1801, Ammi Robbins "at first felt sorry . . . lest all Deists & Infidels would take occasion, yea & *nominal* Christians too, to ridicule all experimental Religion" as mere "Methodist Enthusiasm."[23] Orthodox revivalists hoped to prevent the schisms and altercations which had plagued the First Great Awakening by defining themselves as rational evangelicals, and by strongly condemning noisy disorder. They sought to hold a middle position that would at once distinguish them from the disreputable Methodists and other enthusiasts, as well as from the non-evangelical liberals.

As a consequence Edwardsean revivalists often found themselves being ridiculed simultaneously as cold and spiritless intellectuals and as superstitious enthusiasts. To Methodists, Baptists, and other evangelical dissenters Congregational evangelists were moribund metaphysicians. Giles Cowles, widely regarded as a very effective preacher, led at least four revivals during his ministry in Bristol, Connecticut, and as a missionary in Ohio. One orthodox youth observed in her diary that he was "a plain and intelligent preacher" with the ability "to engage the attention of the young as well as the old." His sermons, she observed, could be "easily comprehended" even by children. But a Methodist rival in Ohio, upon hearing him preach a missionary sermon, criticized his delivery as "lifeless formal."[24]

To the skeptics and universalists in the Connecticut Western Reserve, Cowles and the other Congregational missionaries appeared to be ridiculous fanatics. Nathan Strong and Abel Flint sometimes received scathing critiques of orthodox evangelism from irate liberals in the new settlements. Soon after the first revival narratives appeared in the CEM, a western subscriber reported a conversation with a "respectable clergyman" who regarded the Awakening as a "delusion of the devil" that would soon banish "all *rational* Christianity . . . from our country." The "Connecticut clergy might be honest men," the "respectable clergyman" declared, but they were so grossly deluded that "it behoved all *enlightened* divines to make a stand" against them.[25]

Congregational evangelists were neither the spiritless metaphysicians nor the irrational zealots that their enemies caricatured. In both their doctrines and their piety the men who led the Second Great Awakening in Connecticut's orthodox churches were similar to the Calvinist revivalists of the earlier Great Awakening. They sought to synthesize reason and "vital piety," as had their intellectual mentor, Jonathan Edwards, and decried any attempts to separate experiential religion and knowledge. Like Calvin and their Puritan ancestors, they believed that scripture demanded sustained and rigorous study, and they doggedly affirmed the need for an educated clergy as well as the value of an educated laity. At the same time they insisted upon the need to be "born again of the Spirit," and stressed the complete reorientation of the "affections" which regeneration brought. In their estimation knowledge without zeal was just as deadly as zeal without knowledge.

New England Congregational revivals were probably just as intense as their Methodist counterparts. It would be a mistake to assume that the carefully-worded revival narratives published in the CEM accurately reflected the full range of emotions displayed by the awakened orthodox laity. The lack of falling and shouting, the insistence upon the rationality of the revivals, the "seriousness" and "solemnity" of the meetings, all suggest one dimension of the Awakening that the clergy were particularly eager to display to the public. But in scattered unpublished letters one can sense something of the transforming joy and even rapture which at least some awakened Congregationalists undoubtedly experienced.

In Norfolk, in May 1799, so many people flocked to special services that "not a third" could get into the meetinghouse. Worship was moved out into the town green, and was "attended with extraordinary manifestations of the *Presence* and *Power* of Jehovah." Ammi Robbins observed a variety of responses to this sense of sacred presence. Some people, swept by divine love, commenced "sweetly rejoicing." Others grew "dreadfully distressed with a sense of their horrible guilt," while some passed through a more moderate "time of distress." A portion of the crowd became silently solemn; still others were "filled with astonishment." For more than two months special conferences were held at least twice a week, Ammi reported to Thomas, and the crowd continued "as full as ever." Each day a weary but jubilant Ammi received a stream of visitors "to talk about the state of their souls." By mid-July, he estimated, "upwards 460 among us" had hopes of regeneration.[26]

The transforming power of the revival is beautifully reflected in the correspondence of Sally White Cowles, wife of the Reverend Giles Cowles of Bristol. Prior to the revival Sally apparently wrestled with almost constant melancholy. As the minister's wife she felt she was always on display before a "watching" and "talkative" people, and she suffered a crushing sense of isolation. Secretly she doubted her regeneration, and felt little joy or comfort in religion. However, when the revival broke out in Bristol in the spring of 1799, Sally experienced a profound sense of freedom from her doubts and depression. Her letters clearly reflect the dramatic emotional change she felt as the "joyous, wondrous outpouring of grace" swept through the town. With excitement she wrote to nonprofessing friends, inviting them to come and see for themselves the glory of God, and urging them to surrender themselves to the joy of Christian service. "Trust that I am as much out of my head and talk like a fool as much as you," she wrote to her awakened sister-in-law Clara, ". . . well, happy foolishness."[27]

Sally's transformation did not fade quickly. At the height of the revival she joined together with several other hopeful Norfolk women to form "a little circle of love & harmony" that continued to meet long after the "divine shower" had ceased. In this gathering of "engaged and animated" sisters her feelings of isolation melted. "We have delightful interviews and I would not relinquish their company and conversation for any consideration whatever," she confided to Clara several months later. "There is no fear, distrust or anxiety manifested & I think I may say felt."[28]

Such letters suggest more clearly than the published *CEM* narratives the emotional content of the orthodox revivals in Connecticut. While apparently lacking the physical manifestations that accompanied the Methodist meetings, the same sense of overpowering spiritual presence characterized both. In both instances lay responses ranged from dreadful anxiety to euphoric joy and feelings of liberation. In both cases the revival unleashed a powerful grass-roots organizing impulse that had far-reaching social and ecclesiastical implications. This essential element of the phenomenon is overlooked by most modern commentators, who, like Nathan Hatch, dismiss the Second Great Awakening in New England as "staid, churchly, socially conservative" and "characterized by a 'respectful silence'".[29]

Hatch

III

The New England revivals had a profound impact upon the Connecticut Missionary Society and its operations. By early 1799 missionary leaders were aware "that the *attention* is spreading to the Westward clear to Genesee," information which further fueled their millennial fervor. "I learn that the work of God is spreading rapidly in the towns to the westward," the Reverend Levi Hart of Lebanon, Connecticut, wrote to Nathan Strong in March 1799. "May it become universal, & may we in this eastern quarter not be the last to bring the King back."[30] By the close of 1799 Strong and Flint had received a flood of urgent appeals from awakened migrants in Vermont and New York, begging the Trustees to send them preachers. The Society, eager to promote revivals in the new settlements, instructed missionaries to devote special attention to towns that showed signs of seriousness. Also, additional missionaries were sent to areas where "refreshings" had been reported.

In responding to the demand for evangelists, the CMS faced the same problem that had formerly plagued the Committee on Missions. There were too few ordained pastors available to go on tours. Initially, at least, the outbreak of revivals further intensified the chronic shortage. "The late happy revival of religion . . . renders it improper for pastors of churches to leave their flocks for any length of time," the CMS Trustees observed.[31] This was especially true of the Edwardsean clergy in Hartford and Litchfield counties, where most of the Connecticut revivals occurred. Throughout the 1790s this group of ministers had given the most consistent support to the missionary cause, and were the most likely to accept mission appointments. Thus, ironically, the revivals simultaneously increased the demand for evangelists and temporarily depleted the available supply.[32]

In some ways, of course, the revivals clearly had a positive impact upon orthodox missionary efforts. The treasury of the CMS swelled considerably as convicted sinners and hopeful converts began to donate more generously to the cause. Throughout New England scores of benevolent societies emerged—like Sally Cowles' "little circle of love & harmony"— to pray and to raise money for missions. As a result, CMS Trustees in 1800 optimistically predicted that they could soon increase the number of missionaries in the field, if they could "procure suitable persons to go on missions." In the long run the revivals also inspired many New England youth to enter the ministry; after the War of 1812 the CMS at last had an expanding pool of young evangelists to choose from.[33]

In the short run, however, orthodox missionary leaders had no choice but to be more flexible in selecting men for the field. Initially the CMS planned to rely primarily upon experienced Connecticut ministers, who would continue to serve relatively brief tours in the new settlements. This arrangement was never entirely abandoned by the Society during the period under study, but after 1799 the Trustees also employed dismissed pastors and inexperienced candidates who could itinerate on mission ground throughout the year. Like Seth Williston, many of these licentiates received ordination to the special office of evangelist, and were authorized to perform all pastoral duties in the places they visited.

These early orthodox itinerants did not remain "aloof from the religious movements of the West," as H. Richard Niebuhr asserted. Nor was their style of ministry necessarily out of step with popular expectations. To illustrate this point, we will examine in greater detail the activities of three CMS evangelists who energetically promoted revivals in the new settlements: Jedediah Bushnell, who labored in New York and Vermont from 1798 to 1803; and Joseph Badger and Thomas Robbins, who ministered in western Pennsylvania and eastern Ohio during the height of the "Great Revival" in the Trans-Appalachian West.

IV

Seth Williston later remembered Jedediah Bushnell as "the most success-ful missionary in western New York that I had ever known." He was, probably, the most effective revivalist employed by the CMS. "Mr. Bush-nell highly prized, and intensely labored to promote revivals of religion," the Reverend Thomas Merrill of Middlebury, Vermont, observed in 1849, "and very few pastors have witnessed such a succession of Divine refreshings as fruits of their labours." Between 1798 and 1803, when he itinerated throughout New York and western Vermont for the CMS, Bushnell reportedly led revivals in dozens of towns. Seth Williston be-lieved that Bushnell's work was largely responsible for the awakening in the Genesee region in 1799; Merrill credited the evangelist with sparking "an extensive revival" in Addison County, Vermont, in 1801 and 1802. In 1803 Bushnell, wishing to marry and raise a family, accepted a call to settle in Cornwall, Vermont, but his revival efforts continued unabated. During his thirty-three years as pastor, the Cornwall church experienced fourteen revivals. After his dismissal in 1836 several vacant congregations enlisted his services, and in one of them, New Haven, Vermont, the aging clergyman led his final revival "with his usual devotedness, and with all the energy of a young man."[34]

Bushnell certainly did not fit the standard stereotype of the aristocratic orthodox clergyman. Nothing in his upbringing or style of ministry sug-gested gentility. Born in 1769 in Saybrook, Connecticut, to apparently undistinguished parents, he received only a common school education as a youth. Apprenticed at age sixteen to a tanner and cobbler, he spent the next five years learning the shoemaker's trade. In 1790, at the age of twenty-one, Bushnell opened his own shop. At that time, his friend Thomas Merrill later related, "he had but half a set of shoemaker's tools, and not leather enough to make two pairs of shoes."[35]

Bushnell's first "religious impressions" came in 1791, after a disturb-ing conversation with an evangelical patron awakened him to a sense of his peril. In 1792, at the age of twenty-three, the young shoemaker expe-rienced conversion and felt a call "to become a messenger of salvation to others." He studied for a year to "fit" himself, and in 1793 entered the newly chartered Williams College. A struggling artisan with scant financial resources, he could not defray his expenses without continuing to ply his trade. In addition to shoemaking he picked up work as a school-teacher, and was able to complete his course of instruction in four years because of his "industry and economy." After graduating in 1797 he briefly studied divinity at the home of the Reverend Ephraim Judson of Sheffield, Massachusetts, and in early 1798 was licensed to preach at the comparatively late age of twenty-nine.[36]

Unlike many newly-licensed candidates, Bushnell had no ambition to settle in a prosperous parish in the East. By choice, he spent the remainder of his life in the new settlements, laboring to build up the "vacant waste places." Soon after receiving his license he made his way to Canandaigua, New York, to preach to the "destitute" settlements in that vicinity, and quickly displayed a remarkable aptitude for missionary work. Throughout the spring and summer of 1798 Bushnell received a growing number of invitations from vacant congregations. To the best of his ability he answered every call, often taking no compensation for his services. Wherever he went, Seth Williston observed, "he made a very favorable impression on their minds." Within a few months of his first arrival in Canandaigua, the young evangelist had earned a reputation throughout the Genesee region as an extraordinary preacher "who appeared to have a more than common degree of spirituality and zeal in the cause of Christ."[37]

In 1799 many of the settlements where Bushnell labored experienced revivals. The CMS, eager to nurture these "divine outpourings," commissioned the evangelist to itinerate on their behalf, even though Strong and Flint knew him "only by reputation." The Trustees did not feel altogether comfortable with this departure from normal procedure, and to be on the safe side they instructed Bushnell "to act in concert with and by the advice of Mr. Williston." It soon became evident, however, that Bushnell was the more dynamic and effective evangelist, and possessed an intuitive knack for the missionary enterprise which Williston seemed to lack. Although the two men became close friends and often consulted together, Williston clearly regarded his "brother" as the more gifted and discerning servant.[38]

On November 25, 1799 Williston wrote to Benjamin Trumbull, urging that the Society ordain Bushnell to the evangelical office. Throughout the Genesee country, Williston asserted, "his preaching & conversation has been blessed to stir up saints & sinners." Slumbering Christians had awakened "to righteousness & prayerfulness," and many sinners "are much alarmed." Since Bushnell's arrival they "now pay solemn attention to preaching & religious conferences." The CMS, Williston concluded, "shall hardly find a better missionary. He has a remarkable talent in religious conferences and visits—he engages the attention of children & young people."[39]

The CMS ordained Bushnell the ensuing winter and renewed his appointment to the Genesee country. During the following year Strong and Flint received a steady stream of testimonials to the evangelist's influence. A typical letter from the Union Society of Otego Creek, an interdenominational group, described Bushnell as "a young Timothy" who "did sow the gospel seed in these parts, which was soon followed by a pleasing little harvest." His arrival, the Union Society declared, completely transformed the settlement. "Before Mr. Bushnell came here, people were extremely careless and inattentive . . . of their souls." The Sabbath was desecrated, worship ignored, and "little or no attention paid to God." Bushnell's preaching powerfully aroused the people from their thoughtlessness, and "now, blessed be God, Divine Ordinances are attended with affection, and we hope in union and fellowship with the children of light."[40]

Bushnell's reputation soon spread beyond New York. By early 1801 the Society was receiving appeals from anxious Congregationalists in Vermont, who hoped that Bushnell might visit them and spark a revival. The people in Georgia, Vermont, for example, expressed gratitude for visits from other orthodox missionaries, but "having heard of the uncommon success which has attended the preaching of the Rev. Jeddediah Bushnel," they hoped that the Trustees might send him their way. So, too, did a Committee of the Church in Fairfield, Vermont, which offered to settle Bushnell one-third of the time if the CMS would appoint him to their village.[41]

Bushnell's great popularity and unusual success as a revivalist undoubtedly owed much to his humble origins and his unaffected simplicity. Despite his college education he always retained his identification with common people, and could speak plainly and directly to their concerns. Remembrances penned by Bushnell's friends read much like the tributes written to early Methodist circuit riders. His sermons were simple and clear evangelical exhortations, delivered in a forceful, attention-grabbing manner. "His excellency did not consist in classical learning," Seth Williston recalled, "nor in the elegant composition of his sermons; nor in the rhetorical delivery of them," but rather in his utter sincerity and obvious love. "His preaching was apt to be on subjects which have a very direct reference to the salvation of the soul. It was plain, searching, and pungent. He spoke as one who believes what he says." The Reverend E. C. Wines of Long Island similarly observed that "Mr. Bushnell could not be called an orator. His voice was clear and shrill rather than mellifluous; his action was energetic rather than graceful; and his style of composition had more of strength than of elegance or polish."[42]

Like many Methodist circuit riders, Bushnell also possessed a charismatic presence which commanded reverence. "If it be asked to what cause I impute his extraordinary success," Williston remarked, "I would say . . . his uncommon *spiritual* qualifications." His character, Wines observed, was "pervaded and impregnated by holy love,—a Divine flame, which was fed by everything he saw, heard, read, or studied, and which made his sermons . . . effusions of the heart, and gave them a direct aim toward the hearts of his hearers." When Bushnell "entered the sanctuary, there was an atmosphere of unaffected sanctity about him, that made all feel it was the Lord's day and house; and when he spoke, he commanded and rewarded attention."[43]

In addition to his simplicity and charisma, Bushnell projected a seemingly egalitarian concern for the salvation of his listeners. He approached sinners "with all the meekness and gentleness of Christ," Williston recalled, and made them feel that he desired nothing of them but that they repent and be saved. "He rose far above the bigotry of sect and party, and was willing to receive all as brethren who were received by Christ as disciples." According to Wines, Bushnell constantly aimed "to promote in the highest degree the spirit of piety in himself and others, with a readiness to hope the best of the lowest." He could, Williston agreed, "better than almost any other man I have ever known, approach the sinner, whether in low or high life, and plead with him to be reconciled to God."[44]

Bushnell became famous for his impartiality in dealing with people. Because of his evenhandedness residents of surrounding communities often called upon him to arbitrate conflicts. Wines considered it "remarkable . . . that he would never, not even to his dearest friend, express an opinion about a matter in dispute after hearing but one side of it." This habit of impartiality commanded the respect even of those who sharply rejected his doctrines.[45]

Bushnell's personal qualities made him an ideal bridge between Puritan tradition and the emerging republican culture. In a society that increasingly rejected authority based upon status, wealth, or educational attainments, Bushnell's identification with average people and his ability to communicate easily in the common idiom were tremendous assets. In an era characterized by sometimes fierce social and ideological competition, his skill as a mediator and his ease with folk of varied social backgrounds were surely invaluable possessions. It is no wonder that Nathan Strong, who regarded him as a model evangelist, believed that Bushnell "made a grand mistake in exchanging the missionary field to which he was so admirably adapted, for pastoral duties."[46]

It is noteworthy that Bushnell also embodied many of the attributes of the traditional Congregational clergyman. Far from rejecting the past as a source of authority, as did many evangelicals after the Revolution, he appeared to be very conservative in most matters. Nobody, Thomas Merrill recollected, "preached the doctrines commonly called Calvinistic with more perspicuity, pungency, and fearlessness." Seth Williston once heard Bushnell address a New York gathering about God's retributive justice, an extremely controversial doctrine that even zealous Calvinists conceded to be a "hard truth." Few orthodox beliefs received more scorn from rationalists and Arminian critics than the seemingly tyrannical assertion that God justly punished sinners for crimes which they could not resist. Nonetheless, Bushnell "was very explicit in asserting the righteousness of those claims which God makes on his rebellious subjects." He described God's justice in punishing sin, Williston recalled, as "a *lovely* feature in his character; as though it was but little inferior to mercy itself in its attractiveness."[47]

Bushnell's approach to revivalism was also conservative. The awakening in the Genesee country, at least among orthodox migrants, was apparently free from noise and tumult. Observers described it as solemn and serious, yet deep and powerful. Josiah B. Andrews, a licentiate sent to New York by the CMS in 1800, visited many of the Genesee settlements where Bushnell was laboring. He found "a great revival of religion" in many places and "a solemn expectancy . . . throughout the region." In Freehold the "attention" was "most serious & devout." Bushnell apparently employed no special means to promote these revivals, other than the customary prayer concert. Unlike many Edwardsean revivalists, he disapproved of evening conferences and extended services. "In times of revival," Wines recalled, "he held meetings no longer or later than at other times. To those who wanted to speak before the meeting closed he would say,—'You must speak at the beginning of the meeting; the people will not come again if you keep them too long now.'"[48]

Bushnell steadfastly upheld orthodox tradition against sectarian challenges, and looked askance upon popular movements which opposed his own sense of God's purpose. At times, Wines suggested, this forced him to oppose the wishes of his people. Once, for example, "a certain far-famed itinerant preacher" held a series of meetings "with great apparent success" in a nearby congregation. Many members of Bushnell's church "desired their pastor to invite him to Cornwall," and he agreed "to attend several of the meetings, that he might hear and judge for himself."

Soon, however, "he made up his mind that it would not be for the interest of religion to have such meetings and such preaching" in his own pulpit. Although this decision angered "some of his leading members," he remained "as immovable . . . as the Green Mountains on their everlasting base."[49]

Jedediah Bushnell offers a clear example of a popular evangelist who successfully combined the egalitarian ethos of republican culture with a strong commitment to the traditional doctrines and practices of New England orthodoxy. It was a combination that helped to promote repeated revivals over a career that spanned four decades. His example suggests that many settlers cared more deeply about the style of the minister than about the theological content of the message. An orthodox minister could successfully preach "tyrannical" Calvinism in the new settlements so long as he abandoned external signs of his elite status and addressed the people without condescension.

V

Joseph Badger and Thomas Robbins lacked Bushnell's egalitarian temperament, and had to work harder to bridge the cultural barrier between themselves and the people they served. Unlike Bushnell, who ministered primarily among New England migrants, they routinely worked with Virginians and "Pennamites" as well as Yankees. In both western Pennsylvania and the Connecticut Western Reserve, most settlers were poor Jeffersonian Democrats. In many communities anticlericalism was rampant, even among the leading proprietors, and settlers looked upon orthodox missionary efforts with suspicion.[50] Nonetheless, Badger and Robbins learned to minister effectively in this alien environment, and enthusiastically participated in the camp meeting revivals which occurred throughout western Pennsylvania in the early nineteenth century.

Badger and Robbins displayed some of the same cultural ambiguities exhibited by Bushnell. They were both socially conservative Yale graduates who were passionately committed to Calvinism and to orthodox tradition. Unlike Bushnell, both men had a strong streak of arrogance, and in their letters they sometimes made disparaging comments about the crudeness and doctrinal ignorance of Christians in the new settlements. They also despised democracy, and found frontier politics distasteful. Badger often complained that the Jeffersonian officials in Ohio were "totally void of decency and respectability." Robbins, while passing through western Pennsylvania in 1803, observed a local election, "a spectacle sufficient to sicken republicanism out of the world." In a letter to his father he sarcastically lampooned the democratic process:

> The receivers of votes sit in a house & receive the votes through a small hole in a window. If the voters were admitted in, the house would probably be demolished. Two or three men give votes to all that come, which are put in, generally, without any inquiry. Without, the sovereign people appear in all their majesty. "Jemmy, a'int you a feetheral? Not I." And *possibly* a bad word. "Come then, a glass of whiskey with you." There would certainly be as great a propriety in making the school children in Connecticut choose their instructors.[51]

Despite their strongly elitist impulses, Badger and Robbins both adjusted quickly to frontier life. Although Robbins was the son and grandson of orthodox ministers, and thus had been "born to the study," he was raised in hilly Norfolk, a rural parish that boasted few socially or politically prominent families. Badger, like Bushnell, came from an undistinguished family, and received only a grammar school education until he was in his twenties. He spent his youth farming in Berkshire County, Massachusetts, and during the Revolution served several years as an enlisted soldier in the Continental Army. Both Badger and Robbins could mingle comfortably with the well educated and urbane, and yet readily mix with common people. As missionaries both men developed close friendships with poor families, and freely entered into such community rituals as house and barn raisings, road building, and bridge construction.[52]

Badger, especially, found it easy to assume the role of the backwoods preacher. He was a handy carpenter who not only raised his own cabin and barn, but also made his own furniture, buckets, washtubs, and fences. He often helped settlers with their crops and livestock, assisted them with repairs, and served more than once as a physician. He conscientiously endeavored to fit into frontier society, and became notorious for refusing comfortable lodgings, preferring instead to sleep in the woods several hundred yards away. Because of his eager helpfulness and endearing eccentricities, Calvin Chapin later reported that Badger enjoyed enormous popularity on the Western Reserve until he foolishly involved himself in political controversy.[53]

Badger and Robbins initially shared the common orthodox bias against enthusiasm and bodily exercises. During his first trip to the Connecticut Reserve in 1800, Badger learned that "a pretty general serious awakening" had recently swept through the Presbyterian churches of Washington County, Pennsylvania. In a letter to Nathan Strong, Badger described this outpouring as a western version of the orthodox revivals in Connecticut. The attention was "powerful in humbling the proud heart," but orderly and rational. "By what I can learn," he assured Strong, "the work has been generally free from enthusiasm."[54]

Badger soon discovered, however, that the religious attention in Pennsylvania was quite different from the divine showers in New England. The Washington County awakening was, in fact, the northern extremity of the "great revival" which extended southward to central Georgia. Like the famous camp meetings at Cane Ridge and Gasper River, the Pennsylvania revivals focused upon the Presbyterian "sacramental season," an ecstatic religious ritual that was central to traditional Scots-Irish piety. Throughout the eighteenth century the Scottish immigrants in the Appalachian backcountry had been holding their periodic "holy fairs." Bodily exercises, shouting, and spiritual visions were common occurrences at these events.

According to Leigh Eric Schmidt, from the 1780s down to the 1810s western Pennsylvania was "a preserve for the traditional sacramental occasions of the evangelical Presbyterians."[55] Typically these rituals attracted several hundred or even several thousand worshipers, and lasted four days. The "season" commenced with fasting on the Thursday preceding the sacrament. On Saturday a "preparatory" meeting was held, consisting of alternating exhortations, prayers, and psalm singing that often went on until after midnight. On the Sabbath the sacrament was administered to those regenerate saints who had a right to sit at the communion table, and the alternating exhortations and singing then continued throughout the day. The "season" finally closed on Monday morning with a thanksgiving service.

The sacramental occasion was visually impressive. The number of people who attended these services dwarfed congregations in other mission fields. At the Cross Creek sacrament in June 1803, Joseph Badger estimated that five thousand people were present and that eight hundred communicants came forward to the Lord's table. It was, Badger observed, "the largest by far I had ever seen convened for social worship." To accommodate such huge crowds, residents in the vicinity opened their homes to travelers, but most of the worshipers lived on the grounds in tents, covered wagons, or hastily constructed sheds. Miraculously, it seemed, a large town sprang up overnight in the midst of the Pennsylvania woods. When Badger arrived at Cross Creek on Saturday morning, the "people were gathering from all quarters—probably a thousand were now upon the ground." Around the periphery of the site an encampment was rapidly taking shape: "about twenty five-horse wagons were standing, with as many more large tents pitching around the gathering assembly." In the center of the grounds the people had erected wooden seats "covering nearly an acre of ground," and surrounding these they con-

structed "sheds," or roofed platforms, for preaching. Placed conspicu-
ously in the front of the assembly were several long wooden tables, where
the Lord's Supper would be served to the saints.[56]

At least five ministers and several Presbyterian licentiates were present
at Cross Creek. Once the services began on Saturday afternoon, preaching and singing went on more or less continuously until Tuesday morning, with the preachers and elders "spelling" each other as needed. When
night fell, Badger noted, most of the crowd remained in their places and
candles were placed on trees and posts encircling the grounds, "so as to
give light to the whole congregation." On three consecutive nights "the
greater part" of the crowd refused to retire even after the ministers
reached the point of total exhaustion. "But the elders from several congregations," Badger reported, "tarried with the assembly . . . in this
camp of the Lord through the night." Nothing in the experience of
orthodox Connecticut pastors paralleled the Presbyterian communions,
and the CMS missionaries struggled to find the words to describe the
spectacle. "What we see is not to be told," an amazed Thomas Robbins
concluded. "I might write a week, & you could not obtain an adequate
idea. It is in the highest degree, wonderful & extraordinary."[57]

Among the "extraordinary" things they witnessed at the sacramental
occasions were falling, trances, and people swept up in ecstatic visions.
According to Schmidt such experiences were fairly common at Scottish
and American communions during the seventeenth and eighteenth centuries, especially among the laity. Presbyterian clergymen, like Connecticut Edwardseans, regarded some ecstatic experiences as authentic but
nonetheless remained suspicious of possible enthusiasm. Generally,
Schmidt observes, such experiences played only a minor role in the
communions, but for reasons not fully understood they became a primary
feature of sacramental occasions in the early nineteenth century. Joseph
Badger reported no ecstatic behavior at an 1801 camp meeting east of
Youngstown, Ohio, the first one he ever attended. The following year,
however, at a communion in Elisha Macurdy's Crossroads Congregation
in southwestern Pennsylvania, hundreds of people shouted uncontrolla-
bly and fell helpless from their seats. The phenomenon quickly spread,
and for the next several years was apparently a prominent feature of
Presbyterian communions throughout the Synod of Pittsburgh.[58]

During his tenure with the CMS Joseph Badger observed thousands of
people fall. Though "much opposed for a time to people falling," he soon
altered his opinion and became a strong apologist for bodily exercises. In
an 1803 report on the Cross Creek communion he dismissed the charge
that camp meetings were "enthusiastic," and offered Flint a biblical
defense of falling and shouting. "The enemies of religion," Badger sug-

gested, say that "everything is wild disorder & enthusiasm . . . that awakens up mankind from deep stupidity." The missionary stressed that even though hundreds of people cried out and fell from their seats, including several seated at the Lord's table, the Cross Creek meeting was nonetheless orderly and rational. "I have never seen those who fell left to throw themselves into any indecent situation," he explained. "The ministers, Elders, & pious experienced Christians do watch & strictly guard against every appearance of wildness and disorder."[59]

Furthermore, Badger asserted, those who fell generally possessed a strong sense of their spiritual corruption; their behavior sprang from deep convictions of guilt rather than a false sense of assurance. At Cross Creek he interviewed several people who fell as though dead during his preaching, and "inquired the occasion of their distress." They replied that "it was the apprehension they had . . . of their sins as committed against the Holy God." Badger reasoned that whenever sinful people become powerfully aware of the presence of God it was proper that their strength should fail. The Bible, he reminded Flint, offered many examples:

> When all Israel saw the fire come down and consume the sacrifice & the altar on which Elijah offered sacrifice; they fell on their faces & they said "the Lord he is the God, the Lord he is the God." The disciples in the ships were terrified & cryed out for fear, when they saw Christ walking on the water. Paul fell to the ground, under deep conviction, when going to Damascus. The jailor trembled & fell down before Paul & Silas & said what shall I do?[60]

Thomas Robbins responded to falling and shouting in much the same way. In October 1803, during his initial trip to Ohio, he stopped at Yohogeny, Pennsylvania, to attend a Presbytery meeting and a sacramental occasion held later the same week. Some travelers had arrived for the communion several days early, and they pressed Robbins to preach for them. "I had never seen an instance of falling," the young evangelist wrote, "and if any had fallen that evening while I was preaching, as I have had them many times since, I believe that I should have been so terrified as to be unable to proceed." Just as Robbins closed the service he heard "from the opposite part of the house a very deep crying & sobbing." A small girl had fallen, and was "wholly unable to sit of herself or speak." The excited crowd began to sing hymns, Robbins noted, and soon people throughout the house were tumbling from their seats. "My feelings were exceedingly wrought up," the startled missionary reported to his family. Shouting to make himself heard above the noise, he attempted without success to bring the meeting to order.[61]

During the following week Robbins's initial fear of falling vanished, and he became a wholehearted apologist for the western camp meeting. At the Presbytery meeting he observed many pious and respectable people falling, and the assembled ministers assured him that the phenomenon was common and scriptural. At the Yohogeny sacramental occasion, the first he had ever attended, hundreds fell and shrieked in distress, so that "some of the time the noise was such that the speaker could not be heard." Robbins assisted many who were seized with "the most violent convulsions," and was startled to learn that despite their agitations, "their minds are never more lively & active. . . . They think upon divine things more intensely than at any other time." The scene, he imagined, was much like "Judgment Day," when there would be "groans and sighs expressive of the greatest anguish, shouts of joy & praise, the deepest sobs & cries which can be made, inarticulate noises expressive only of agitation and distress."[62]

The camp meeting at Yohogeny demolished many of Robbins's preconceptions, and at the close of the meeting he publicly announced his change of heart. Asked to preach at the final thanksgiving service on Monday morning, he delivered from memory a revival sermon he had written in Danbury, Connecticut, in 1799. The audience, he noted, "by this time . . . all knew who I was," and listened to him attentively. To his delight, many fell under views of divine glory. At the close of his sermon he expressed joy and gratitude that God had permitted him "to witness the glorious work . . . among them." Filled with emotion, he promised to send an accurate account of the meeting to "our dear fellow Christians in New England," so that they might pray for the continuation of the Awakening in Pennsylvania. The saints in New England and the saints of the West, he announced, were essentially one body, "servants of the same common Lord, brethren of the same church of the Lord Jesus, enlisted in the same glorious cause, hoping in the same divine Redeemer," and destined "to sit down together with the church triumphant above, never to be separated more."[63]

True to his word, Thomas penned a detailed account of the Yohogeny communion for his father, and asked that it be read to the congregation in Norfolk and shared with other ministers. The letter focused primarily upon the topic of falling and enthusiasm, and clearly was designed to dispel orthodox misconceptions about western camp meetings. Thomas suggested two separate explanations for the prevalence of falling. First, like Badger, he reasoned that pious sinners quite properly faint at the approach of the Holy God. "Do you wonder that they fall?" he asked of his family. "Ought we not to wonder that any person in that situation ever can stand?" Indeed, Thomas suggested, truly pious souls found the work all but irresistible: "If my Mamma had been present . . . I question whether she would not have fallen with those who did."[64]

Secondly, Thomas speculated that God intended to arouse the general populace as well as hopeful converts, and therefore employed different tactics depending upon the state of society. Refined people were more easily awakened than rough frontier folk, so that revivals in the West necessarily took a different form than those in New England parishes. "For the highly privileged people of Connecticut," he explained, God could speak in "the still, & as you would say, decent & glorious manner which you have witnessed." In order to impress "the hardened, stupid, ignorant people of these backcountries," however, God wisely "ordered those striking visible appearances which attended the present work."[65]

Thomas's letter evoked mixed responses from his family. His sister Sally worried about his obvious zeal for enthusiastic exercises, and scolded him for dwelling too much upon the subject. "Tho I make no doubt but it is a good & glorious work," Sally complained, "yet I think that part of their exercises is *too* much made of in the . . . letters we have received." "Don't you think in many instances," she anxiously inquired, "those fall down, who have ever been & continue to be strangers to the wicked & total corruptions of their hearts?"[66]

Given the spread of Methodism in Connecticut, and the efforts of orthodox revivalists to forge a middle ground between enthusiasm and liberalism, the letters of Thomas Robbins and Joseph Badger may indeed have seemed dangerous to cautious Congregationalists. Nevertheless, Ammi Robbins obligingly read the Yohogeny narrative "to many of our people in concerts & conferences," as well as to a circle of clergymen that included Judah Champion of Litchfield, Jeremiah Day of New Preston, Peter Starr of East Greenwich, Asahel Hooker of Goshen, Ebenezer Porter of Salisbury, Zephaniah Swift of Roxbury, and Dan Huntington of Litchfield. "Hooker & Huntington," Ammi noted, became "much animated—said they had now a number of things answered wh[ich] they wanted to know." After discussing the narrative at great length, "all agreed it was a work of divine grace."[67]

VI

At first glance it seems remarkable that Badger and Robbins so readily endorsed the intensely tumultuous Pennsylvania camp meetings. Several factors worked together to overcome their culturally-conditioned preconceptions. For one thing, both missionaries observed that the preachers were thoroughly "Calvinistic in sentiment." Also, at least a few of the Presbyterian revivalists had earned college degrees, a fact noted by both men in their reports to the CMS. Although Badger and Robbins considered many of the Pennsylvania clergy to be crude and unlettered, they could not help but be impressed by such men as the Reverend James Hughes, "an excellent preacher" educated at Princeton. Surely, they would have denounced the camp meetings as enthusiastic delusion had they been led by unlettered Methodist exhorters.[68]

More importantly, the sacramental occasion embodied values that powerfully appealed to Connecticut Edwardseans. As proponents of the "pure church," Badger and Robbins believed that only regenerate Christians had the right to partake of the Lord's Supper. Not surprisingly, therefore, the Presbyterian custom of "fencing the tables" deeply impressed them. In this most solemn ritual of the sacramental season, a minister reminded the assembly "that none, who have no right to the table and Children's Bread, may come near it." He then proceeded to enumerate the many "profane sins" which barred people from communion. When this lengthy litany was finished, an invitation was given to all repentant Christians to come forward to the feast. The saints—those who had experienced conversion and had been received into the Church— then rose from their seats and separated themselves from the crowd. Each communicant had already received a small lead token, to be presented to the elders who carefully guarded the communion tables. No one without a token dared to approach the sacred meal.[69]

This elaborate process mesmerized Badger and Robbins. The use of communion tokens and the practice of fencing gave concrete expression to the invisible distinction between the saints and the unregenerate. As Leigh Schmidt has observed, "this ritual . . . proclaimed to the world in precise detail who the unclean and the wicked were and conversely who were the pure and godly." The "pure churches" of Connecticut embraced a similar theology, but they had no parallel ritual for visibly expressing the boundaries of their sacred community.[70]

The first time that Badger and Robbins officiated at a Presbyterian communion, they felt intense elation. Never before, Badger reported to Abel Flint, had he experienced such love and intimate union at the Lord's Supper. "It helped me to get some faint idea of what the saints will enjoy, when they come to see the King in his beauty, & be present at his table without sin or flesh to interrupt their sight." Robbins freely wept as he administered communion at his first sacramental season. "I never witnessed an occasion in which it appeared so much that God was there," he explained to his family. The meal itself especially impressed him:

Conceive a large number of the visible people of Christ sitting around his table, contemplating his sufferings & love, weeping in silent tears at the consideration of their imperfection & his boundless compassion. . . . Conceive them surrounded with two or three thousand beholders of every character, in silent astonishment at the view of scenes they cannot understand, in the midst of whom are scores weeping, groaning & begging for mercy. Your minds will then be much below the reality.[71]

The tangible sense of evangelical community generated by the sacramental occasions exerted an almost magnetic force upon the missionaries. Most historians have regarded the camp meetings of the "Great Revival" as anti-institutional events which promoted individualism and democracy. There was, however, a strongly conservative dimension to these rituals during the eighteenth and early nineteenth centuries. The sacramental occasion was an intensely communal celebration that helped to forge bonds of "mutual love and unity" among the saints, and to reinforce personal and collective commitments to Presbyterian tradition.

Leigh Schmidt has demonstrated that these community revivals followed carefully prescribed forms that effectively bound the people together. Sacramental seasons, occurring only once or twice a year in each congregation, were gala events intended to attract visitors throughout the Presbytery and beyond. Often people from dozens of congregations traveled as far as fifty or sixty miles to participate in the meetings; along the way to the communion, travelers socialized, sang hymns together, and began to establish the friendships that would be cemented by the sacramental rituals. Throughout the "season" they would live together, pray together, weep together, sing together, and perhaps sit together at the table of the Lord. Through this festal gathering, Schmidt has written, "broad geographical communities could thus be forged out of isolated farms and hamlets. . . . Summer-in, summer out, these Presbyterians assembled and reaffirmed the bonds that made them a covenanted people."[72]

Badger and Robbins longed to duplicate this communal experience among the New England migrants in the Connecticut Reserve. As we have already seen, the erosion of New England's traditional communal ethic was the primary impulse behind the Congregational missionary movement. The sacramental occasion seemed to embody a sense of unity, harmony, and mutuality that was notably lacking among many Yankee settlements in New York and Ohio. Badger and Robbins were awestruck by the spectacle of thousands of scattered Calvinists joyously coming together to reaffirm their unity in Christ and their commitment to one another. "Oh how different," Badger lamented, "is the state of things in this county [Trumbull, Ohio] in general. Many of our New England people, when they get here, show themselves to be the most bitter enemies to the Christian religion, & do all in their power to injure the cause."[73]

In 1804 Badger and Robbins attempted to introduce the sacramental occasion among the Congregational settlers in the Reserve, but were quickly disappointed by the lukewarm response. The first recorded attempt was at Smithfield, Ohio, in late September. Robbins's diary suggests that the missionaries faithfully followed the broad outlines of the Presbyterian ritual. They secured "a pleasant place in the woods" to hold the meeting, and gave notice to all of the churches in the region that "public communion" would be observed. The Thursday before the meeting may have been designated a fast day; Robbins notes that he spent much of it "in providing for the sacrament." On Saturday afternoon Badger opened "the exercises of a sacramental occasion." If there was any of the rapture which characterized the Presbyterian gatherings, Robbins failed to record it.[74]

Many people did not arrive until Sunday morning, when the sacrament itself was to be administered. Robbins noted that the Sabbath day crowd was "a large collection of people" who remained "very attentive and solemn" throughout the ceremony. It is unclear whether or not the missionaries adopted the practice of fencing the table, but the service otherwise resembled the Presbyterian practice. Two large tables were placed in the center of the clearing, and "about sixty communicants" came forward in response to the invitation. Robbins administered at one table; Badger at the other. The service continued throughout the day, and on Monday morning a crowd "most as large as yesterday" convened for the closing Thanksgiving service. No dramatic revival had accompanied the event, and no extraordinary physical manifestations of the Spirit had appeared. "I hope," a tired and somewhat disappointed Thomas Robbins noted in his diary, "it received the divine blessing."[75]

The following week, when the missionaries attempted another sacramental occasion at Canfield, the meeting turned into a fiasco. Canfield was a Jeffersonian stronghold, and the missionaries frequently received rough treatment from Democrats in the area. Perhaps unwisely, Badger and Robbins chose to hold the communion less than two weeks before the state elections, when the town was "in a great ferment on account of a town quarrel and the approaching election." On Saturday "very few people attended" the opening service, and some of those who came to the meeting were "quite disorderly." Again, many folks did not arrive until the Sabbath, a day so cold that the meeting had to be moved indoors to "an open new house." Although "a good number of people" attended the communion service itself, by Sunday afternoon the audience had dwindled away. Discouraged, the missionaries "concluded not to have any meeting" on Monday since "there is so little prospect of having any number to attend."[76]

Historians often portray the Congregational clergy as reactionary elitists who attempted to check the populist impulses of the laity. From this standard perspective we might hypothesize that the average Yankee emigrant was more open to innovative modes of worship than the staid clergy. Badger and Robbins, however, clearly wanted to copy the popular communion ritual of the Scots-Irish Pennsylvanians, hoping to revitalize community among the orthodox settlers in the Reserve. To their dismay, the laity themselves showed little inclination to embrace the camp meeting. Both at Smithfield and Canfield many people would come only to the traditional Sunday morning service. In general, Connecticut settlers displayed little interest in preparatory meetings or thanksgiving services. Perhaps because New Englanders had no familiarity with the traditional Presbyterian rituals they did not respond to the sacramental occasion as Badger and Robbins had hoped. Thus, the camp meeting failed to take root in the Reserve, but not because orthodox missionaries opposed its introduction.

Significantly, however, shouting and falling did spread throughout the Reserve in the wake of the camp meetings. Between 1802 and 1805 Badger and Robbins often encountered "extraordinary external manifestations" of the Spirit during preaching engagements and family visits. An especially strong "work of divine grace" broke out in northern Trumbull County in the autumn of 1803 and continued throughout the spring and summer of 1804. The phenomenon seemingly cut across social boundaries, affecting poor settlers as well as wealthy property holders. "Scarcely a family [is] passed over," Robbins reported, "they fall generally, but make very little noise."[77]

The revival was strongest in Smithfield, where Robbins observed that the common "bodily affection is a constant twitching and frequent falling without any cessation. . . . Some pretty violently exercised." In March 1804, Badger visited "Esquire Smith" and "Esquire Brockway," two large landowners in the town. Smith had a five-year old daughter who was "so exercised as frequently to fall helplessly." Brockway also had a young daughter who "frequently falls helplessly under views of Divine Glory."[78]

The missionaries did not denounce such incidents as wild enthusiasm; instead they calmly accepted the behavior as normal in the new settlements. Indeed, Robbins feared that doubting settlers might cause the Holy Spirit to withhold further blessings. Some people in Smithfield were disturbed that "about eight or ten fall almost every meeting," Robbins noted, and "some few people have doubts of the genuineness of the present work of grace." On January 29, 1804 he delivered a sermon defending the convicted subjects against the charge of enthusiastic delusion. "Endeavored to show," he noted in his diary, "that the present work of religion in these back countries is a work of the true spirit. I hope it satisfied many doubting minds."[79]

In differing ways Bushnell, Badger and Robbins combined within themselves a commitment to traditional orthodox values as well as an openness to new modes of thinking and ministering. Despite their conservative social and theological convictions, they recognized the need to adjust to changing circumstances. Their efforts to promote revivals in the new settlements clearly reflected the dual nature of Congregational evangelism in the early republic. On the one hand, they looked back to the covenanted communities of the New England past, and clung tightly to the corporate values they had inherited. On the other hand they embraced innovative means to advance these values, means which could potentially blur the distinction between themselves and the sectarian enthusiasts they opposed. CMS missionaries were certainly traditionalists, but not the one-dimensional reactionaries caricatured by their anticlerical enemies.

CHAPTER

SIX

The CMS and the Republican Frontier

As CMS missionaries fanned out across the northern frontier in the 1790s and early nineteenth century, they encountered a society that in many respects differed from the world they knew in Connecticut and Massachusetts. From northern New England to the Ohio territory, the American backcountry was populated primarily by marginal farmers who were land-rich but cash-poor. Many of these settlers had purchased their land on credit, and looked with deep suspicion or even open hostility upon the elite creditors who seemed to control their economic destiny.

The egalitarian ideology of the Jeffersonians flourished in such an environment, as did the most stridently anticlerical religious movements in the young republic. Backcountry insurgency, Nathan Hatch reminds us, expressed itself not only in such political upheavals as Shays's Rebellion and the Whiskey Insurrection, but also in a host of anticlerical religious movements that competed for the loyalty of New England migrants. The frontier was filled with popular preachers who simultaneously proclaimed Jeffersonian democracy and evangelical Christianity, as though the two were inseparable elements of the same holy gospel.[1]

The Congregational response to the "disorganized" frontier was filled with ambiguity. As we have already seen, orthodox missionaries clung to the communal ideals of the New England past, and most of them found Jeffersonian politics distasteful. Initially, at least, they typically regarded the frontier as an alien and potentially dangerous environment, urgently in need of transformation. At the same time, however, CMS employees remained remarkably open to new ways of thinking and ministering, and quickly learned to compete aggressively with the more democra-

103

tic sectarians for popular favor. In short, orthodox clergymen who labored in the new settlements were themselves transformed by the experience.

The process of adaptation was in many ways hampered and in some ways facilitated by common orthodox preconceptions about frontier existence. When CMS missionaries headed for the mission field, they carried with them a set of deeply-held expectations about "wilderness living" which colored their perceptions of frontier society and powerfully influenced their ministry. Migrants who lived in "wilderness" conditions, they assumed, were peculiarly subject to heresy and temptation, and far harder to awaken to the truth than folk in Connecticut. This parochial myth had important consequences—positive as well as negative—for Congregational missionary efforts in the new settlements.

The concept of wilderness, Roderick Nash has observed, is highly subjective and can be applied to widely divergent environmental conditions. For the Puritans who first settled New England, the wilderness began at the edge of the clearing. God, they believed, had ordained that humans live together in well-organized communities, where man's natural inclination toward sinfulness could be held in check by the influence of laws and civilizing institutions. In the Puritan understanding all unorganized land, that is land not yet cleared and brought under the authority of godly laws and customs, constituted "the wilderness."[2]

Although all European colonizers shared to one degree or another an antipathy toward wilderness, the concept occupied an especially important place in the thinking of New England's founders. The Puritans, whose typological exegesis of the Old Testament led them to identify themselves with ancient Israel, regarded their own migration to the new world as a reenactment of the Exodus. Just as the Israelites had fled from bondage in Egypt, they had fled from the oppressive wickedness of England. And like the children of Israel they expected to sojourn in the wilderness for a time before God would permit them to possess the promised land in America. New Englanders, Edward Johnson believed, were like "the ancient Beloved of Christ, whom he of old led by the hand from Egypt to Canaan, through that great and terrible wildernesse."[3]

Puritan ministers derived from scripture a clear image of what the encounter with the wilderness entailed. In Hebraic thought wilderness connoted the harsh and seemingly barren desert land, the special abode of demons. Furthermore, the Garden myth associated wilderness with sin and immorality. When Yahweh became angry with his rebellious children, he threatened to curse Israel by turning it into a desolate wilderness; when he blessed Israel, the wilderness became a fruitful garden. Because man was peculiarly subject to attack from evil while in the wilderness, the biblical writers believed that God often used the cursed land to test the faith of his chosen ones. In the Exodus narrative God leads the Israelites through forty years of wilderness trials in order to purge them and to prepare them to fulfill their priestly function. After his baptism Jesus is led by the Spirit into the wilderness, where he endures forty days of temptation in preparation for his ministry. While these stories clearly demonstrated that evil was under the sovereign rule of Yahweh, they also underscored the dark and terrifying character of the wilderness. From such accounts, as Nash has noted, European Christians came to associate the conquest of wilderness with moral progress.[4]

Early modern Christians often employed wilderness as a metaphor for fallen humanity, and the subjugation of wilderness as a symbol for redemption. Anglo-American Calvinists were quite familiar with such literary and rhetorical devices. John Bunyan's *Pilgrim's Progress,* for example, a favorite devotional text among New Englanders as late as the nineteenth century, begins with the phrase, "As I walk'd through the wilderness of this world." According to Roger Williams, "the wildernesse is a clear resemblance of the world, where greedie and furious men persecute and devoure the harmless and innocent as the wilde beasts pursue and devoure the Hinds and Roes." Thus the famous Puritan "errand into the wilderness" involved not only the literal penetration of the "wild" New England forests, but also a metaphorical encounter with evil and a typological victory over the sinful world. Like the Old Testament Exodus, Puritans believed, the establishment of their city upon a hill offered tangible proof to all mankind that God was redeeming a fallen humanity from its wilderness condition.[5]

In the early republic orthodox New England clergymen continued to embrace this negative understanding of wilderness, and consistently applied it in their analysis of the new settlements. Their forefathers had made the wilderness "blossom as the rose" through the establishment of covenanted communities. The cities and villages of New England constituted a new world Zion, and the Congregational clergy had inherited the task of safeguarding the covenant upon which it rested. Orthodox leaders viewed the frontier to the North and West as dark and foreboding. Until the new settlements were blessed by the creation of covenanted churches and godly institutions they would remain in a wilderness condition, and the migrants would be continually subject to the dangers peculiar to wilderness sojourners. It mattered not that many settlements were only a few days' ride from Connecticut, or that some townships had already passed beyond the frontier phase before they received their first visit from a Congregational missionary. To the orthodox mind all communities that lacked a "regular ministry" and a properly gathered church were prone to the licentiousness and sloth that Puritan evangelist John Eliot once referred to as "wilderness temptations."[6]

In this regard the attitude of Congregational missionaries differed markedly from that of Methodist circuit riders. Methodist preachers in the new settlements generally possessed little formal schooling, and were less attached to the intellectual traditions that dominated Yale and other orthodox centers of learning. This fact probably helps to explain their greater receptiveness to the new Romantic attitude toward nature which began to appear in the late eighteenth century. Methodist circuit riders typically inverted the orthodox understanding of wilderness; for them the frontier constituted a sanctuary from the degenerate towns and cities of the East, where church and state were dominated by an arrogant learned elite who had turned society into a moral wasteland.[7]

It is striking that Methodist memoirs rarely referred to frontier settlements as "wilderness," a term that appears frequently in the journals of orthodox evangelists. Francis Asbury, who suffered many privations as he journeyed tirelessly through the backcountry from Georgia to Maine, nonetheless felt perfectly at home in what he sometimes called his "solitary" surroundings. But visiting Connecticut in 1794, Asbury could "scarcely find a breath of living, holy, spiritual religion here, except amongst a few women in East Hartford." "Will Methodism ever live in such whited walls and painted sepulchers as these people," Asbury asked of orthodox Connecticut churchmen a few years later, "who delight to dwell insensibly to the life of religion, and closed up in their own formality and imaginary security?"[8]

The contrast between virtuous frontier folk and demoralized city dwellers became a standard theme of Methodist literature in the nineteenth century. According to the circuit rider Peter Cartwright, frontier Methodists were models of piety precisely because they were free from the influence of elite institutions and man-made laws and traditions. Thus unfettered, God's Spirit could more easily lead them in the ways of righteousness. As Methodism gradually became more institutionalized in the nineteenth century, Cartwright feared that the movement would perish. "Multiply colleges, universities, seminaries, and academies," he warned, "multiply our agencies, and editorships, and fill them . . . with our best and most efficient preachers, and you localize the ministry and secularize them too." Then, he prophesied, "we plunge right into Congregationalism, and stop precisely where all other denominations started."[9]

The anti-institutionalism expressed by Cartwright made no sense from the perspective of Congregational evangelists. From their vantage point schools, academies, colleges, and literary institutions aided in the propagation of revealed truth, and thus helped to elevate society above the barbarous state toward which mankind naturally inclined. Without such institutions a covenanted community could not be maintained for long. With such institutions, properly governed, society would reap both material and spiritual blessings. "Look at some parts of New England," the orthodox missionary Giles Cowles observed in the early nineteenth century, "& you may see the durable effects of the good civil and religious institutions which were introduced by our wise and pious ancestors." Because of the civilizing efforts of the Puritan fathers, "good effects have continued down amidst all revolutions of time for . . . two hundred years." The task confronting Congregational evangelists, at least in part, was to carry this civilizing mission forward.[10]

Some orthodox leaders viewed the migration of New Englanders to the new settlements as a reenactment of the original Puritan migration to the wilderness. New England's sons and daughters had gone forth, as had their ancestors, "to make the wilderness rejoice and blossom as the rose." The Reverend Ammi Robbins believed that God planned to use "those precious scattering emigrants" to establish "His name & praise in those wilds which have for ages been only the dwelling places for beasts of prey & savages as ignorant as they." Before this could occur, however, migrants would be tested and tempted to the limits of their endurance, just as their ancestors had been before them. Nathan Perkins, riding through Vermont in 1789, observed that destitution, famine, and disease were the universal lot of frontier inhabitants. The terrified evangelist lost his way while passing through "ye wilderness on ye Lake Champlain" and "expected every step to be killed." Such trials led him to meditate upon the sacrifices made by earlier saints. "I can now realize," the urbane clergyman reflected, "what our forefathers suffered in settling America!"[11]

Throughout the early republican era Congregational leaders repeatedly urged New Englanders to take pity upon "their fellow Christians in the Wilderness," who confronted extraordinary trials without the comfort and guidance of the "common means of grace." Pious church members, the Connecticut General Association asserted in 1793, ought to place themselves in the "circumstances of their brethren in a wilderness," who lived without the benefit of proper churches or schools and "in a great measure without good books." In such destitute circumstances even the most faithful migrants could succumb to the spiritual lassitude fostered by wilderness living. Only prompt missionary action, the General Association believed, could prevent the corruption of myriad souls by vice and "gross heresy."[12]

During the 1830s Giles Cowles summarized for his "young brethren" the importance of orthodox evangelism. In a missionary sermon Cowles reminded prospective evangelists that they were "in a peculiar manner responsible" for the moral condition of the nation. Missionaries labored in "new and destitute" regions where schools, churches, and literary institutions were virtually nonexistent. The "manners and habits" of frontier settlers, Cowles believed, reflected the crude conditions in which they lived. Missionaries promoted godly habits and discouraged wilderness vices, not only by their preaching and praying, but also by encouraging "schools & all institutions calculated to promote the cause of Christ and the good of the community." The "religious sentiments & practices . . . which you may be means of introducing or confirming," the old evangelist insisted, "will probably continue for years and generations yet to come, & be means of lasting good or evil for years after you are moulding in dust."[13]

So strong was the influence of the wilderness myth upon orthodox thinking that Congregational missionaries had a difficult time perceiving frontier society accurately until they had lived in the mission field for an extended time. Beginning missionaries typically regarded missionary service as an epic adventure. The call to mission initiated a dangerous journey which wrenched the heroic missionary out of his customary world and placed him in an exotic environment filled with deadly enemies. Not only could the missionary expect to encounter wild beasts and a host of natural dangers, but also satanic adversaries in various human guises. The wilderness harbored robbers and murderers and scoundrels of all types. Giles Cowles warned young missionaries that "the enemies of Christ's cause" would come out "boldly in their opposition." Missionaries must expect to encounter "many infidels" and "open opposers and scoffers," as well as "many ministers of Satan, transformed as ministers of rightness, who under their hypocritical garb are propagating gross & dangerous errors." Ministers who accepted the call to "travel in the lonesome paths of the wilderness," the Reverend Cyprian Strong observed in a sermon delivered at the ordination of Jedediah Bushnell, must expect to find no comforts or consolations other than the knowledge that "the cause . . . is the cause of God."[14]

In light of these preconceptions it is not surprising that new missionaries often approached their tours with mounting apprehension. In the orthodox imagination the new settlements were a world apart from the villages of southern New England, an alien land where inconceivable trials and potential disaster awaited pilgrim Christians. When Ammi Robbins was commissioned to tour the Mohawk Valley in 1793 he harbored doubts about his safe return, even though his trip took him only a few hundred miles through well-charted territory. "Daddy has returned from his tour verry well," a relieved Sally Robbins later informed her worried brother Thomas, "which I did not expect." Several years later, when Thomas followed his father into the mission field, he experienced similiar apprehensions upon reaching the Hudson River, the Rubicon separating his familiar world from the uncertain wilderness. "Crossed the Hudson to Catskill," he noted in his diary. "Will a holy God preserve me and enable me to recross it with joy?"[15]

For at least some Congregational ministers the prospect of confronting physical hardship and spiritual danger was itself a powerful motive for undertaking missionary labor. Joseph Conforti has perceptively suggested that Edwardsean clergymen needed opportunities to test their own disinterested benevolence. Missionary work provided an ideal outlet for this need. By sacrificing familiar comforts and voluntarily exposing themselves to "satanic" attacks, young evangelists could gain a measure of assurance that they had experienced regeneration.[16]

The blessedness of heroic suffering was perfectly illustrated by the eighteenth-century Indian missionary David Brainerd, whose journal became required reading for Edwardsean students during the early republic. In actual life Brainerd's accomplishments had been negligible. Employed in 1742 by the Society in Scotland for Propagating Christian Knowledge, the young evangelist worked ineffectively among the Indians of New York, New Jersey, and Pennsylvania for only a few years before he succumbed to consumption. During this period he became a close friend and protégé of Jonathan Edwards, and was engaged to wed Edwards's daughter at the time of his death. Edwards regarded Brainerd's diary as a masterpiece of Christian piety, and after the young man died he edited the manuscript for publication. Published as the *Life of Brainerd,* the work eventually became Edwards's most popular book.[17]

Edwardsean pastors regarded Brainerd as the perfect model of disinterested benevolence. His journal conjured up vivid images of wilderness privations and terrifying encounters with savage humans. The saintly missionary endured chronic physical illness, unrelenting opposition, and repeated failure. In the face of these trials he seemed to exhibit total dependence upon God, unfailing self-denial, and a willingness to suffer with joy for the spread of God's kingdom. To many orthodox ministers the emulation of such a hero seemed a worthy ambition.[18]

Brainerd's example inspired missionary efforts on two continents. In 1798 John Love, Secretary of the London Missionary Society, expressed his hope that New England might produce "a host" of Brainerds, "by whose exertions the whole American wilderness may become a field of blessings, a vineyard of red wine, a garden of heavenly pleasures and fruit." At the time many young men in New England embraced the same lofty vision. David Bacon, a licentiate who traveled to Detroit in 1800 for the CMS, first decided to become a missionary after reading Brainerd's journal as a youth. Like many other Connecticut evangelists Bacon carried a copy of Brainerd's *Life* with him on his journey, and struggled to match the piety of his hero. So, too, did Seth Williston, who avidly read Brainerd as he toured central New York during the 1790s, seeking to embody the same "fervor of soul which distinguished that eminent servant of God."[19]

With Brainerd's example before them, missionaries like Samuel P. Robbins renounced comfortable callings and "worldly objects" in order to "follow the church into the wilderness." Such missionaries took literally Christ's commandment to leave everything behind for the sake of God's kingdom. The call to missionary service, Robbins declared, was a call to forsake all worldly ambitions for "things of a sublimer nature." Seth Williston agreed. "O Lord, thou knowest my heart," he wrote in his diary. "Thou knowest whether I am a volunteer in the service of the new settlements, or whether I have a secret desire to be accommodated in a rich, gay parish" with a "painted church and a bell." In true martyr spirit, Williston petitioned God for the grace "to preach all my days in loghuts & never again ascend a pulpit if it is most for the glory of thy Kingdom."[20]

The drive toward heroic suffering probably accounts for the tendency of new Congregational missionaries to exaggerate the degree of destitution and hardships experienced on their tours. In their journals they often lamented the terrible food they were forced to consume, the "rough & miry roads" they followed, the life-threatening rivers they crossed, and the cold houses they slept in. Everyday aspects of frontier existence assumed epic proportions fraught with eternal significance. Inconveniences and difficulties became terrifying tests of their spiritual condition. In the face of these trials, they believed, they were to submit themselves faithfully to God's protection and to suffer gladly like their hero Brainerd.

The desire to suffer heroically could take bizarre form. Joseph Badger became notorious throughout the Western Reserve for his tales of hairbreadth escapes from accidents and wild beasts. His most famous story involved a ferocious bear who supposedly attacked him while he was returning home from a preaching engagement. The evangelist escaped by climbing a tree, but the bear refused to leave, so that Badger was obliged to spend the entire night clinging to a limb and praying for deliverance. It is impossible to determine what degree of truth lay behind such stories, but almost certainly they were exaggerated. The Reverend Calvin Chapin, a Trustee of the Connecticut Missionary Society, toured the Western Reserve in 1806 and found people throughout the area joking about Badger's bear. The missionary also gained notoriety for refusing invitations to sleep in private homes, preferring instead to spend the night sleeping in the nearby woods.[21]

Seth Williston brooded over his seeming inability to match Brainerd's heroism. Deprived of the large meals that he was accustomed to eating at home, he experienced chronic hunger throughout his 1797 missionary tour of New York. Williston regarded his appetite as "a dark symptom" of spiritual corruption. "Mr. Brainerd said that eating & drinking was a low kind of happiness for him," he noted in his journal. "I wish that I could say so!" Nor was this the only dark symptom which disturbed him. Many aspects of missionary life frightened the young evangelist, who seemed unable to dispel from his mind a foreboding of disaster. Unlike Brainerd, he sadly realized, "I am afraid to die."[22]

Throughout the 1790s and early 1800s the Connecticut General Association routinely published portions of missionary journals in magazines and annual reports. These narratives did much to perpetuate the belief that the new settlements were moral wastelands, and that orthodox Christians who migrated must anticipate severe attacks upon their faith. Such accounts served several useful purposes. They undoubtedly helped to generate enthusiasm for domestic missions among New England congregations, and probably inspired at least some ministers to take up missionary work. They may also have strengthened the determination of at least some migrants to resist sectarian attacks upon their faith.

But the wilderness myth could also be a liability to orthodox efforts. Nineteenth century Methodist publications delighted in lampooning the exaggerated fears of New England missionaries, and their apparent ignorance of frontier life-styles. Circuit rider James B. Finley told the story of a young orthodox missionary, fresh from his theological studies, who resolved to preach "in the wilds of the West" after reading accounts of frontier destitution in New England religious periodicals. Although the prospect of encountering robbers and murderers terrified the young evangelist, he determined with "a martyr spirit" to preach the gospel "and to introduce the meliorating influences of civilization" among his perishing countrymen in the wilderness.

The young man had been on mission ground only one day, Finley related, before he found himself lost and hungry. Toward nightfall he encountered "an uncouth specimen of humanity" whose "personal appearance, dress, and equipage, manifested no friendly design." The stranger's head "was covered with the skin of the prairie wolf, with tail hanging behind." His hunting shirt, with "the cape and side-strips curiously notched and fringed," had an "alarming aspect," as did the "formidable knife" thrust into his leather belt. His unkempt black beard, swarthy countenance, and "rough, stalwart frame" were equally shocking. "Every indication painted most vividly on the perturbed imagination of the missionary the danger that hung over his head."

Thinking that he had been accosted by a murderer or robber, the orthodox evangelist at first thought to flee. But second thought "convinced him of the hopelessness of the attempt," and praying to heaven for protection he submitted himself to his fate. The stranger led the terrified missionary to his rough cabin and fed him a coarse meal. But "bewildered and confused" the young man could not eat, still expecting at any time to be robbed of his few possessions. Among these was a "small package of neatly-written sermons, which had cost him several months labor," by which he hoped "to disperse the clouds of ignorance" that brooded over the poor frontiersmen.

Soon after dinner the supposed ruffian and his wife struck up "the favorite hymn of the followers of Wesley," and then proceeded to pray "with several audible groans," affectionately remembering the missionary "at the throne of mercy." Only then did the startled young man relax, ashamed that he had mistaken the "kind-hearted local Methodist preacher" for a robber. To the missionary's surprise, Finley reported, he "found a field of labor in a new and growing village, among a population quite as intelligent and virtuous as the people of his native state."[23]

Peter Cartwright also criticized the "newly-fledged missionaries" from New England who undertook "to civilize and Christianize the poor heathens of the West." Although they would encounter hundreds of spirit-filled gospel preachers on their tours, Cartwright complained, they nonetheless would "write back to the old states hardly anything else but wailings and lamentations over the moral wastes and destitute condition of the West." When "the ignorant and uninformed thousands" read these letters, the Methodist observed, they "would melt into tears, and . . . liberally contribute their money to send us more missionaries." The backwoods preacher was outraged by orthodox evangelists, who would accept invitations to preach "in large and respectable Methodist congregations" and then "write back and give those doleful tidings."[24]

Cartwright asserted that the missionary narratives published in New England served to assist Methodist circuit riders in the new settlements. "Now, what confidence could the people have in such missionaries," he queried, "who would state things as facts that had not even the semblance of truth in them?" Through their exaggerated stories, Cartwright claimed, orthodox preachers often destroyed their own usefulness, "and cut off all access to the people." Once, he recalled, the citizens of one frontier community became so outraged by false reports about their

spiritual condition that they offered him "a thousand dollars per an-
num . . . if I would go as a missionary to the New England States, and
enlighten them on this and other subjects."[25]

We should not accept such stories as accurate representations of frontier Congregational evangelists. As we shall see, most orthodox missionaries differed markedly from the Methodist caricature. It is important to
note that these reminiscences were penned during the 1850s by elderly
Methodist statesmen, at a time when Methodism was rapidly losing its
sectarian quality and becoming a more institutionalized organization.
Pioneers like Finley and Cartwright feared for the future of their denomination, and had strong reason to emphasize the radical distinction between the early Methodist heroes and their "genteel" Congregational
competition.

Despite the apocryphal quality of these Methodist memoirs, there
nonetheless was a kernal of truth in their observations about orthodox
missionary narratives. The editors of the *Connecticut Evangelical Magazine* sometimes received hostile letters from readers who were outraged
by distorted narratives. Many migrants understandably felt angry when
they read reports that portrayed them as licentious heathens. In 1798
Joshua Leonard, a Connecticut minister who had migrated the preceding
year to Cazenovia, New York, warned the General Association that "the
missionaries journals published in New England would not bear reading
in this country." When New Yorkers read the narratives, Leonard advised, they suspected that orthodox missionaries "designedly misrepre-
sented" frontier conditions. The "impression which their contents . . .
make on your mind," he observed, "is far different from what you would
learn were you located in this country one year."[26]

Such letters lend some credence to Methodist claims that New England missionaries alienated frontier settlers by their arrogance and their
ignorance. Clearly, orthodox evangelists had to relinquish their preconceptions about "wilderness living" before they could effectively minister
to migrants who resided in the new settlements.

But acclimatization took time. The earliest Congregational missionaries, who generally were settled pastors like Nathan Perkins, traveled
only briefly through frontier communities before returning to comfortable parishes in Connecticut. Their exposure to frontier conditions was
too brief, and their intimacy with the settlers too superficial, to challenge
their preconceptions significantly. They were likely to find most aspects
of frontier existence crude and distasteful, and to come away from their
tours fortified in their prejudice against wilderness living. "The Lord has
carried me out & brought me in," the Reverend David Higgins of Lyme,
Connecticut, reflected characteristically at the close of his 1794 trip

through Vermont. "I have seen . . . his way in the wilderness & blessed be his name."[27]

As Leonard's letter suggests, however, orthodox ministers who remained long enough in the new settlements gradually began to feel more at home in their adopted environment. Many soon began to acquire the same habits and manners as the "destitute" folk they had come to save and civilize. The seasoning process took varying lengths of time, and different ministers adapted to different degrees. But most orthodox preachers, once settled in the new settlements, learned to minister effectively in social conditions far different from Hartford or New Haven. Their transformation could be so complete as to shock those new missionaries who still thought of the ministry as a dignified, scholarly office. David Higgins, after his return from Vermont in 1794, lamented the "wretched creatures" who served as clergymen in frontier communities. "And I am sorry to say," he reported to his friend Benjamin Trumbull, "our own denomination suffers on this account as much as any."[28]

Nathan Perkins felt a similiar disgust upon meeting Vermont's orthodox clergy. For all their piety and educational advantages, he reported, they appeared as "rustic" as any other migrants. Perkins considered the Vermont association of congregational ministers to be an "[i]lliterate, miserably appearing body," and complained that there was "scarcely any sensible preaching in the state." The Reverend Mr. Swift, "ye Apostle of Vermont," supervised a household that was "unpolished,—countrified in manners, and without any elegance." The Reverend Mr. Beebe, from a fine genteel family, had sacrificed "honor & ye prospects for wealth" to become a frontier preacher. Now, Perkins observed, he appeared to be "destitute of neatness" and displayed only "little reading."[29]

The "inelegant" appearance of Vermont's orthodox pastors undoubtedly reinforced Perkins's fears about wilderness temptations. Clearly, it seemed to the dignified clergyman that not even the staunchest Congregational migrants could resist the corrupting influence of the disordered frontier. In reality, however, these backcountry ministers were learning to accommodate the democratic aspirations that permeated the new settlements. It was a necessary adjustment if orthodox preachers were going to transmit their message successfully beyond the established towns and cities of New England. As we shall see, many Congregational missionaries made the adjustment without great difficulty.

CHAPTER SEVEN

The CMS and Republican Religion

The Congregational missionary movement was not designed to prop up an embattled orthodoxy. As we have seen, orthodox missionary leaders were driven by a desire to keep covenant with New England migrants in "the wilderness," as well as by millennial expectancy. The creation of the CMS constituted a positive, forward-looking response to social change, not primarily a negative reaction against sectarian competition or the threat of disestablishment.

Nonetheless, confrontation with preachers of other denominations was necessarily a major concern of Congregational missionaries in the field. From northern New England to the Ohio country, CMS employees came into constant contact with Methodist circuit riders, regular and freewill Baptist preachers, Universalists, freethinkers, and vocal proponents for a host of other sects. In the absence of any meaningful checks on religious expression, republican Americans were free to reject the authority of traditional creeds and platforms, and to espouse virtually any set of beliefs that conscience and personal taste might dictate. Post-revolutionary Americans experienced, as Robert Wiebe has observed, a dramatic "revolution in choices" that made the early republic a fertile environment for the growth of new religious movements of remarkable diversity. "Whenever someone discovered new nooks and crannies on the spiritual landscape," Martin Marty has written, "they quickly developed new movements or sects. The message of the aggressors to the uncommitted was 'be saved!' and to each other, 'Adapt or die!'"[1]

Many scholars have concluded that Congregationalism declined after the Revolution because orthodox ministers could not adapt to this fluid new environment. Most assessments of orthodox evangelism share the assumption, clearly stated by Roger Finke and Rodney Stark, that Congregational ministers in the early republic were "men of learning and elegance," who were "recruited from and moved most comfortably within . . . the social and financial elite." These genteel clerics "flocked to Harvard and Yale but . . . would not serve churches outside the settled and comfortable towns and cities." While "rough and ready" sectarian upstarts made "immense strides . . . in churching America," Finke and Stark conclude, the Congregational clergy complacently "dozed."[2]

According to Finke and Stark, Methodists and Baptists could compete for "shares" in the free "American religious market" far more effectively than Congregationalists. Well-paid, well-educated, and "highly professional" clergymen, the sociologists observe, "dominated" the orthodox churches. They preached a "sedate and learned" gospel, offering metaphysical discourses that had little to say about "sin and salvation, or hellfire and redemption." Methodist and Baptist preachers, in contrast, were "common folk" who preached to their neighbors for little or no compensation. They spoke extemporaneously in the vernacular, "stressing spiritual conversion" and the need for personal "experience with the sacred." They "looked like ordinary men because they were," Finke and Stark assert, "and their sermons could convince ordinary people because their message was direct and clear." Unlike orthodox ministers, who read "carefully drafted, scholarly, and often dry sermons" from notes, the Methodist and Baptist exhorters proclaimed a message that "seemed to issue directly from divine inspiration."[3]

Furthermore, the orthodox clergy supposedly failed to understand the need for aggressive competition in a free market. According to Finke and Stark, the Congregationalists never successfully developed a "marketing technique" because they were "accustomed to gentlemen's agreements limiting competition." Unlike the Methodists and Baptists, they did not see a need to use aggressive means to gather souls, nor did they take decisive steps to counter the inroads made by sectarian challengers. "In contrast," Finke and Stark observe, "when Baptists and Methodists collided in pursuit of flocks, no holds were barred and no quarter was asked or given."[4]

Finke and Stark pursue a supply-side approach in their analysis of Congregationalist declension and sectarian success. They focus upon the purveyors of the gospel rather than the audience, and locate the source of religious change in what the churches did correctly—or incorrectly—in their efforts to convert the American people. Historian Terry Bilhartz takes a similiar approach in his study of Baltimore during the Second Great Awakening. Baltimore Methodists succeeded better than any other sect at sparking revival, Bilhartz concludes, "because they labored so diligently to promote it." While other churches desired "an enlarged and invigorated congregation," they were "unwilling to risk disrupting either the dignity of religion or the status profile of the church to reach these ends." Unlike Presbyterians and Episcopalians, for example, "Methodists made evangelism their top priority and unhesitatingly pursued all means available to achieve this goal."[5]

Although Bilhartz does not examine the Congregationalists, who did not venture as far south as Baltimore, his work may be regarded as the standard supply-side explanation for Methodist success vis à vis the more established denominations. Methodists expected converts, and to get them "they preached at camp, town, and convention meetings, in worship houses, public places, and forest groves, before bishops, artisans, and slaves." The Methodists "sang and shouted, prayed and praised, and while others complained of declension, they counted their converts by the thousands."[6] Presumably, had other churches made the same energetic efforts at evangelism they would have grown as well.

Nathan Hatch also asserts that Methodists and other sectarian evangelists were unlettered, simple folk who addressed the common people more zealously and effectively than the genteel Congregational clergy. In addition to this common supply-side argument, he also emphasizes broader social and ideological currents that apparently worked against the old colonial establishments. According to Hatch, the egalitarian ideals of the Revolution permeated every dimension of popular culture in the early republic, creating a grass-roots demand "for a theology of the people." Most citizens rejected Calvinism as outdated and elitist, and stridently insisted upon the right of all persons to interpret scripture for themselves, without the guidance of creeds, educated clergymen, or abstract theologies. From Hatch's perspective, orthodox Congregationalism had ceased to be culturally relevant. Republican citizens did not want to buy the message that the aristocratic orthodox preachers had to proclaim; no amount of evangelism would have made the Calvinistic New Englanders more popular.[7]

Although these standard interpretations of orthodox declension capture elements of historical reality, they badly distort the nature of Congregational evangelism in the early republic. As suggested in the preceding chapter, orthodox missionaries in the new settlements underwent a seasoning process. They soon abandoned many of their preconceptions about wilderness living, embraced as much as possible a popular style of ministry, and attempted to adapt to their new surroundings. As a result Congregational ministers who served communities in the new settlements—the men most responsible for the growth or declension of

Congregationalism—quickly developed an outlook and style quite different from the clergy who remained in the long established parishes of New
England.

Historians have failed to observe this regional dichotomy because they
have focused upon the wrong ministers. Perhaps because settled pastors
in southern New England were much more likely to attain social promi-
nence and to publish their sermons and memoirs, they have received far
more attention from scholars than the Congregational ministers who
joined the frontier migration. Thus Lyman Beecher, Timothy Dwight,
and Jedediah Morse are familiar names to most students of the early
republic, while the equally important Joseph Badger, John Seward, and
Seth Williston remain unknown.

Careful analysis of the 148 ministers employed by the CMS between
1798 and 1818 clearly reveals the inadequacy of existing interpretations
of orthodox declension. Most scholarly assumptions about post-
revolutionary Congregational evangelism are either patently false or misleading half-truths. Congregational evangelists cannot accurately be described as genteel scholars, unless we employ this term to define everyone
who received at least some college education during the early republic.
They generally were as well-suited for life in the new settlements as most
other settlers. They did not force metaphysical sermons upon unwilling
audiences, read dry discourses from notes, confine their efforts to comfortable settlements, nor shy away from aggressive confrontation with
sectarian competitors. Accounts of Congregational evangelism penned
by nineteenth-century Methodists, as well as twentieth-century scholars,
typically exaggerate the social distance between orthodox and sectarian
preachers in the early nation. They invariably exaggerate, too, the "competitive edge" enjoyed by Methodist and Baptist exhorters, and under-
estimate the ability of Congregational missionaries to build up large
followings in the new settlements.

II

Congregational missionaries did not generally come from "the social and
financial elite," as Finke and Stark suggest. It is perfectly true, of course,
that the orthodox churches continued to rely primarily upon college-
educated pastors, and that the possession of a "liberal education" automatically placed one within a small, select class of citizens. Attainment of
a college degree traditionally marked one as a gentleman, and therefore

held powerful symbolic significance, particularly for the majority of people who never went beyond common school. In this restricted sense only can we speak of the Congregational evangelists as an elite group.

Despite their college training, CMS missionaries did not come from socially or politically influential families. While possession of a liberal education might make one a gentleman, not all gentlemen in early America came from equally exalted stations in life. Harvard and Yale, for example, both offered numerous scholarships for pious poor youth; approximately 12 percent of the eighteenth century New England clergy came from this class. Among their number was Joseph Badger, who obtained admission to Yale through the patronage of his friend, the Reverend Jeremiah Day. According to the Reverend Nathan Perkins, Badger could not have attended the school without the assistance of his "poor—homely—kind" wife, who "helped to defray ye expenses of his Education by her own industry."[8]

Within the ranks of those admitted to Yale and Harvard there was a broad gradation of status and wealth, from promising "charity cases" to the sons of New England's political scions. A minority of the students who passed through these schools entered the ministry, and these generally came from the poor or middling families rather than the very wealthy. According to Donald Scott, only 28 percent of Yale graduates between 1750 and 1800 became clergymen, and the percentage declined during the nineteenth century. In short, the ministry was not the occupation of choice for wealthy youth with ambitions for social or political leadership.[9]

Scott has demonstrated that the number of poor and marginal youth entering the Congregational ministry dramatically increased in the early republic. To help ease the shortage of clergy, orthodox ministerial associations in the late eighteenth century began aggressively recruiting pious "hopeful" youth for ministry, and numerous organizations were established to assist those who could not afford a liberal education. Although Finke and Stark assert that the Congregational clergy "flocked to Harvard and Yale," the vast majority of these ministerial recruits attended one of the newer "provincial" colleges, such as Amherst, Bowdoin, Dartmouth, Hamilton, Middlebury, or Williams. "In many ways," Scott notes, "these provincial colleges bear a stronger resemblance to the community colleges of the twentieth century than they do to eighteenth century Yale and Harvard." They offered a basic liberal education at one half to two- thirds the cost of Yale, and attracted primarily youth from the surrounding agricultural communities, not the elite. Typically these students were the first members of their families to attend college. Like the shoemaker Jedediah Bushnell, they generally worked their way through school, and often had to wait until they were in their twenties before they had saved enough money to enroll.[10]

Prior to the creation of the CMS in 1798, all the men sent out on brief tours by the Connecticut General Association were older men who had graduated from Yale or Princeton. They generally did not spring from the social elite, however. As we have seen, most of those who accepted commissions were New Divinity pastors settled in the rural backcountry of Connecticut. These New Divinity men, Joseph Conforti observes, were often ridiculed as "farmer metaphysicians" by more urbane clergymen. "The vast majority" of them, he writes, hailed "from modest or obscure social backgrounds."[11]

An exception to this rule was Nathan Perkins, West Hartford's New Divinity pastor, who was one of the first orthodox missionaries to tour the new settlements in Vermont. Perkins's wealthy Norwich family controlled substantial landholdings, and his father stood near the top of the town's social elite. As a youth Nathan received a strong classical education, and at Princeton College he quickly distinguished himself as a Latin scholar. In 1770 he graduated at the top of his class and was selected salutatorian. Throughout his life Perkins rubbed shoulders with the rich and powerful, and played a leading role in many of Hartford's educational and cultural institutions, including the Connecticut Academy of Arts and Sciences.[12]

In many ways Perkins epitomized the arrogant, genteel orthodox missionary so often lampooned by the Methodists. Throughout his 1789 tour of Vermont he complained about the ignorance of the people and the vileness of their manners and lifestyle. He delivered long, polished sermons filled with classical allusions, and swelled with pride when the less educated Vermont ministers praised him as "philosophical—Deep—penetrating—a great scholar." Such praises did little to ease his constant longing for home, however, and "a table richly furnished & elegantly set." He felt himself always to be a stranger sojourning in a strange land, even though he invariably lodged with the most respectable families that he could find.[13]

Perkins, however, was a truly exceptional case. Most Congregational missionaries had less exalted social and educational backgrounds. Of the 148 men who received CMS commissions between 1798 and 1818, only thirty-five (23 percent) attended Yale. None of the missionaries graduated from Harvard; a few, at most, matriculated from Princeton. Thus, more than 70 percent of the men who itinerated for the CMS in this period received their liberal educations from provincial institutions. Moreover, at least four of the evangelists educated at Yale commenced their studies at Dartmouth or Williams before transferring to the more expensive Connecticut school to complete their degrees. Another, Thomas Robbins, followed his grandfather and father to Yale, but transferred to Williams in his senior year and is officially listed as an alumnus of both schools.[14]

The twenty-nine evangelists who served in the Western Reserve between 1798 and 1818 probably constitute a fairly representative sample. They were a remarkably varied lot. Nine of them attended Yale (31percent), and five of them graduated from Williams College. As already noted, Thomas Robbins may be regarded as the tenth Yale graduate since he matriculated from both schools. One missionary came from Middlebury College in Vermont; another attended Hamilton in New York. Significantly, the Trustees employed four men who were trained at backwoods Jefferson College, an institution that attracted primarily Scots-Irish Presbyterians from the Trans-Appalachian counties of Pennsylvania. Another missionary received his liberal education from the fledgling Greensburgh Academy, a Presbyterian school in Westmoreland County, Pennsylvania. Remarkably, the CMS commissioned at least three men—David Bacon, Jonathan Beer, and Alvan Coe—who never received a college diploma. The academic background of five of the missionaries is unknown.[15]

In light of these considerations we must carefully qualify the characterization of Congregational evangelists as an elite cadre by virtue of their education. What of their property holdings or income levels? Finke and Stark assert that orthodox evangelists were recruited from the ranks of the "financial elite" and preferred to move within high society. This assumption echoes a popular anticlerical cliché of the early republic: that the Congregational clergy were "covetous hirelings," who preached only to maintain their comfortable lifestyle. Sectarian preachers often warned the people to beware of "the literary men," one Connecticut-reared New Yorker observed to Abel Flint in 1809. "Those bellowing teachers fill all ears with that the literrary preachers preach only for filthy luker, and many have been told it till they are persuaded that it is so." According to Finke and Stark, the "privileges" enjoyed by the "well-paid" orthodox evangelists naturally alienated Americans as "democratic convictions grew." Moreover, the high salaries demanded by the prosperous Congregational ministers supposedly made it all but impossible for orthodoxy to spread to the frontier, where most people were poor.[16]

At first glance the Congregational clergy do appear to be "well-paid" compared to sectarian exhorters. The typical Baptist preacher was a layman who supported himself by subsistence farming, and preached without compensation to his neighbors. Methodist circuit riders also received little remuneration; as late as 1834 they were officially allowed an annual stipend of only $100. In contrast, Finke and Stark observe, orthodox ministers in the early republic earned between $1,000 and $4,000 in large towns, and in "small country towns" $400 to $1,000.[17]

Most settled Congregational ministers, however, clearly earned salaries on the low end of this scale. While they were employed by the CMS many of them received much less than the lowest figure cited by Finke and Stark. To the best of their ability the Trustees attempted to adjust missionary wages to the cost of living in the various mission fields. Their goal was to provide a salary sufficient to meet the basic needs of the evangelist, but nothing in excess of a subsistence life-style. Prior to 1806 the Society paid employees between five and seven dollars per week, with the average wage being six dollars per week. Hence, a full-time itinerant like Joseph Badger could expect to earn between $260 to $364 per year. In 1806 the Trustees raised the wage to a uniform eight dollars per week, comparable to what the typical settled pastor might receive in Connecticut. This remained the standard missionary wage for the next quarter century.[18]

Unmarried missionaries without family responsibilities could live comfortably, although not opulently, on the wages paid by the Society. In the new settlements, however, the cost of living was much higher than in Connecticut, and some missionaries had difficulty defraying various unforeseen expenses that frontier evangelists sometimes incurred. David Higgins complained to Nathan Strong in 1801 about "the extraordinary ware & tare of clothing, harness, & horse-flesh" which rendered his mission much more expensive than he had anticipated. Higgins agreed with many other missionaries that the Society paid its employees too little. "Whether I again become a laborer in that field or not," he wrote, "I hope to see those who are faithful servants of the Most High reaping in every way the rewards of their labor."[19]

Such complaints suggest that the orthodox itinerants perhaps had different material expectations from the Methodist circuit riders. The Methodist itinerants undoubtedly incurred the same "extraordinary ware & tare" as the Congregational missionaries. Yet they rendered their services without complaint for less compensation, and they seemingly possessed all that they needed. Methodists and Congregationalists perhaps had different definitions of a subsistence wage. Congregational missionary journals suggest one major reason for the discrepancy: orthodox evangelists replaced their clothing, tack, and horses whenever they became frayed and worn out. When a Methodist preacher's clothing became tattered, however, he was likely to wear shabby clothes; when his horse wore out, he would ride a tired or lame mount.[20]

Nonetheless, we should not accept sectarian warnings about "hirling" ministers. Congregationalist missionaries did not demand high wages to support an unnecessarily refined and luxurious lifestyle. At best, the CMS paid wages comparable to what the average settled minister could expect to receive in Connecticut. This amount traditionally would support a "middling" lifestyle, but not extravagance.

As Donald Scott has observed, moreover, ministerial wages in the early republic did not keep pace with the cost of living. Congregational pastors increasingly found themselves in a genuine financial squeeze as the ministry rapidly developed into an impoverished profession. Sectarian preachers generally believed that ministers ought to live at a bare subsistence level, and thus saw nothing amiss in this trend. But Congregational ministers were fond of the maxim that "the laborer is worth his hire." Orthodox clergymen expected to be paid on par with other vocations; that congregations proved unwilling to provide them with an equitable support indicated misplaced spiritual priorities on the part of the people.[21]

During the early nineteenth century many New England ministers found themselves trapped by conflicting cultural forces in a most uncomfortable dilemma. Their people would not increase their salaries. This trend in part reflected latent anticlerical tendencies; in part it stemmed from the shrinking population and eroding tax base suffered by many parishes as migration drew folks away to the frontier. From mixed motives orthodox lay leaders determined to keep both the minister and his salary under tight control. To support their families, many Congregational clergymen took up farming or other outside employment, much as the Baptist preachers did. At the same time, however, their people still expected them to perform the myriad duties traditionally incumbent upon a faithful shepherd. The result was mutual resentment and an unprecedented wave of clerical dismissals.[22]

Congregational ministers like Giles Cowles felt embittered by the situation. In 1810, after seventeen years as pastor, Cowles sadly left his Bristol congregation over a salary dispute. In one of his final sermons he described the plight facing many New England clergymen. Foolish congregations, he proclaimed, out of a false sense of economy were forcing their pastors to "lay aside reading, study & meditation, in a great measure . . . that they might get their bread by instructing youth, laboring in the fields, & by such employment as they can find." This was not the lot "of one or a few individuals who might be thought inordinately covetous, or to have less economy than men have in general," he observed, "but it is considerably general." Despite their added responsibilities these overworked ministers struggled to maintain the "many

intimate bonds uniting pastors & people." They visited families, catechized youth, prayed with the anxious, consoled the grieving, sat with the
sick, and studied to proclaim God's word faithfully. The burden, Cowles
concluded, ate away at their spiritual life and threatened the health of the
entire flock:

> By means of this, they can't do the service of the Lord so well as they
> otherwise might, their sermons are not enriched with so much instruc-
> tion, they themselves are not so apt to teach, nor so affectionate nor
> feeling in their ministry, are ofttimes weary in body, & more exposed to
> the intrusions of worldly cares on the Sabbath than if their worldly
> circumstances were otherwise.[23]

Cowles, like many other dismissed clergymen, applied to the CMS for a
commission. Some of these men, like Abner Benedict of Greenwich,
apparently saw missionary work as a temporary source of income until
they could secure another settled pastorate. Others, like Joseph Badger,
planned to become full-time evangelists in the new settlements. Still
others accepted calls from frontier congregations that could not afford to
hire a permanent pastor. In such cases the church typically would pay
anywhere from 20 to 50 percent of the minister's salary, and the remainder would be paid by the CMS. Giles Cowles, for example, agreed to settle
as half-time pastor of the church in Austinburgh and Morgan, Ohio; for
six months each year he itinerated throughout the Western Reserve for
the CMS.[24]

Such evangelists did not arrive in the new settlements with great wealth
or property. When Giles Cowles left Bristol he was indebted to several
"poor mechanics and day laborers," whom he had been unable to pay
because his salary was too scanty. Joseph Badger was also struggling to
make ends meet when he accepted a CMS commission, and had to ask the
Trustees for a large loan in order to move his family to Ohio.[25] Unfortunately, missionary employment did nothing to improve their financial
woes.

The Trustees of the CMS paid the same salary to both married and
unmarried evangelists. Single men like Seth Williston could live quite
easily on this income, but the many married pastors who accepted CMS
commissions often suffered real hardship. It is not surprising that in 1803
Jedediah Bushnell left the mission field when he wished to marry and
raise a family, nor that Joseph Mills could not "continue long in the
business" because he was "anxious to provide a convenient home & the
means of support" for his aged mother.[26]

Some missionaries believed that the CMS was unreasonably parsimonious. "That the funds of the Society should be well husbanded is certainly desirable," David Higgins complained, "but is it not of as much consequence that faithful services should be well compensated?" In 1803 William Lyman turned down a commission because he feared for the material welfare of his family should he accept the appointment. "I find by conversing with missionaries," Lyman informed Flint, "that their tours have been attended with expenses to themselves to a considerable amount beyond their wages." Among these personal expenses was the need to secure a pulpit supply out of their own resources, at a cost of seven or eight dollars per week. Although this was a common source of aggravation for many short-term missionaries, the missionary society never assumed any responsibility for supplying vacancies or assisting the families of those who went on tours. David Higgins probably spoke for many evangelists when he concluded that "for anyone who has a large family to support, & to support with the avails of his daily labor, to undertake a missionary tour . . . appears inconsistent with the gospel order for a man to provide for his own house."[27]

The cases of Joseph Badger and David Bacon seemed to confirm this assessment. When Bacon traveled to Detroit as a CMS evangelist in 1800, the Trustees paid him only two hundred dollars per year. Bacon, who preached both to Indians and white settlers, not only had to pay living expenses for himself, his new wife, and infant son, but also had to hire a translator. His expenditures quickly exceeded his salary, and he was forced to purchase many necessities on credit. Although he repeatedly informed the Trustees of his plight, he did not receive a salary increase for three years. To help make ends meet, Bacon's wife opened a boarding school for Detroit children, managed "a large Dairy on shares," and attempted to learn the Ojibwa language so that they could dispense with the translator.[28]

Joseph Badger initially received seven dollars per week as an itinerant in the Western Reserve, but in 1802 the Trustees voted to reduce his pay to six dollars per week. This action was prompted by anticlerical rumors that the missionary was using CMS funds to acquire "fortune & large tracts of land" in Ohio. The Trustees, while giving no credence to these charges, nonetheless feared that donors might regard Badger's slary as "extravagant." The action deeply hurt the dumbfounded missionary, who years later was still trying to put to rest the false rumors about his property. Far from acquiring wealth, he later reflected, his family was

> barely comfortable without the least degree of affluence. It is true we
> have not been in a state of painful hunger; but many times in straight-
> ened circumstances for daily bread. For clothing both myself and fam-

ily suffered. I often rode in frosty weather in storms of snow & heavy rains destitute of necessary clothing. My wife & children severely felt the want of clothing for decency & comfort.[29]

Orthodox evangelists typically became more "destitute" and "unpolished" the longer they remained in the new settlements. Those who chose to settle permanently in the vacant "desert places" lived much like their neighbors. Unlike Nathan Perkins, who dined upon sumptuous meals and rode about Hartford with his "elegant lady" in a chaise, frontier Congregational preachers lived in log cabins, worked farms, kept schools, and relied heavily upon family labor and the charity of friends to support their ministry. "You may ask how we are supported," the Reverend Alvan Coe's wife wrote to her friend Sally Cowles from a Michigan schoolhouse:

> Our support for years past has been mostly through the channel of benevolent individuals. . . . We have received many favors from the people here. My school will do a little more than pay our house rent, perhaps get our wood. I sometimes fear we shall want, although I know what a kind provider we have. Mr. Coe has full confidence in the promise 'Trust the Lord & do good & verily thou shalt be fed.'[30]

In light of these facts we must reject easy generalizations about the "well-paid" and comfortable genteel clergy. During the early republic there was no "typical" Congregational pastor; orthodox preachers varied as markedly as the circumstances in which they ministered. There were refined and haughty scholars like Nathan Perkins and Benjamin Trumbull, who by training and temperament were best suited for life in the study. But there was also the indigent Reverend Seth Noble, more than seventy years old and "in his dotage," who worked his farm in Franklin County, Ohio, six days a week and on the Sabbath held forth against the Baptists, Methodists, and Episcopalians "in a fashion that would disgust serious people." There were well-placed pastors like Nathan Strong, of Hartford's First Church, whose pews each week were filled with the most powerful members of the Connecticut standing order. But there was also the Reverend Luther Leland, of Derby, Vermont, whose principal financial support came from impoverished settlers "who would much prefer another doctrine," and who paid him less than half his promised salary each year.[31]

III

Despite the modest social and financial attainments of most Congregational missionaries, nonetheless they were far better educated than the average citizen of the republic. Not only did they usually possess a liberal education, but all of them had formally studied theology either in a seminary or more often under the tutelage of a teaching pastor. In this regard they differed significantly from their sectarian competitors, who almost never attained college degrees and who generally eschewed theological training as an unnecessary and dangerous waste of time.

According to nineteenth century Methodists and many modern scholars, this distinction was a crucial factor in the decline of orthodoxy. The common people, Hatch tells us, wanted nothing to do with ancient creeds and theological abstractions. Post-revolutionary America witnessed a remarkable "individualization of conscience," as populist leaders successfully proclaimed the absolute right to think for oneself. One potent expression of this new American gospel was a plethora of religious sects and movements that insisted on every person's right to interpret scripture privately, without the benefit of theological training or knowledge of ancient languages. Elias Smith, leader of the so-called "Christian" movement, expressed the essence of this radically individualistic view of Christianity when he asserted the "unalienable right" of all people to interpret the New Testament for themselves, even though their "principles may, in many things, be contrary to what the Reverend D.D.'s call Orthodoxy."[32]

In Smith's opinion, theologically trained clergy constituted threats to religious freedom and authentic Christianity. The early Methodists also attacked the educated orthodox clergy, deriding the notion that a man could become a preacher by study and elocution. God called men simply to preach the word, and the Holy Spirit brought the convicting power. An unlettered saint, humble and pure, could better preach the gospel than a proud scholar caught up in his own conceit.[33]

Peter Cartwright offered the classic Methodist caricature of the orthodox evangelist, "a fresh, green, live Yankee from down East" who knew nothing about frontier life. Cartwright's stereotypical Congregational preacher "had regularly graduated, and had his diploma, and was regularly called, by the Home Missionary Society, to . . . throw us poor upstarts of . . . Methodist preachers, into the shades of everlasting darkness." The arrogant missionary was, of course, "very forward and officious," wanting to take charge of Cartwright's meetings as soon as he arrived upon the scene. One night the knowing Methodist champion "put him up . . . to read his sermon." Wind blew hard through the unplastered building, the "candles flared and gave a bad light," and

> our ministerial hero made a very awkward out in reading his sermon. The congregation paid a heavy penance and became restive; he balked, and hemmed, and coughed at a disgusting rate. At the end of about thirty minutes the great blessing came: he closed, to the great satisfaction of all the congregation.

After the "little hot-house reader" closed "his paroxysm of a total failure," Cartwright mercifully saved the meeting with a spirit-filled exhortation, and "solemn power rested on the congregation." The orthodox greenhorn, Cartwright observed, never bothered his people again.[34]

Finke and Stark, as well as Nathan Hatch, seem to confirm Cartwright's one-dimensional caricature. While Baptists and Methodists delivered without notes a simple message of conversion that spoke to peoples' hearts, the orthodox preachers supposedly preferred learned discourses that lacked spiritual conviction. Frontier audiences could easily grasp what the simple sectarians had to say, while the orthodox preachers lost them in an intellectual haze. "If the goal was to arouse faith," Finke and Stark conclude, the carefully prepared lectures of the scholarly ministers "were no match for the impromptu, emotional pleas of the uneducated preachers."[35]

Contrary to standard assumptions, Congregational missionaries in the new settlements clearly emphasized "heart religion" more than abstract doctrine. Moreover, they had little time to study texts or carefully prepare theological discourses while they were itinerating. They did not read from "old, musty, worm-eaten sermons," as Peter Cartwright charged, nor generally preach from notes. Many Congregational clergymen conscientiously attempted to adapt their style of ministry to suit popular tastes. For some this proved a difficult task; others adapted easily.

As early as 1789 the Congregational clergy living in the new settlements already differed sharply from the men who held pastorates in Connecticut. When Nathan Perkins visited Vermont he was startled by the rusticity of the state's orthodox preachers. Although he considered many of them to be honest, pious souls, for the most part they had "no acquaintance with books." Furthermore, despite the benefits of education, they expressed themselves in an unrefined manner. After listening to many Vermont sermons, Perkins concluded that there was "scarcely any sensible preaching in the state."[36]

Orthodox ministers like Perkins expected sermons to be coherent. The classical English sermon was divided into three units: the text, the explication, and the application or "improvement." Orthodox preachers customarily read the scripture, explicated the meaning of the text, and then attempted to apply the message to the concrete situation of the listeners. Each sermon was to have one essential point, and the various parts were to fit together logically to bring the point clearly home to the people. Thus the sermon was designed not only to convict sinners and stir the soul, but also to instruct the people.

One of the most common criticisms leveled against sectarian preachers by orthodox Congregationalists was that their sermons did not logically hang together. "I have not heard a sermon preached since you left Middlebury," a Vermont friend wrote to Thomas Robbins in 1799, "altho' have been two Sabbaths to hear Mr. Sawyer the Baptist preacher." The orthodox Vermonter apparently did not consider Sawyer's performances to be sermons because "the man gives a word of exhortation but is not able to raise a Doctrine from any perticular text. His ideas are scattering and consequently very unconnected."[37]

Moses Welch described a Baptist preacher in his Mansfield, Connecticut, parish in a similar fashion. In his "public exhibitions" there was "the want of system, or connection in the parts of his discourse." In addition to this deficiency, Welch observed, he had a "superficial knowledge of the most obvious import of passages of scripture." Welch was offended, too, by his "inability to support by arguments drawn from scripture or reason" the points upon which he declaimed, as well as his "frequent grammatical incorrectness, and fondness for the use of uncommon words, which is done with great impropriety." All in all, the orthodox critic concluded, the Baptist gave "an empty, incoherent performance," although "ignorant" townspeople undoubtedly considered him "captivating."[38]

Orthodox evangelists could not effectively proclaim the gospel in the new settlements without coming to grips with the fact that many people enjoyed the emotional, "incoherent" exhortations of the sectarians. To some extent Nathan Hatch is surely correct about the spreading populist impulse in post-revolutionary Protestantism. Many people demanded preaching that seemed to spring from the Holy Spirit rather than human artifice. Congregational missionaries, therefore, had to modify their conception of "sensible preaching" in order to gain popular favor.

Although it was not necessary to altogether abandon the classical sermon structure, it *was* necessary to dispense with written notes. Congregationalists had to appear to proclaim the gospel under direct divine inspiration, just as the sectarians did. In 1804 a committee from several towns in Luzerne County, Pennsylvania, made this point clearly in a request for CMS assistance. They needed a "man of real piety, talents, erudition and experience," the committee informed the Trustees, someone who would hold up "upon public trial" in the face "of backwardness and diversity of opinions." Above all, it was "vital" that he be "one who could perform without notes, as most of the people are prejudiced against the use of notes in the pulpit."[39]

Extemporaneous preaching was in fact standard practice for most Congregational evangelists during the period under study. Orations designed for special community observances, such as Independence Day or fast days, were general exceptions to this rule. Also, when missionaries accepted part-time calls from Congregational churches, they usually would not speak extemporaneously when they preached from their home pulpit. Whenever they were on their evangelical tours, however, orthodox itinerants usually preached either without notes or with only the roughest sermon outline.

For Connecticut Edwardseans, the adoption of an extemporaneous mode of preaching was perhaps not a drastic leap. Revivalists during the Great Awakening had often preached without notes, as they sought to stir the religious affections with their simple, direct calls for repentance and conversion. Throughout the eighteenth century Edwardsean pastors had stressed the importance of plain evangelical preaching of the "great doctrines of salvation." Ministers, Nathan Strong typically exclaimed in 1794, must plainly and clearly proclaim three essential truths to their people: the natural depravity of every human, the absolute necessity of being born again, and the impossibility of rebirth except through the action of God's sovereign Spirit.[40]

Orthodox missionaries received instructions to preach these basic evangelical doctrines wherever they journeyed. "Preach plainly and faithfully . . . the great doctrines of the gospel," Thomas Robbins was twice charged during his ordination to the "evangelical office":

> Warn the wicked, & sound the alarm to the secure, stupid sinner—
> Reprove the vicious with a spirit of meekness—Instruct the ignorant, &
> endeavor to convince the erroneous. Guide the doubting,—comfort
> the desponding—Invite the weary & heavy laden to Christ.[41]

There was nothing particularly learned or abstract about these instructions. Finke and Stark are wrong when they assert that Congregational evangelists "offered a message that was literate and intellectual, but . . . said little about salvation, hellfire or the principal themes of the Baptist and Methodist sermons."[42] In their public addresses Connecticut missionaries stressed moral duties and fundamental evangelical doctrines that most Protestants could readily accept. Seth Williston, for example, preached constantly about the need to be born again. He served for more than a year in the Chenango settlements before he first ventured to preach on the controversial doctrine of predestination, a subject, he confessed, upon which he "felt a little confused." Randolph Stone, a missionary to the Western Reserve, also focused his efforts upon the need to repent. "In my preaching," Stone declared, "I endeavor to keep close to my guide, the *Scriptures*—& never to lose sight of the great object, *Christ crucified.*" Although Methodist circuit rider Robert Hanna did not care for Giles Cowles's delivery, he nevertheless found that he could readily "approve of his doctrine."[43]

Several of Ammi Robbins's missionary sermons have survived. The striking contrast between these and his numerous surviving occasional sermons is most illuminating. When Ammi delivered election sermons or ordination sermons, he adopted a "high style" that reflected the dignity of the occasion and the learning of the audience. In 1800, for example, he delivered the annual Yale Address to the clergy of Connecticut, a learned discourse that filled sixteen 7" x 4" pages. His "ad clerum" sermon was a well-constructed, polished essay, replete with theological arguments and Latin phrases. Obviously, Robbins had expended a great deal of time and effort composing the piece, and probably intended it for publication.[44]

For standard evangelical proclamation, however, Ammi employed a "plain style." We have more than twenty of his nonoccasional sermons from the years 1793 to 1800, including several delivered during his missionary tour of New York. These focus upon basic evangelical themes, such as the need for regeneration, the importance of holiness, the dangers of infidelity, and the necessity of praying for revivals. Ammi scratched the rough outline of his sermons in a tiny, barely legible hand on small 3" x 4" pieces of paper that would easily fit into his palm. The outlines followed the classical three-part structure, but consisted only of chapter and verse references and abbreviated topic sentences. Clearly he could not read from these sketchy notes; the outlines functioned as simple aids to memory, helping him to order his thoughts and develop his argument as he delivered the message extemporaneously.[45]

Ammi's son Thomas almost always preached without notes when he itinerated for the CMS. The Robbins Papers contain hundreds of extant sermons delivered by Thomas in the years before and after his mission to Ohio, but no missionary sermons. In his diary entry for August 28, 1803, the day after he crossed the Hudson River on his way to the Western Reserve, we find the following explanation: "Where I do not mention the mode I shall preach without notes, as I have today." For the next three years Thomas employed notes to preach on only a handful of occasions. One of these was the ordination of his cousin Samuel, who had accepted a call from the Congregational church in Marietta, Ohio. This sermon, which was published at the request of the congregation, evoked the admiration of his surprised father:

> but how you could prepare your sermon in so short a time & under such embarrassing circumstances seems almost incredible—Your sermon is full of energy & your style very unexpected—for as Sally has observed, we expected, by living in the woods & preaching often extempore, your language would be accordingly.[46]

Thomas probably had a natural flair for extemporaneous preaching, for he seemed to suffer no discomfort in adopting this mode of address. His sermons, of course, were not all original products of divine inspiration. On several occasions, such as the Yohogeny, Pennsylvania, camp meeting in 1803, he preached from memory a revival sermon written earlier in Connecticut. As he itinerated from place to place he customarily kept to the same text for several consecutive appointments, so that soon he could recite the message with ease. There were, of course, dangers in this method. Sermons that succeeded in one village did not necessarily inspire folks in other settlements. Moreover, sermons delivered from rote memory could easily lose the aura of spontaneity that extemporaneous preaching was supposed to produce. "Mr. Strong says he knows of no instance wherein a missionary has not contracted a tone of sameness in preaching," Sally Robbins wrote to her brother. "I mention this, that you may guard against it."[47]

Sometimes "extemporaneous" preachers undoubtedly plagiarized the sermons of other ministers. Although itineration offered precious little time alone for study, a surprising number of families in the new settlements possessed at least a few volumes of published sermons. For example, both Robbins and Williston routinely came across the works of John Flavel, the renowned seventeenth-century British preacher, as well as the works of Jonathan Edwards, Samuel Davies, Nathaniel Emmons, and a host of other evangelical luminaries. Often, after their hosts had retired for the night, the missionaries browsed through the books of the house seeking illumination. "I was fed with a sermon of Mr. Flavel's upon crucifying the flesh," Williston recorded, "I preach to others & Mr. Flavel preaches to me." Surely many missionary sermons germinated during these late-night episodes.[48]

Although Williston and Robbins do not say explicitly that they took their sermons directly from these sources, the practice was not uncommon. In 1804 G. H. Tower, of Westmoreland, Pennsylvania, reported to Thomas that a local orthodox evangelist "is gone out on the frontier, [and] is thought to improve fast." The reason was obvious, Tower reflected. Previously his productions had been his own, but now he was preaching from George Whitefield. Tower, a transplanted New England schoolteacher, had recently heard the evangelist deliver an extemporaneous sermon that was "Whitefield's . . . verbatim." Although the frontier audience was apparently none the wiser, and approved of the effort, Tower believed "that Whitefield, had he been present, would be much displeased at the uncouth delivery."[49]

For some missionaries, of course, no amount of preparation or repetition made extemporaneous preaching easy. The Reverend John Field, who itinerated in the Western Reserve for almost a decade, could not organize his thoughts without a written sermon. Nonetheless, he had to make the attempt. Once, while he was preaching extemporaneously in Ravenna, Ohio, a small child began to cry. The distracted evangelist "stopped to make observations" to the mother, Giles Cowles reported, "& by this means lost his ideas & so was obliged to break off his discourse." Sadly, Cowles observed, such incidents had occurred before when Field preached, so that the poor missionary became an object of derision "among the loose & irreligious" folk in the region.[50]

Although it was his usual mode of preaching, Seth Williston never felt completely comfortable with extemporaneous delivery. Unlike Badger and Robbins, who seemed ready to speak whenever the need arose, Williston was more self-conscious and often at a loss for words. He preferred to carefully organize his ideas before proclaiming the gospel, and relished the rare opportunities he had to prepare his Sabbath sermons in advance. Once, while left alone for an evening by a blazing fire, he reminisced nostalgically about the "old times when I had a study by myself." He was tired of itinerating, he noted in his diary, "more for want of a room by myself & opportunity to study than on any other account."[51]

Despite his scholarly proclivities, however, Williston could preach extemporaneously with good effect. Like Ammi Robbins, he frequently constructed brief outlines of his sermons to help him organize his thoughts, but he did not generally read from his notes when he preached. His goal, he noted, was "to have my sermons transcribed upon my heart, that I might deliver them warm from thence. To preach from paper is no preaching for me . . . I do not seem to myself to preach unless I can feel what I utter."[52]

When he first became a missionary, however, Williston sometimes found it difficult to successfully "transcribe" his sermons on his heart. Plagued by insecurities, he sometimes gave in to the temptation to preach from notes; invariably, he discovered, his audience responded coolly. Shortly after his arrival in the Chenango settlements, for example, he spent two entire days preparing a sermon that he hoped would be a powerful instrument of revival. But when the Sabbath morning dawned he "was so cold in body & mind . . . that it seemed to be lost labor." The congregation was obviously bored by Williston's carefully prepared discourse, so the disappointed missionary "determined to preach without notes" in the afternoon. Taking Matthew 22 for his text, he stumbled his way through "an incoherent sermon, but a plain one," all the while feeling embarrassed and angry. To his surprise, the "hearers gave better attention," even though it was "not so correct a sermon as I delivered in the morning."

On the following Sabbath, Williston again tried to deliver a carefully prepared revival sermon, and again he "was pretty dull, till I had done with my notes." Thereupon, he noted, God assisted him "to add a few words" extemporaneously, and these appeared "to have some impression upon my hearers." Little by little, such experiences built up Williston's self-confidence, and gradually he was able to preach readily with virtually no preparation.[53]

IV

No matter what preaching style they employed, Congregational missionaries were unmistakably Calvinistic in sentiment. According to many modern scholars, this fact made them anachronisms in a society which wanted nothing more to do with Calvinism. Moreover, unlike their sectarian competitors, they steadfastly upheld the authority of ancient creeds and confessions of faith, at a time when many people demanded the right to think for themselves. In a democratizing culture, the masses were increasingly making their own subjective feelings and opinions the ultimate criterion of truth.

To some extent the experiences of CMS evangelists confirm Hatch's thesis about the individualization of American Christianity. Wherever they traveled Connecticut missionaries encountered sectarian opponents whom Hatch would define as populist insurgents. Orthodox clergymen in northern Vermont faced stiff competition from "Preachers, self-authorized, ill-informed, of vagrant life, . . . and erroneous principles," who seemed to be everywhere "disaffecting the minds of people to a regular ministry." The same situation existed in New York and the Old Northwest. In the Western Reserve it was commonplace for hecklers to disrupt public worship, rising in the midst of missionary sermons to denounce "priestcraft" and "Connecticut priests." For example, when CMS evangelist Randolph Stone visited the settlement of Kingsville, Ohio, a Methodist preacher stood up as he was beginning a religious conference. "This," the Methodist charged, "is *our ground,* & I claim it, & come with authority to oppose you."[54]

But there is another dimension to the American religious scene which clearly emerges from the CMS Papers: many Americans in the new settlements rejected the sectarian insurgents and continued to support orthodoxy. Far from being uninvited guests in the republican frontier, CMS missionaries were warmly welcomed wherever they went by folk who longed for "regular stated orthodox preaching."

There is no reason to suppose, as is sometimes suggested, that only the wealthy elite of frontier communities were receptive to Congregational evangelism. In December 1799, Nathan Strong received an appeal from Black River Town #4 in New York, begging the CMS to send a missionary for as long as possible. The town had only recently been settled, and was still quite poor. Nonetheless the appeal was signed by fifty-eight men, including most of the family heads in the community, who contributed more than thirty-nine dollars as a sign of their good faith. They were eager, they wrote, to secure orthodox preaching quickly, aware "of the unhappy & dangerous situation of bringing up families, when the Sabbath & divine things are greatly neglected."[55]

In 1811 Joel Bennedict traveled through Meredith, New York, an impoverished village in the Catskills. A few years earlier a small Congregational church had been established in Meredith by CMS missionaries, consisting of about twenty members. The church had been visited only occasionally by orthodox evangelists since 1808, and the surrounding area was filled with "Methodists and confirmed Arminians." Nonetheless, the people continued to meet regularly on their own for worship, and had grown to seventy members. When Bennedict visited them he admitted an additional fifteen members, administered the Lord's Supper to over sixty communicants, and preached to a congregation numbering in the hundreds. Most impressive of all, however, was the thoroughness of their discipline, and the care with which they scrutinized candidates for membership:

> The inhabitants of this place are low in property, not able as yet to support the preaching of the gospel statedly among them. Yet they constantly maintained the worship of God on the Sabbath, and on strict evangelical discipline. Tho' poor in this world's goods, yet the church as such appears rich in grace, but few more orthodox in sentiment or evangelical in their lives.[56]

In 1818 the CMS evangelist Randolph Stone accepted a call to settle over the small church in Morgan, Ohio. The church had only thirty members; the entire Society some fifty families. The region was filled with sectarians of every stripe, from Methodists to Universalists. Yet people flocked to hear Stone, a graduate of Yale, preach his sermons. Each Sabbath between three to four hundred worshipers sat in Stone's congregation:

> They all seem anxious to come to the sanctuary, & rather than not attend, are conveyed in sleds & carts drawn by oxen. Their attention too is serious & solemn: sometimes all are bathed in tears, & it seems as if the Spirit of God was truly among them in its quickening & awakening power.[57]

Hundreds of similar examples of orthodox commitment could be given. Despite the real hostility directed at them by anticlerical foes, and the obvious presence of sectarian competitors, CMS evangelists found a warm reception and willing audiences in hundreds of frontier communities. If orthodox Congregational missionaries had stood outside the mainstream of American culture, across an ideological chasm from the people they served, we should expect to find strong evidence of this in the missionary records. Such evidence, however, seems lacking. Instead, the Connecticut missionaries consistently reported that they preached Reformed doctrines plainly and fearlessly wherever they went, that many people bitterly opposed these "doctrines of grace," and that many others gladly received them. There were those who mocked and hurled insults, and those who apologized for the bad behavior of their neighbors. There were those who refused to hear "hireling preachers," and those who gladly walked ten miles or more for "the faith of the fathers."

Above all, however, there were many settlers who exercised their republican freedom by listening intently to whatever evangelists came their way. In the Western Reserve, Calvin Chapin reported in 1806, ministers of every denomination confronted a divided and confused people who were hungry for preaching but uncertain about many doctrinal matters. This created a serious challenge for orthodox missionaries, but also for the sectarian exhorters: "They preach to people of all denominations & they cannot defend the peculiar tenets of *one,* without giving offence to *many.*"[58]

Congregational clergymen could compete successfully in this open environment so long as they possessed an appropriate style of ministry. The personal qualities of the preacher mattered far more to many people than his theology. What settlers wanted, the Presbytery of Geneva, New York reported to Abel Flint in 1810, was ministers

> who are firm in the faith, distinguishing in their communications—of a fervent & pious cast—apt to teach—of considerable experience in all

practical concerns of the ministry—& capable of adapting themselves in all their transactions, to the different grades of men in society.[59]

A man who possessed these traits could minister successfully in the republican frontier, regardless of his doctrinal position.

Congregational missionary leaders well knew that evangelism in the new settlements required a special set of gifts. The effective missionary had to be capable of interacting tactfully with all classes of people, and had to be able to confront sectarian opposition coolly but forcefully. It was important to preach and teach in a popular fashion, and yet not compromise with the essential tenets of Reformed Christianity in order to gain popularity. Simeon Parmele, a missionary who itinerated in northern New York in 1814, believed that evangelism demanded a fine balance of special qualities. Because frontier settlements "are much divided into sectaries," Parmele wrote,

> [i]t requires men for missionaries as wise as serpents and as harmless as doves. A man of skill will hew down opposition and strengthen the feeble band grounded upon the truth; while an inexperienced person will make wider the divisions and bring a reproach upon the Society. . . . Coming from different parts of the country, and bringing all their habits and prejudices with them, it needs someone to go among them who can become all things to all men, and yet maintain the fundamental truths of the gospel.[60]

Not every missionary possessed these gifts. Ezekiel Chapman, a young licentiate sent to the Western Reserve in 1802, was renowned for his humility and piety, but was unable to handle sectarian challengers. Hecklers often disrupted his meetings, attacking Calvinism, the CMS, and at times Christianity. The inexperienced Chapman refused to dispute with his detractors, believing that it would be more effective to ignore their calumnies. His meek approach, Joseph Badger observed, rendered him "totally unfit for the place he is in now." Well-known enemies of the missionary society gleefully attended his services, sometimes pretending to be subjects of hopeful conversion in order to arouse public laughter at the expense of the timid young evangelist. Despite repeated humiliations, Chapman refused to confront them. In a highly confidential letter, Badger urged the Trustees to recall Chapman and to send missionaries who could boldly confront all types of settlers: "There is a necessity of talking to a hoard of babblers in this country, on their own ground; with arguments drawn from the plain simple voice of nature & Reason, showing them the absurdity of their talk." This, Badger observed, "requires more time & labour than that of preaching."

While acknowledging that Chapman possessed all the qualities of a fine pastor, "and would make an excellent minister in some Connecticut congregation," Badger insisted that frontier evangelists needed the additional ability to engage readily in sometimes heated sectarian warfare:

> If you send missionaries into this country they ought to be men of experience & acquaintance with men & things: human nature must be met in every shape, & missionaries must know something about it & how to combat it, grasping the weapon at the time & place for the encounter. If one should get up after preaching & tell the congregation he did not believe any of those doctrines, the Bible is nothing but priestcraft, etc. he must be made to feel he is a blockhead, & the bystanders will feel so too.[61]

Many other missionaries agreed with Badger that opposition should be confronted. "This western country," Joel Bennedict observed a few years later, "is so overrun with arminianism and universalism, that a missionary who is not prepared to wage & defend a war with these destroyers of souls will have but little success at best." To refrain from confrontation with sectarian preachers, Bennedict believed, only reinforced the oft-repeated accusation that orthodoxy could not hold up to rational inquiry. As a case in point, he might well have cited the example of Abner Benedict, who in 1813 refused a challenge from a Chenango Universalist to a public debate on Calvinism. Benedict declined because he "was not sent to dispute—but to preach the gospel." His refusal, however, was regarded by his opponents as cowardice. In a society that carefully watched the competing purveyors of religious truth for signs of strength or weakness, such apparent timidity could be fatal to the cause.[62]

Most missionaries clearly understood the need to confront their opponents; missionary reports provide many examples of such confrontation. CMS evangelists routinely attended the meetings of "irregular" preachers, and often engaged in heated dialogue with their hosts after the exercises had closed. They visited the homes of sectarian families, and routinely accepted invitations to preach to Methodist classes or Baptist congregations. They invariably went out of their way to visit towns touched by revival, even when sectarian preaching had been responsible for sparking the excitement. They especially attempted to influence children and youth, and made a special effort to visit whatever schools they encountered on their tours. Wherever they went they passed out Calvinist tracts to the people, pushed subscriptions to the *CEM,* and attempted to establish public libraries stocked with Edwardsean titles.

Congregational evangelists could in truth be formidable competitors for the loyalty of frontier settlers. Missionary letters chronicle many instances when CMS efforts checked the growth of rival churches, saved besieged orthodox congregations from destruction, or successfully planted new Congregational churches in the midst of sectarian strongholds. In many communities orthodox missionaries lured Methodist or Baptist proselytes back into the Congregational fold, and in other cases converted unchurched folk to the faith of the fathers. During times of revival their presence posed a genuine threat to the interests of sectarian competitors.[63]

In 1811 a Freewill Baptist writer complained that whenever humble Baptist preachers sparked revivals, Congregational missionaries soon appeared upon the scene to gather the harvest. The orthodox evangelists had "a sly way of getting along," the Arminian critic fumed. "They generally fall in with the work, and own the reformation, and try to proselyte the converts; but degrade the preachers who were the instruments of their conversion." The Congregational missionaries cast aspersions upon the unlettered preachers, and frightened awakened sinners with talk of heresy:

> These men deny the doctrine of eternal, particalar, unconditional election, and the doctrine of original sin! says one. They have no foundation, nor articles of faith, but the Bible! says another. They deny the final perseverance of the saints, and hold that men can save themselves! says another. These men deny infant sprinkling, and go about breaking up churches! says another.

Soon, the sectarian writer asserted, orthodox missionaries had so confused and alarmed the converts with their dire warnings and their theological jargon, that many feared to fall in with the Baptists.[64]

The CMS Papers provide strong evidence to confirm the Baptist complaint. Congregational missionaries typically devoted special attention to places where the people were "unusually serious," or where they showed signs of revival. Such "works of grace" generally attracted preachers of competing sects as well. At these times it was common for Congregational evangelists and various rival exhorters to appear together at religious conferences, and to follow each other from place to place. In family visits, especially, orthodox evangelists attempted to undercut the teachings of their foes.[65]

Orthodox missionaries believed that sectarian preachers had to be challenged during revivals, since freshly convicted sinners were most easily led astray by false teachers. If not checked by sound ministers, "irregular" revivalists would promote enthusiastic delusion and instill in awakened persons a premature sense of assurance. To prevent this, orthodox evangelists sought out those who were under conviction—regardless of their denominational affiliation—and labored to protect them against error and false hopes.

Passing through Euclid, Ohio, on the way home from a missionary tour, Randolph Stone once found that "a universal spirit of prayer" had gripped the townspeople. "The hopes of false professors are breaking up," Stone reported. "Backsliders are beginning to return—Deists begin to feel their foundation giving way, & are crying for mercy." Because the only settled minister in Euclid was an "irregular" Arminian, Stone feared that the newly awakened "sheep are in danger of being led astray." Accordingly, he spent several days in conference with the people, and "scarcely found time to rest, being thronged with sinners enquiring what they should do to be saved." Before departing he sent an urgent appeal to fellow CMS missionary John Seward, requesting him to "bend your course this way as soon as possible" for a more extensive visit. "You know how eager awakened sinners are for comfort," Stone observed, "& how easy it is to settle them on false foundations. This is at present the danger to which the people in Euclid are exposed."[66]

In 1812 a powerful revival broke out in Delaware and Otsego counties, in the Catskills of New York, and soon spread to Chenango and Schoharie counties. The "work" continued for more than a year, touching virtually every denomination in the region. In addition to the dominant Methodists and regular Baptists, Universalists, Freewill Baptists, Lutherans, Dutch Reformed, and Congregationalists were also active in the area. The CMS commissioned Joel Bennedict and David Harrower to protect the small Congregational churches against sectarian invaders, to fan the flames of the revival, and to gather as many of the converts as possible into orthodox congregations. Wherever they went the two labored to turn the people away from the irregular preachers, and repeatedly came into face to face conflict with their foes.

During the month of July 1813, Harrower preached almost every day before crowds of Methodists, Baptists, or Universalists. At a revival meeting in Norwich, New York, he addressed a very large gathering that was "greatly unacquainted with sound doctrine." His sermon provoked intense hostility from rival leaders, but succeeded in stirring debate. The next two days he was "employed every hour of the day in . . . conversation with opposers, & with people who wished for information." A couple of days later he attended a "very large assembly" led by "three Methodist preachers & one Arminian Baptist minister." One of the Methodist exhorters "entered into a close vindication of their plan." Harrower followed him on the platform, "& entered largely into the doctrine of election." Again his actions provoked opposition, yet "many visited me in the evening, with whom I conversed until midnight." Some of these sectarians, he reported, accepted "the truth of the doctrines of grace" and manifested a deep awareness of "their guilt & danger."[67]

Joel Bennedict, too, provoked both opposition and honest inquiry when he appeared at meetings appointed by the sectarian preachers. The two missionaries also convened numerous Congregational conferences, often attracting hundreds of visitors. Almost invariably, after the meetings closed, flocks of anxious sinners came to their quarters, inquiring the way to salvation.

Bennedict and Harrower added dozens of new members to existing Congregational churches in the region, but also planted new congregations in several places where the Methodists or Baptists already had a strong presence. In Norwich, for example, they gathered a church of twenty members in June 1814. By August approximately four hundred worshipers were attending services at the new church each week. At Punch-Kill a large assembly of Dutch settlers urged them to gather an "English" church after the revival swept the town. In late 1813 Bennedict established a Congregational church of twelve members, and soon the weekly attendance numbered between two and three hundred souls.[68]

Such examples could easily be multiplied. Congregational missionaries did not complacently doze while the "upstart" sects made "great strides in churching America." Nor did people generally close their ears to the Calvinist preaching of the New England missionaries. CMS employees usually had no difficulty drawing large audiences in the new settlements, even in places where sectarians far outnumbered loyal orthodox settlers. In short, to adopt the terminology employed by Finke and Stark, Congregational evangelists aggressively competed for "shares" of the religious market, and they consistently found a healthy demand for the message they proclaimed.

CHAPTER

EIGHT

Congregational Declension Reconsidered

Explanations for Congregational declension after the American Revolution generally focus either upon the inability of orthodox missionaries to adjust to republican culture, or upon the culture's rejection of orthodoxy. Both approaches to the problem are flawed. This study suggests that Congregational leaders adjusted to the democratization of American society in various ways, and embraced innovative means to evangelize their fellow citizens. Moreover, this study indicates that there was an openness to the message which Congregational evangelists proclaimed; when offered a choice between orthodoxy and populist insurgency, many frontier Americans found orthodoxy the more attractive alternative.

It is impossible to sustain the argument, advanced by William Warren Sweet and many others, that Congregational leaders were "more or less indifferent" to expansion into the frontier. Fueled by fervent millennial hopes, a profound sense of their covenant obligations, and a strong commitment to evangelism, post-revolutionary New Light Congregationalists broke with generations of orthodox tradition by creating dozens of missionary agencies. As we have seen, the Connecticut Missionary Society alone sent 148 evangelists into the new settlements during the first two decades of its existence. Many more were employed by smaller Congregational organizations such as the Berkshire Missionary Society, the Hampshire Missionary Society, the Massachusetts Missionary Society, the Vermont Missionary Society, and a host of other state and local agencies. Many of these missionaries regarded the "evangelical office" as a special calling, distinct from the traditional Congregational pastorate.

It is also impossible to sustain the argument that Congregational evangelists wished to recreate the New England standing order and to promote Federalism in the new settlements. In the late 1790s Connecticut missionary leaders conscientiously backed away from public controversy, eschewed party politics, and enjoined evangelists to abstain from partisan behavior. Furthermore, they sought to build a base of financial security that was independent of legislative assistance. They attempted to mobilize popular support and to shape public opinion through the press, and sought to advance their cause through competition and moral suasion. In short, missionary leaders embraced the principles of religious voluntarism long before the final disestablishment of Connecticut's Congregational churches.

Contrary to the standard assumption, articulated most recently by Roger Finke and Rodney Stark, Congregational ministers in the new settlements were not particularly genteel. For the most part they came from poor or "middling" families; many had been reared in the New England backcountry. They generally attended affordable provincial schools, possessed little wealth or property, and wielded virtually no political influence. Those who remained in the new settlements as full-time itinerants or settled pastors lived much as their neighbors lived. They entered into community rituals, farmed, and adjusted to the expectations of the people they served.

There is little evidence to support the hypothesis that Calvinism had become culturally unacceptable. Anti-Calvinist preachers clashed with Calvinist preachers; both sides hurled insults at the other. Large audiences turned out to hear ministers of every stripe, listened attentively, and followed their consciences and personal tastes. This fluidity was, as Hatch suggests, a revolutionary change that challenged orthodox authority. But it also challenged the authority of "populist" leaders. Often, people chose to reaffirm their traditional allegiances when they had the opportunity to do so.

Why, then, did Congregationalism suffer a relative decline in the early republic? Why did the largest and most prestigious colonial denomination fail to maintain its dominant position? An obvious answer, of course, is that no single denomination could dominate post-revolutionary society. Baptists and Methodists, as well as the Congregationalists, had to be content with sharing social influence with their theological foes. This situation was probably more traumatic for the once-dominant orthodox clergy than for their upstart competitors, but the circumstances were hardly as desperate as Finke and Stark imply when they speak about the "crumbling" of orthodoxy. The Congregationalists were down, but they certainly could not be considered a marginal religious body.[1]

This obvious answer, however, begs the important question posed in the introduction to this book: why did Methodists and Baptists grow at a much more dynamic rate than the Congregationalists? This study suggests that several factors capped orthodox growth potential. Some of these factors have long been recognized by scholars; others have hitherto been ignored.

The often cited shortage of Congregational clergymen was, in fact, a significant obstacle to orthodox growth. The rapid expansion of the frontier after the Revolution created an unprecedented demand for new clergymen that the sectarians were able to fill. Congregational missionaries could compete with the Methodists and Baptists only in the settlements they served. Hundreds of communities, however, lacked orthodox preaching all or much of the time. Even after the creation of Congregational missionary societies the demand for orthodox preachers always far exceeded the supply.

Scholars often note that the shortage of Congregational ministers stemmed from the orthodox insistence upon a college-educated clergy. The sectarians relied primarily upon untrained exhorters, and thus were able to raise up ministers wherever they were needed. This is an accurate generalization, of course, but it identifies only one dimension of a more complex problem.

Orthodox missionary leaders themselves contributed greatly to the shortage of Congregational evangelists in the new settlements. The CMS Papers clearly reveal that there were many more orthodox ministers available to go on missions than the number that actually went forth. Throughout the early history of the CMS, the Trustees complained about the chronic shortage of suitable missionaries. All the while, however, Strong and Flint rejected one applicant after another because they were uncertain about their doctrinal purity or personal character. Generally they offered commissions only to men they personally knew, or to those who came highly recommended by trusted friends. This cautious policy, designed to insure the purity of the infant churches, in fact had negative consequences for their cause. Many orthodox settlers waited and waited for missionaries who never arrived, while neighboring sectarian preachers busily drew away the potential Congregational flock.

The pure church ideals of the Edwardsean missionaries capped Congregational growth in other ways as well. As this study has argued, orthodox evangelists could draw large audiences in many settlements. They preached a basic evangelical message that powerfully appealed to many settlers. They could lead revivals, producing hundreds of anxious inquirers asking, "What must I do?" But they would not compromise upon their pure church principles and admit these awakened sinners to communion without satisfactory evidence of their regeneration. Nor would they establish new churches without going through the rigorous, clumsy "gathering" process formulated by their pious ancestors.[2]

Joel Bennedict offers an excellent illustration of this problem. During his missionary tour of 1812–1813, Bennedict often addressed crowds of hundreds, many of them "deeply impressed" and anxious about their spiritual state. He spent countless hours counseling convicted sinners who were seeking salvation. Yet he admitted only a handful of these awakened settlers to full communion. At Punch-Kill, where he gathered a church, hundreds of people came to his services, but only twelve were admitted to communion. He demanded not only a clear conversion account of those he admitted, but also a thorough understanding of Calvinist doctrine. "The examination was very lengthy & particular," he explained, "as·I considered it of vast importance that they should be well informed, as well as pious, to become a *chh.* in such a polluted place."[3]

Literally hundreds of missionary letters bear testimony to this phenomenon. The zealous orthodox evangelists would go forth to save the new settlements. They would preach to thousands of settlers, many of them solemn and "seriously hopeful." Perhaps they would counsel a crush of anxious visitors, seeking spiritual assurance. Typically, however, by the close of their tours, they had admitted no more than a dozen or so new members to the churches they visited. In light of this fact, it is small wonder that "heterodox disorganizing preachers" followed orthodox missionaries like Joel Bennedict "into almost every place" they traveled.[4] Surely many awakened sinners who could not give satisfactory evidence of regeneration must have been eager to receive preachers who offered salvation on easier terms.

Pure church principles also dictated baptism decisions. Missionaries were instructed to baptize only the children of "visible believers" who could present evidence of their regeneration. The best evidence was church membership, but frontier settlers sometimes migrated without obtaining letters of dismissal from the churches they had left behind. Some people had experienced conversion only after arriving in the new settlements, but had no orthodox church to join; in many cases they were complete strangers to the missionaries, as well as to other settlers who might vouch for them. As a result, "truly pious" Congregationalist parents could be turned down when they requested that their children be baptized.[5]

The "infant seed" of unregenerate parents, of course, could not receive baptism from Edwardsean evangelists, a fact which infuriated some settlers. Anxious parents routinely approached CMS missionaries, desperately wanting their children to be baptized according to the well-known "Half-way" covenant. Often they presented arguments based upon egalitarian principles to justify their request. One common sentiment, Thomas Robbins noted, was "that one child is as good as another & therefore has as much right to baptism." Another popular argument was that "many persons, who are not professors of religion, appear as real Christians as some who are, & therefore have as good a right . . . to give their children in baptism." Each time the missionaries would explain to the confused and angered parents the covenantal nature of baptism and the worthlessness of the sacrament to the children of the unregenerate. Surely, such spurned parents must have been especially open to sectarian attacks upon the Congregational "elitists."[6]

Unlike their Methodist counterparts, Edwardsean evangelists could not help but think of the church first and foremost as a covenanted community of regenerate saints. Although they longed for the salvation of individuals, they could not conceive of the lone, solitary Christian. Always, their goal was to gather converted souls into new communities of faith that could successfully support the stated preaching of the gospel. Consequently, they were very hesitant to establish small churches that had little or no prospects for self-sufficiency. Instead, scattered orthodox settlers were encouraged to gather together informally for scripture reading, hymns, and prayers, and to prepare themselves for the future day when they would be better able to support the gospel.[7]

Many isolated folk rarely received visits from orthodox missionaries, who generally concentrated their efforts upon areas where viable churches could be easily gathered. The scattered, solitary individuals were left by default to their own devices or to the "irregular" preachers who *did* visit them. In an incredibly mobile frontier society, where large numbers of Congregational professors were isolated from other orthodox professors, this was a critical error.

The early Congregational evangelists successfully accommodated many aspects of the democratizing republican society, but their accommodation was always limited by their commitment to the ideal of the pure church. While they desired conversions, and undoubtedly *could* have gained more converts than they did, they steadfastly refused to alter their ecclesiology to permit themselves to compete more effectively with the sectarian upstarts. In 1808 the General Association of Connecticut published a statement that beautifully illustrates this fundamental aspect of their thinking:

> The loss of members from our churches by desertion, ought, in no measure, to deter the followers of Christ from the straight path of his commandments. Better is it that the church should be a small select band, cemented by ardent love to the Master and his interest, than a discordant multitude, without harmony of sentiment and affection.[8]

To a remarkable degree the Congregational clergy of the early republic deliberately chose for themselves the path that they followed. This choice underscores the conceptual distance separating the Edwardsean evangelists from many modern scholars and church leaders who write about religious declension. It seems almost inconceivable today that evangelists would turn people away from the church. Yet this is precisely what many Congregational missionaries chose to do. Presented with a choice between doctrinal purity and tradition on the one hand, and a loss of adherents on the other hand, Edwardsean missionaries chose to uphold doctrinal purity.

Roger Finke and Rodney Stark, in their market analysis of American religious history, identify the Congregational clergy as a prime example in support of their thesis that denominations inevitably decline when they lose the tension between themselves and the secular world. According to Finke and Stark, the Congregationalists lost out to the upstart Methodists and Baptists because they had become too worldly, too secular, too accommodated to the social and intellectual environment around them.[9] Clearly, this characterization of the post-revolutionary Congregational clergy is highly misleading.

The Edwardsean ministers who dominated the orthodox missionary movement were fiercely conservative in matters of doctrine and religious practice, and ever critical of secularizing tendencies in the church. An examination of the confessions and bylaws of the churches they gathered clearly shows that they would tolerate no significant deviation from pure church ideals.[10] In their sermons they constantly asserted the total depravity of human nature; the need for repentance; the need for the new birth; and strict conformity to the laws of God. "If we expect the blessings of the Christian covenant," Nathan Strong characteristically proclaimed, "we must on our own part keep it." For Edwardsean ministers, keeping covenant meant reverently upholding "the word of God, and our old institutions of piety, which made our fathers blessed in life."[11]

The conviction that the true Church lived according to an inviolable covenant with God led Congregational missionary leaders to assume a countercultural role in the face of the apparent growing apostasy of the Church in America. From their perspective, Christians were buffeted by heresy on every hand. Freethinkers attacked the truth from the rationalist side, thoughtlessly elevating reason above the word of God "so as to reject all evangelical holiness, faith in Jesus Christ . . . and the ministration of the Spirit in the heart."[12] But sectarian preachers corrupted the Church as well. They attacked the truth by exhibiting a "fanatical zeal, which is not according to knowledge," foolishly repudiating vital Reformed traditions and accommodating too much to popular democratic tastes.

We should not dismiss the Congregationalist critique as simply a reactionary response to declension, as generations of historians have tended to do. Unlike the Puritans, Harry Stout has cogently observed, the emergent evangelical sects "had no colonial or European past they wanted to emulate." The Methodists, Baptists, and other sectarians were often fierce antitraditionalists, who "incorporated into their theology and sociology the new American gospel that change was, by definition, change for the better."[13]

Nathan Hatch has demonstrated that the Methodists, Baptists, and a host of other early republican sects blatantly integrated ascendant Jeffersonian political values into their presentation of the gospel. A great deal of their popular appeal lay precisely in their ability to assure people that God heartily endorsed the dominant values of the new nation, and was, in fact, a most democratic deity. They also gained popular appeal by proclaiming the absolute right of all people to interpret the scriptures for themselves, and by denouncing creeds, confessions, and ancient expressions of doctrinal orthodoxy as man-made religious cant. Finally, they tended to elevate the authority of subjective religious experience over propositional truth.[14]

In an age of rising democracy and individualism, these were not costly positions to adopt. The growing evangelical groups in many ways mirrored the prevalent values of early republican America, and they greatly benefited from this ideological match. Contrary to Finke and Stark, their status as a countercultural force was ambiguous at best.

Congregational evangelists, on the other hand, constantly risked alienating people by denouncing what they regarded as the faithlessness of the church and of American society. The "religious upstarts," Edwardseans believed, achieved popularity at the expense of doctrinal truth and the inheritance bequeathed by the colonial founders. Rationalists and populist exhorters alike pointed the people not to the sovereign, holy, and inscrutable God of the Bible, but to popular idols of their own construction. The daily discourse of the orthodox leadership was peppered with the old rhetoric of the Puritan jeremiad. Like Old Testament prophets, they repeatedly warned about the wrath which would inevitably fall upon the nation if the people did not return with their whole hearts to the faith of their ancestors. In short, Congregational evangelists maintained perhaps a greater level of tension with republican society than their competitors.

These conclusions challenge much conventional wisdom about church growth and religious declension. Ever since 1972, when Dean Kelley published his landmark *Why Conservative Churches are Growing,* many historians, sociologists, and church-growth experts have argued that churches grow *because* they are stricter and more sectarian. In his richly nuanced analysis Kelley persuasively argued that people look to religion for *meaning,* and that meaning is generated only within communities that place very high demands upon members. Kelley presented a model of "strong" religious movements that included undivided commitment to group goals, strict discipline, and missionary zeal. Exclusivist organizations, he concluded, are inherently better at providing meaning than inclusivist, pluralistic, liberal bodies.[15]

Roger Finke and Rodney Stark build much of their interpretation of American religious history upon Kelley's hypothesis. Although their single-minded adherence to market analysis tends to become reductionist, depriving their study of the subtlety and complexity which characterized Kelley's work, they reach essentially the same conclusion. Religious movements prosper when they place high demands upon members in terms of commitment, discipline, and adherence to doctrine. Churches grow when they maintain a high degree of tension with society; when they adopt exclusivist membership requirements; and when members are stigmatized for their commitment.[16]

By these standards post-revolutionary Edwardsean evangelists should have been stellar successes. They clearly had an extremely high regard for purity in doctrine and practice. They adhered doggedly to exclusivist admission standards, and they possessed an evangelistic fervor fueled by millennial expectancy. They prophetically critiqued the dominant social and political trends in their society, and they maintained at least as much tension with the world as their competitors. Finally, they were stigmatized by their enemies and faced determined opposition in many communities. Nonetheless, they experienced declension, in part precisely *because* they were too strict and too unyielding in their commitment to the pure church.

These findings remind us that we must be extremely cautious about the application of sociological models, even models as eminently useful as Kelley's. It is axiomatic that history is not monocausal; nevertheless, the axiom deserves to be repeated. Congregationalism declined in the early republic due to many interlocking factors. Formulaic explanations, such as those Finke and Stark offer, fail to do justice to the complexity of historical reality.

Students of American religion often explicitly or implicitly assume that church growth is a vitally important goal and that increasing membership rolls are a valid indicator of spiritual health. There is a marked tendency to universalize our own modern preoccupation with numbers, and to speak of growing churches as "successful," "effective," "healthy," or "winners." Conversely, we often refer to churches that do not grow, or which experience declining membership, as "stagnant," "ineffective," "dying," or "losers."

Clearly, however, if we uncritically project these assumptions upon the past, we will fail to understand many historical religious movements. Post-revolutionary Congregationalism offers a case in point. In contrast to the assessment of many modern scholars, Congregational leaders in the early republic did not regard themselves as "losers." Quite simply, they did not think in terms of "market shares" or adherence rates. In the face of a drastic reversal of their fortunes, Congregational evangelists did not try very hard to maintain numerical or political dominance, not because they lacked conviction or zeal but because they had other concerns which they considered more urgent.

Indeed, as Finke and Stark themselves recognize, most Congregational leaders confronted their apparent declension with optimistic equanimity.[17] The whole structure of Edwardsean thought was radically God-centered. God, they knew, was providentially directing the cosmos, including all the ups and downs of human history. It was inconceivable to them that anything evil could ultimately befall those whom God had elected, and who faithfully maintained the ancient covenant bequeathed by countless generations of saints before them.

Edwardseans embraced an eschatological understanding of history that gave them immense reassurance. In the last days, they believed, Satan would apparently be stronger than ever before and the saints would face bitter opposition. Indeed, the world would be most black just before the long-awaited dawn. Every apparent reversal of fortune only served to confirm this expectation. Infidelity and widespread apostasy from the traditional faith were not a cause for alarm to Christians who felt certain that the game was almost over and that they were on the winning team.[18]

Nathan Strong, in a sermon at the ordination of Thomas Robbins to the "evangelical office," observed that the world was nearing its final days. It was urgent, therefore, that missionaries like Robbins go forth to minister to those who had no orthodox pastor. This task, he observed, "is the most difficult to perform," and undoubtedly Robbins must expect "to meet trouble and affliction for the sake of our Lord." Although the universal reign of Jesus was near at hand, Strong asserted,

> We have yet to fight with beasts at Ephesus, and there are many Alexanders who will do much evil to us and the cause of our Lord. We have to wrestle with flesh and blood, with principalities and powers and spiritual wickedness in high places. It is yet a time for wrestling and

prayer and much tribulation. The beast is yet making war against the saints, and the dragon continues to cast waters out of his mouth after them.

In the face of all obstacles and setbacks to the cause, Strong advised Robbins, ministers must devote themselves to prayer, earnestly study the scriptures, and "seek communion with our Lord, and wisdom and fidelity from him to do our duty." God is faithful to his promises, Strong reminded the young missionary, "and if we thus do he will not forsake us."[19]

The growth of competing sects could not convince ministers with such a mindset that they needed to make any fundamental changes in their ecclesiology. Indeed, it simply reinforced their commitment to stand firmly on the side of their traditions, to proclaim the gospel as faithfully as they could, and to trust that a sovereign God had the situation in hand. Let others follow madly after innovation; they would keep the covenant.

And who can say with any assurance that their efforts were unsuccessful? For the early evangelists commissioned by the CMS, success could not be measured by the number of persons they admitted to communion, the size of their congregations, or the degree to which they provided settlers with a sense of meaning. Success or failure would be revealed only at the end of time, when God at last separated the true church from the world and called his faithful servants to their eternal reward.

Notes

CHAPTER ONE

1. Elias Smith, *The Loving Kindness of God Displayed in the Triumph of Republicanism in America: Being a Discourse Delivered at Taunton (Mass.) July Fourth, 1809; at the Celebration of American Independence* (n.p., 1809), p. 32.

2. Robert Wiebe, *The Opening of American Society: From the Adoption of the Constitution to the Eve of Disunion* (New York, 1984), pp. 159–60. An outstanding brief survey of Christianity in post-revolutionary America is Nathan O. Hatch, "Christianity and Democracy: From the Revolution to the Civil War," in Mark Noll, ed., *Christianity in America: A Handbook* (Grand Rapids, Mich., 1983), pp. 158–276.

3. Martin Marty, *Pilgrims in Their Own Land: 500 Years of Religion in America* (New York, 1985), pp. 169–75; Hatch, "Christianity and Democracy," p. 166; Rodney Stark and Roger Finke, "American Religion in 1776: A Statistical Portrait," *Sociological Analysis* 49 (1988): 39–51; Roger Finke and Rodney Stark, "How the Upstart Sects Won America: 1776–1850," *Journal for the Scientific Study of Religion* 28 (1989): 27–44.

4. See Sydney Ahlstrom, *A Religious History of the American People*, 2 vols. (New York, 1975), 1:551–70, for a lucid discussion of New England migration and the failure of orthodoxy to compete with the "popular denominations."

5. W. P. Strickland, ed., *Autobiography of Peter Cartwright, the Backwoods Preacher* (New York, 1856), p. 358; W. P. Strickland, ed., *Autobiography of Rev. James B. Finley; or, Pioneer Life in the West* (Cincinnati, 1853), pp. 299–300, 330–36.

6. Strickland, *Autobiography of Cartwright*, pp. 358–60, 370–72.

7. William Warren Sweet, *Religion on the American Frontier*, vol. 3, *The Congregationalists* (Chicago, 1939), p. 11; Marty, *Pilgrims In Their Own Land*,

pp. 169–70; Clifton Olmstead, *Religion in America: Past and Present* (Englewood Cliffs, N.J., 1961), pp. 57, 62.

8. Sweet, *The Congregationalists,* pp. 10–11; J. F. Thorning, *Religious Liberty in Transition* (New York, 1931), p. 47; H. Richard Niebuhr, *The Social Sources of Denominationalism* (New York, 1957), pp. 152–54; Malcolm Rohrbough, *The Trans-Appalachian Frontier: People, Societies, and Institutions, 1775–1850* (New York, 1978), pp. 150–51.

9. William W. Patton, *The Last Century of Congregationalism; or the Influence on Church and State of the Faith and Polity of the Pilgrim Fathers* (Washington, 1878), p. 7; Sweet, *The Congregationalists,* p. 12. Donald M. Mathews, "The Second Great Awakening as an Organizing Process, 1780–1830: An Hypothesis," *American Quarterly* 21 (Spring 1969): 23–43, does not directly address the problem of Congregational declension. Mathews does, however, suggest that Methodism spread rapidly because Methodists recognized that the church "must be an organizing impulse reaching throughout society rather than a stabilizing institution located in one place." The Congregationalists organized their churches according to theological abstractions, while Methodists were led by "pragmatic necessity" to conceive of their entire communion as a vast missionary organization. Indeed, Mathews believes that Congregationalists eventually organized missionary associations in imitation of the Methodists, and only after Methodist itinerants had made heavy inroads into Congregational parishes: "In New England the establishment was taught the powers of persuasion before it was taught the necessity of it." Congregationalists, Mathews clearly implies, failed to creatively adapt to changing circumstances, developing missionary organizations only in defensive reaction to the success of the Methodist system of evangelism. See pp. 36–37, 41. Finke and Stark also stress the organizational weaknesses of Congregationalism *vis à vis* the Methodists and Baptists in "How the Upstart Sects Won America," 33–34.

10. Wiebe, *The Opening of American Society,* p. 159; Gordon S. Wood, "The Democratization of Mind in the American Revolution," *Leadership in the American Revolution* (Washington, 1974), pp. 63–89; Hatch, "Christianity and Democracy," pp. 166–67. J. Franklin Jameson observed as early as 1926 that the Revolution altered Americans' theological preferences, noting that the fastest-growing denominations of the post-revolutionary era were anti-Calvinistic: "In a period when the special privileges of individuals were being called in question or destroyed, there would naturally be less favor for that form of theology which was dominated by the doctrine of especial election of a part of mankind, a growing favor for those forms . . . based upon the idea of the natural equality of all men." See J. Franklin Jameson, *The American Revolution Considered as a Social Movement* (Princeton, 1926), p. 157.

11. Nathan O. Hatch, "The Christian Movement and the Demand for a Theology of the People," *Journal of American History* 67 (December 1980): 566–67. Also see Nathan O. Hatch, "The Triumph of Vernacular Preaching in the Early Republic," paper presented at the Conference on Faith and History, Washing-

ton, D.C., December 30, 1987; Nathan O. Hatch, *The Democratization of American Christianity* (New Haven, Conn., 1989).

12. William G. McLoughlin, *Revivals, Awakenings, and Reform: An Essay on Religion and Social Change in America, 1607–1977* (Chicago, 1978), pp. 108–12. This interpretation of the revivals rests heavily upon the memoirs of Lyman Beecher, who ascribed the awakening among Congregational churches to orthodox efforts to stave off democratic revolution and disestablishment. See Barbara M. Cross, ed., *The Autobiography of Lyman Beecher,* 2 vols. (Cambridge, Mass., 1961) 1:190–93, 251–56. Beecher's account has been accepted by most students of the era. See, for example, Stephen Berk, *Calvinism versus Democracy: Timothy Dwight and the Origins of American Evangelical Orthodoxy* (Hamden, Conn., 1974), pp. 161–93; Winthrop Hudson, *Religion in America: An Historical Account of the Development of American Religious Life* (New York, 1965), pp. 78–96; F. H. Littell, *From State Church to Pluralism: Protestant Interpretation of Religion in American History* (New York, 1962), p. 30; Sidney E. Mead, *Nathaniel William Taylor, 1786–1858: A Connecticut Liberal* (Chicago, 1942), pp. 38–53; Cushing Strout, *The New Heavens and New Earth: Political Religion in America* (New York, 1974), p 114. In his pioneering monograph, *The Second Great Awakening in Connecticut* (New Haven, Conn., 1942), pp. 56–69, Charles Roy Keller long ago challenged Beecher's account, noting that few orthodox ministers appeared concerned about disestablishment, and that the revival narratives and sermons of the Awakening fail to reflect any political motivation. More recently, Richard D. Shiels has presented a strong case against Beecher's account in "The Second Great Awakening in Connecticut: Critique of the Traditional Interpretation," *Church History* 49 (1980): 401–32. Joseph Conforti has also challenged the standard political interpretation of the revivals in *Samuel Hopkins and the New Divinity Movement: Calvinism, the Congregational Ministry, and Reform in New England Between the Great Awakenings* (Grand Rapids, Mich., 1981), pp. 183–84.

13. Harry S. Stout, *The New England Soul: Preaching and Religious Culture in Colonial New England* (New York, 1986). See also Sacvan Bercovitch, *The American Jeremiad* (Madison, Wis., 1978), for a brilliant analysis of the evolving Puritan concept of errand during the colonial and early national periods.

14. Stout, *New England Soul,* pp. 312–19, discusses the Congregational clergy's difficult adjustment to republican culture. Stout, p. 316, succinctly summarizes the contrasting mentality of orthodox ministers and their sectarian competitors: "Unlike their Puritan predecessors, the new evangelicals had no colonial or European past they wanted to emulate. Instead they incorporated into their theology and sociology the new American gospel that change was, by definition, change for the better."

15. Sweet, *The Congregationalists,* pp. 13–14. On New England emigration see Ray Allen Billington and Martin Ridge, *Westward Expansion: A History of the American Frontier* (New York, 1982); Dixon R. Fox, *Yankees and Yorkers* (New York, 1940); Lois Kimball Mathews, *The Expansion of New England: The*

Spread of New England Settlements and Institutions to the Mississippi River, 1620–1865 (Boston, 1909); Randolph A. Roth, *The Democratic Dilemma: Religion, Reform, and Social Order in the Connecticut River Valley of Vermont, 1791–1850* (Cambridge, Mass., 1987); Lewis D. Stilwell, *Migration From Vermont (1776–1860)* (Montpelier, Vt., 1937).

16. An excellent analysis of "the failure of the covenanted community and the standing order" in the Connecticut River Valley of Vermont can be found in Roth, *The Democratic Dilemma,* pp. 41–79.

17. See, for example, Conforti, *Samuel Hopkins and the New Divinity Movement;* Frank H. Foster, *A Genetic History of New England Theology* (Chicago, 1907); Edwin Scott Gaustad, *The Great Awakening in New England* (Chicago, 1968); Charles C. Goen, *Revivalism and Separatism in New England, 1740–1800* (New Haven, Conn., 1962); Allen C. Guelzo, *Edwards on the Will: A Century of American Theological Debate* (Middletown, Conn., 1989); Joseph Haroutunian, *Piety versus Moralism: The Passing of the New England Theology* (New York, 1970); James Walsh, "The Pure Church in Eighteenth Century Connecticut," Ph.D. diss., Columbia University, 1967.

18. On the Plan of Union see William Warren Sweet, *Religion on the American Frontier,* vol. 2, *The Presbyterians* (New York, 1936) and *The Congregationalists,* especially pp. 13–42. See also R. H. Nichols, "The Plan of Union in New York," *Church History* 5 (1936): 29–51, and Samuel C. Pearson, "From Church to Denomination: American Congregationalism in the Nineteenth Century," *Church History* 38 (1969): 67–85.

19. Two old studies provide brief introductions to the major Congregational missionary organizations: Oliver W. Elsbree, *The Rise of the Missionary Spirit in America, 1790–1815* (Williamsport, Pa., 1928) and Colin B. Goodykoontz, *Home Missions on the American Frontier* (Caldwell, Idaho, 1939). Sweet, *The Congregationalists,* reproduces many missionary letters, but provides little analysis. Chapter 4 of Keller, *The Second Great Awakening in Connecticut,* discusses the organization of the Connecticut Missionary Society, but does not throw much light on the work of the missionaries themselves. Paul Jeffrey Potash has written an informative article on CMS missionaries in eighteenth and early nineteenth century Vermont: "Welfare of the Regions Beyond," *Vermont History* 46 (1978): 109–28, and there are occasional glimpses of orthodox evangelism in Whitney R. Cross, *The Burned–Over District: The Social and Intellectual History of Enthusiastic Religion in Western New York, 1800–1850* (Ithaca, N.Y., 1950).

CHAPTER TWO

1. R. Pierce Beaver, "Missionary Motivation Through Three Centuries," in Jerald C. Brauer, ed., *Reinterpretation in American Church History* (Chicago, 1968), p. 117.

2. Connecticut General Association (CGA), *An Address of the General Association of Connecticut, to the District Associations on the Subject of a Missionary Society; Together With Summaries and Extracts from Late European Publications on Missions to the Heathen* (Norwich, Conn., 1797), p. 8.

3. Lois Banner, "The Protestant Crusade: Religious Missions, Benevolence, and Reform in the United States, 1790–1840," Ph.D. diss., Columbia University, 1970, pp. 24–25.

4. The Dedham covenant is analyzed by Kenneth Lockridge, "The History of a Puritan Church, 1637–1736," in Alden T. Vaughan and Francis J. Bremner, eds., *Puritan New England: Essays on Religion, Society, and Culture* (New York, 1977), pp. 93–95.

5. Winthrop is quoted in Alden T. Vaughan, *New England Frontier: Puritans and Indians, 1620–1675*, rev. ed. (New York, 1979), p. 235. See pp. 235–308 of Vaughan's study for a general overview of seventeenth-century Puritan missions. See also Henry Warner Bowden, *American Indians and Christian Missions: Studies in Cultural Conflict* (Chicago, 1981), pp. 96–163; and Francis Jennings, *The Invasion of America: Indians, Colonialism, and the Cant of Conquest* (New York, 1976), pp. 228–53.

6. Jonathan Edwards, *Some Thoughts Concerning the Present Revival*, in Perry Miller and John Smith, gen. eds., *Works of Jonathan Edwards* (New Haven, Conn., 1957–) 4:353. For Miller's description of Edwards, see Perry Miller, "The End of the World," in *Errand Into The Wilderness* (New York, 1964), p. 233.

7. On Edwards's eschatological thinking, see C. C. Goen, "Jonathan Edwards: A New Departure in Eschatology," *Church History* 38 (1959): 25–40; Ruth Bloch, *Visionary Republic: Millennial Themes in American Thought, 1756–1800* (Cambridge, Mass., 1985), pp. 16–21; James West Davidson, *The Logic of Millennial Thought: Eighteenth–Century New England* (New Haven, Conn., 1977), pp. 16–19. The influence of Edwardsean eschatology upon British missions is discussed in Johannes Van den Berg, *Constrained By Jesus' Love: An Inquiry Into the Motives of the Missionary Awakening in Great Britain in the Period Between 1698 and 1815* (Kampen, 1956), pp. 120–22.

8. Jonathan Edwards, *Dissertation on the Nature of True Virtue* in *Works of Jonathan Edwards,* 2:261–99. The scholarship bearing upon the *Dissertation* is extensive, but see especially Douglas Elwood, *The Philosophical Theology of Jonathan Edwards* (New York, 1960) and Clyde A. Holbrook, *The Ethics of Jonathan Edwards: Aesthetics and Morality* (Ann Arbor, Mich., 1973).

9. My treatment of Hopkins relies heavily upon two works by Joseph Conforti: *Samuel Hopkins and the New Divinity Movement,* especially pp. 109–40, and "Samuel Hopkins and the New Divinity: Theology, Ethics, and Social Reform in Eighteenth Century New England," *William & Mary Quarterly* 34 (1977): 572–89. See also George M. Marsden, *The Evangelical Mind and the New School Presbyterian Experience* (New Haven, Conn., 1970), pp. 31–58.

10. In addition to the works by Conforti and Marsden, Ahlstrom, *A Religious*

History of the American People, 1:489–503, provides an excellent brief synopsis of the New Divinity and scholarly assessments of the movement.

11. Beaver, "Missionary Motivation," pp. 120–22, discusses the centrality of the *gloria dei* theme in traditional Puritan missionary thought.

12. Charles Backus, *The Benevolent Spirit of Christianity Illustrated; in a Sermon Delivered at the Ordination of the Rev. Thomas Snell to the Pastoral Care of the Second Church in Brookfield, Massachusetts* (Worcester, Mass., 1798), pp. 14–15.

13. Franklin B. Dexter, ed., *The Literary Diary of Ezra Stiles, D.D. LL.D,* 3 vols. (New York, 1901) 3:247, 463–64.

14. Conforti, *Samuel Hopkins and the New Divinity,* pp. 6, 122–23.

15. Robert Gross, *The Minutemen and Their World* (New York, 1976), p. 189.

16. Stout, *New England Soul,* pp. 282–311, brilliantly analyzes the Congregational clergy's response to the Revolution. Emerson is quoted on p. 290.

17. Williston Walker, *A History of the Congregational Churches in the United States* (New York, 1894), p. 311; Sweet, *The Congregationalists,* p. 44; Horace Hooker, "Congregational Home Missions In Connecticut," in Leonard Bacon et al., eds., *Contributions to the Ecclesiastical History of Connecticut,* vol. 1 (New Haven, Conn., 1861), p. 163.

18. J. William T. Youngs, Jr., *God's Messengers: Religious Leadership in Colonial New England, 1700–1750* (Baltimore, 1976), pp. 66–67.

19. Walker, *The Congregationalists,* pp. 311–12; Fairfield West Association Minutes, 1774–75, Folder 1, Records of the Fairfield West Association, Congregational House, Hartford, Conn.

20. The records for this period are very sketchy, and few details can be known with certainty. In 1788 the General Association commissioned the Rev. Jeremiah Day to tour western Vermont, and recommended that the district associations send out missionaries as well. At least a few pastors made brief tours of the area. Among these was Nathan Perkins of West Hartford, who vaguely mentions in his 1789 journal other "Connecticut brethren" who preceded him. Some of these were certainly ministerial candidates, but at least two, Gideon Hawley and John Avery, were ordained clergymen. The total number of ordained Connecticut pastors sent out prior to 1793, however, was probably fewer than ten. See Nathan Perkins, *A Narrative of a Tour Through the State of Vermont* (Woodstock, Vt., 1930), pp. 25, 28, 35.

21. John Comstock, *The Congregational Churches in Vermont and Their Ministry, 1762–1942* (St. Johnsbury, Vt., 1942); Potash, "Welfare of the Regions Beyond," pp. 111–12.

22. Potash, "Welfare of the Regions Beyond," pp. 112–15. Quotation is from Billington and Ridge, *Westward Expansion,* p. 107.

23. Potash, "Welfare of the Regions Beyond," pp. 112–15.

24. Perkins, *Narrative of a Tour,* pp. 18, 32.

25. Monkton Committee to General Association, 14 September 1793, Con-

necticut Missionary Society Papers, Congregational House, Hartford, Conn. Hereafter cited as CMS Papers.

26. Youngs, *God's Messengers,* pp. 27–29. See also Donald M. Scott, *From Office to Profession: The New England Ministry, 1750–1850* (Philadelphia, 1978), pp. 4–6.

27. Mary Ives to Benjamin Trumbull, 1 April 1800, Benjamin Trumbull Papers, Beinecke Library, Yale University, New Haven, Conn. Hereafter cited as Trumbull Papers (Yale).

28. "Lady in Virginia" to Abel Flint, 6 August 1814, CMS Papers.

29. Perkins, *Narrative of a Tour,* p. 33.

30. James Andrews to Thomas Robbins, 4 October 1799; Nathaniel Munger to Thomas Robbins, 26 October 1799, Thomas Robbins Papers, Connecticut Historical Society, Hartford, Conn. Hereafter cited as Robbins Papers.

31. Perkins, *Narrative of a Tour,* pp. 26, 30.

32. CGA, *A Narrative of the Missions to the New Settlements, According to the Appointment of the General Association of the State of Connecticut. . . .* (New Haven, Conn., 1794), p. 15.

CHAPTER THREE

1. CGA, *A Continuation of the Narrative of the Missions to the New Settlements . . .* (New Haven, Conn., 1795), pp. 19–20.

2. Billington and Ridge, *Westward Expansion,* p. 248.

3. Ibid., pp. 253, 256–58.

4. CGA, *A Continuation of the Narrative of the Missions to the New Settlements . . .* (New Haven, Conn., 1795), p. 21.

5. This and the following paragraph are both based upon the *Connecticut Gazette,* May 2, 1793.

6. Ibid.; CGA, *A Narrative of the Missions to the New Settlements . . .* (New Haven, Conn., 1794), pp. 2–4; Minutes, Connecticut General Association Committee on Missions, Trumbull Papers (Yale).

7. My discussion of the Appropriation Act is based largely upon James R. Beasley, "Emerging Republicanism and the Standing Order: The Appropriation Act Controversy in Connecticut, 1793 to 1795," *William & Mary Quarterly* 29 (1972): 587–610.

8. Ibid. Quotations are on p. 604.

9. Committee on Missions, Minutes, Trumbull Papers (Yale).

10. Sidney E. Mead, "The Rise of the Evangelical Conception of the Ministry in America (1607–1850)," in H. Richard Niebuhr and Daniel D. Williams, eds. *The Ministry in Historical Perspectives* (New York, 1956), pp. 207–49.

11. Youngs, *God's Messengers,* pp. 68, 138–41; Stout, *New England Soul,* p. 19; Scott, *From Office to Profession,* pp. 2–3.

12. For an excellent analysis of clerical dismissals in one New England state, see George B. Kirsch, "Clerical Dismissals in Colonial and Revolutionary New Hampshire," *Church History* 49 (1980): 160–77.

13. Sally Robbins to Thomas Robbins, 13 December 1793, and Nathaniel Robbins to Thomas Robbins, 29 December 1793, Robbins Papers.

14. Elmer C. Clark, ed., *The Journal and Letters of Francis Asbury,* 3 vols. (Nashville, Tenn., 1958) 2:58; Moses Welch to Jonathan Edwards, Jr., 1 July 1793, CMS Papers. For a suggestive discussion of Methodism's early impact see Richard D. Shiels, "The Methodist Circuit Rider in the Second Great Awakening in New England," paper presented at Asbury College, June 10, 1988.

15. See Committee on Missions, Minutes, Trumbull Papers, for the routine operations of the committee.

16. CGA, *A Narrative of the Missions to the New Settlements* . . . (New Haven, Conn., 1794), pp. 4–5.

17. Jeremiah Day to Jonathan Edwards, Jr., 6 January 1794, 7 July 1794; Cyprian Strong to Jonathan Edwards, Jr., 30 June 1794; William Robinson to Committee on Missions, 27 August 1794; Theodore Hinsdale to Jonathan Edwards, Jr., 27 June 1793, CMS Papers.

18. Moses Welch to Jonathan Edwards, Jr., 1 July 1793, CMS Papers.

19. Azel Backus to Jonathan Edwards, Jr., 7 July 1794, CMS Papers.

20. Noah Merwin to Ezra Stiles, 19 August 1794; Samuel Nott to Jonathan Edwards, Jr., 10 October 1793, CMS Papers.

21. William Lyman to Jonathan Edwards, Jr., 18 July 1794, CMS Papers.

22. Nathan Williams to Benjamin Trumbull, 21 June 1793, CMS Papers.

23. Jonathan Edwards, Jr. to Benjamin Trumbull, 19 October 1796, CMS Papers.

24. CGA, *An Address to the Inhabitants of the New Settlements in the Northern and Western Parts of the United States* (New Haven, Conn., 1795), pp. 1–6.

25. Jonathan Edwards, Jr. to Benjamin Trumbull, 12 July 1796, CMS Papers.

26. Benjamin Trumbull to Abel Flint, 18 October 1798, CMS Papers.

27. Hatch, *Democratization of American Christianity,* pp. 23–33.

28. The thirteen missionaries and their churches were as follows: Jeremiah Day (New Preston)*; Samuel Ells (North Branford); David Higgins (Lyme); Asahel Hooker (Goshen)*; David Huntington (Marlborough); Aaron Kinne (Groton); Samuel J. Mills (Torringford)*; Ammi Robbins (Norfolk)*; John Shepherd (North Stamford); Cotton Mather Smith (Sharon)*; Peter Starr (Warren)*; Noah Williston (West Haven) and Benjamin Wooster (South Britain)*. An asterisk (*) denotes a Litchfield pastor. Biographical information about these men was gleaned from the following sources: Bacon et al., *Contributions to the Ecclesiastical History of Connecticut;* Conforti, *Samuel Hopkins and the New Divinity Movement;* Franklin B. Dexter, *Biographical Sketches of the Graduates of Yale College,* 6 vols. (New York: 1885–1912); James McLachlan, *Princetonians, 1748–1768: A Biographical Dictionary* (Princeton, 1976); William B. Sprague, *Annals of the American Pulpit,* 6 vols. (New York, 1969); Walsh, "The Pure Church in Eighteenth Century Connecticut," pp. 248–64.

29. On Stiles's hostility toward the New Divinity see Edmund S. Morgan, *The Gentle Puritan: A Life of Ezra Stiles, 1727–1795* (New Haven, Conn., 1962), p. 176; and Richard D. Birdsall, "Ezra Stiles versus the New Divinity Men," *American Quarterly* 17 (Summer 1965): 257. Dana's theological views are discussed in Sprague, *Annals* 1:565–71.

30. William Lyman to Abel Flint, 28 November 1803, CMS Papers.

31. CGA, *A Narrative of the Missions to the New Settlements* . . . (New Haven, Conn., 1794), pp. 4–10.

32. Journal of Aaron Kinne, 30 January 1794, CMS Papers.

33. Most of the missionaries spent approximately two months in the field on each tour, while a few spent only four to six weeks.

34. CGA, *A Narrative of the Missions to the New Settlements* . . . (New Haven, Conn., 1794), pp. 6–8.

35. Ibid., pp. 8–9; Samuel Ells to Committee on Missions, n.d., CMS Papers.

36. CGA, *A Narrative of the Missions to the New Settlements* . . . (New Haven, Conn., 1794), pp. 7–8.

37. Committee of the Walton Society to David Huntington, 28 November 1793, CMS Papers.

38. CGA, *A Narrative of the Missions to the New Settlements* . . . (New Haven, Conn., 1794), pp. 10–11.

39. David Higgins to Benjamin Trumbull, 19 February 1795, CMS Papers.

40. Ammi Robbins to Jonathan Edwards, Jr., 24 January 1794, CMS Papers.

41. Ibid.

42. Ibid.

43. Samuel Ells to Committee on Missions, n.d., CMS Papers.

44. Journal of Aaron Kinne, 30 January 1794, CMS Papers.

45. Terry Bilhartz, *Urban Religion and the Second Great Awakening: Church and Society in Early National Baltimore* (Rutherford, N.J., 1986), pp. 138–39.

46. Jeremiah Day to Jonathan Edwards, Jr., 10 November 1794, CMS Papers.

47. David Higgins to Benjamin Trumbull, 19 February 1795, CMS Papers.

48. Isaac Babbit and James Evarts to the General Association of Connecticut, 30 August 1793; Committee of Monkton Society, 14 September 1793; Committee of Addison Society to Ezra Stiles et al., 21 September 1793; Committee of Peacham Society to Ezra Stiles, 2 September 1794, CMS Papers.

49. On Ogden see Richard A. Harrison, *Princetonians, 1769–1775: A Biographical Dictionary* (Princeton, 1980), pp. 93–97; Dexter, *Biographical Sketches of the Graduates of Yale College,* vol. 5 (New York, 1911), pp. 316–17; and Alan V. Briceland, "The Philadelphia *Aurora,* the New England Illuminati, and the Election of 1800," *The Pennsylvania Magazine of History and Biography* 100 (January 1976): 4–36.

50. John C. Ogden to Benjamin Trumbull, 6 July 1795, CMS Papers.

51. Asahel Hooker to Jonathan Edwards, Jr., 28 January 1795, CMS Papers.

52. For Hooker's comments, see ibid.

53. Clark, *Journal of Francis Asbury,* p. 23.

54. Trumbull scribbled his opinion of Ogden in the margin of the latter's letter of 6 July 1795, CMS Papers.

CHAPTER FOUR

1. Williston noted many of these "wondrous" developments in his Diaries. See John Q. Adams, ed., "The Diaries of the Rev. Seth Williston, *Journal of The Presbyterian Historical Society* 7–9 (December 1913–March 1917), Parts I through IV. Hereafter cited as Williston, "Diaries." Williston refers to the New York City awakening in Part III, p. 45, and to the Somers revival in Part IV, p. 127. The fullest account of the Somers revival is by Charles Backus, "An Account of the Revival in Somers, Connecticut," *Connecticut Evangelical Magazine* 1 (1801): 20–23.

2. CGA, *A Continuation of the Narrative of the Missions* . . . (New Haven, Conn., 1797), p. 12.

3. See Susan O'Brien, "A Transatlantic Community of Saints: The Great Awakening and the First Evangelical Network, 1735–1755," *American Historical Review* 91 (October 1986): 816–20.

4. Ibid, pp. 829–30. See also R. Pierce Beaver, "The Concert of Prayer for Missions," *Ecumenical Review* 10 (1957–58): 816–20.

5. O'Brien, "A Transatlantic Community of Saints," 830–31, rightly emphasizes that the Concert was "purposefully instrumental," suggesting a gradual "shift in position by evangelicals" toward an unabashed use of "means" to promote revivals. Despite this growing instrumentalism, however, eighteenth-century American Calvinists continued to insist that awakenings and revivals were purely products of divine grace, which could not be advanced through any human effort. The implicit contradiction between the traditional Puritan understanding of salvation and the instrumentalism of the United Concert was clearly reflected in the thinking of Connecticut evangelicals. Throughout the late eighteenth century Edwardsean New Lights prayed for revivals and anticipated another awakening. But when the revivals actually broke out in Connecticut during the 1790s, they stressed that these "divine works" were altogether unexpected. This theme appeared in virtually all the published accounts of the revivals of the Second Great Awakening. Richard D. Shiels cogently analyzes these narratives in "The Connecticut Clergy in the Second Great Awakening," Ph.D. diss., Boston University, 1976, pp. 226–44. Not until the 1810s, several generations after the first appearance of the Concert, did Congregational evangelicals unabashedly embrace the use of means and begin to self-consciously consider themselves to be a revivalistic movement.

6. On the revival of the Concert see O'Brien, "A Transatlantic Community of Saints," 831; Archibald Fawcett, *The Cambuslang Revival: The Scottish*

Evangelical Revival of the Eighteenth Century (London, 1971), pp. 223–33; Ernest A. Payne, *Prayer Call of 1784* (London, 1941); and Michael R. Watts, *The Dissenters: From the Reformation to the French Revolution* (Oxford, 1978), pp. 456–61.

7. The origins of the Baptist Missionary Society and the London Missionary Society are discussed by Johannes Van den Berg, *Constrained By Jesus' Love*, pp. 126–31, and Stephen Neill, *Christian Missions* (Grand Rapids, Mich., 1964), Chapter 9.

8. Bacon et al., ed. *Contributions to the Ecclesiastical History of Connecticut,* 1:308. The minutes of the North Hartford Association note that "several proposals" for a United Concert were already circulating throughout the nation, apparently initiated by ministers "without any public authority." The North Hartford clergy asked all Connecticut churches to join behind these proposals. See Minutes, Folder 2, Records of the North Hartford Association.

9. Ammi Robbins to Thomas Robbins, 31 December 1794, Robbins Papers; George Leon Walker, *History of First Church in Hartford, 1633–1883* (Hartford, Conn., 1884), p. 344; Edwin Pond Parker, *History of the Second Church of Christ in Hartford* (Hartford, Conn., 1892), p. 166.

10. Ms. sermon on "United Prayer," 2 December 1794, Robbins Papers. Thomas later recalled the origins of the Concert in Norfolk in an 1844 Century sermon, excerpted in Theron Crissey, *History of Norfolk* (Everett, Mass., 1900), pp. 149–50.

11. Shiels, "The Connecticut Clergy in the Second Great Awakening," p. 21.

12. Chandler Robbins to Thomas Robbins, 25 July 1797, Robbins Papers.

13. Ibid. At the time Thomas was studying theology under West.

14. Williston records visits to Stockbridge and letters from West throughout his diary. West, who was a close friend of Joseph Bellamy and Samuel Hopkins, preached to both whites and Indians at Stockbridge. He had an especially keen interest in missionary work, and apparently kept up an extensive correspondence with evangelists in both America and Britain. He also prepared many students for the ministry, and was an influential proponent of the New Divinity. See Conforti, *Samuel Hopkins and the New Divinity Movement,* pp. 178–79, 232.

15. Ahlstrom, *A Religious History of the American People,* 1:505, reflects the standard position, noting that despite "earlier signs of refreshing" the "first phase of the Second Great Awakening proper took place between 1797 and 1801, when many towns from Connecticut to New Hampshire felt refreshing showers." At first glance New Light rhetoric seems to support this interpretation: even as millennial hopes mounted throughout the 1790s and Edwardseans rejoiced at the awakening in Britain, they often insisted that their own parishes remained spiritually dead. We should not, however, accept this assessment at face value. Observations about "deadness" prior to the revivals must be placed within the context of Edwardsean eschatological thinking, which stressed that authentic revivals cannot be predicted, that the movement of God's Spirit invariably provokes Satan to increased opposition, and that the millennium must be preceded immediately by a period of great darkness. Hence Connecticut New

Lights often contrasted the "dullness" of the present time with the anticipated glory of the millennial future when God would act decisively to revive his people.

16. Baptist historian J. Edwin Orr adopts this interpretation in his informative book *The Eager Feet: Evangelical Awakenings, 1790–1830* (Chicago, 1975). Orr, a conservative evangelical, defines an awakening on p. vii as "a movement of the Holy Spirit bringing about a revival of New Testament Christianity in the Church of Christ and in its related community." This definition, which would probably have been acceptable to eighteenth-century New Lights, has distinct advantages, although many historians may be inclined to reject it as analytically meaningless. Clearly, the "awakening" which New Lights announced in the 1790s was not a concrete historical event which may be empirically investigated, so much as an intellectual construct and perhaps a numinous experience that lay at the core of New Light reality. We may well come closer to understanding the course of the Awakening if we accept at least provisionally evangelical categories of thought. Unfortunately, we do not fully understand what the term "awakening" signified to New Lights; more research into the rhetoric of eighteenth-century revivalism is badly needed. At present the best treatment of this knotty problem is Shiels, "The Connecticut Clergy in the Second Great Awakening," pp. 164–380.

17. McLoughlin, *Revivals, Awakenings, and Reform,* p. 108.

18. Williston, "Diaries," Part I, p. 205.

19. Williston makes millennial references throughout his diary. Quotations may be found in "Diaries," Part I, p. 205; Part IV, p. 125; Part VII, p. 320.

20. Ibid., Part II, pp. 239–41.

21. Ibid., Part II, p. 241.

22. Ibid., Part II, pp. 246–47.

23. Williston had numerous encounters with Methodists prior to his decision to seek ordination as an evangelist, and he occasionally lodged with Methodist families. Although he does not record any direct contact with Methodist preachers prior to this time, he undoubtedly was familiar with their system of evangelism.

24. Ibid., Part II, p. 254.

25. Ibid., Part IV, pp. 131–32, describes the details of his ordination.

26. Ibid., Part IV, p. 140.

27. Minutes, Folder 4, Records of the South Hartford Association; Minutes, Folder 2, Records of the West Fairfield Association; Recordbook, p. 50, Records of the New London Association, Congregational House.

28. Bacon et al., *Contributions to the Ecclesiastical History of Connecticut,* 1:166; General Association of Connecticut, *An Address of the General Association of Connecticut, to the District Associations on the Subject of a Missionary Society; Together With Summaries and Extracts From Late European Publications on Missions to the Heathen* (Norwich, Conn., 1797).

29. John Love to Dwight, Dana, and Trumbull, 23 February 1798, Trumbull Papers (Yale).

30. Minutes, Folder 4, Records of the North Hartford Association; Walker,

History of First Church in Hartford, pp. 349–50; "Subscription Paper and Address of the North Association of Hartford County," CMS Papers.

31. The lay Trustees of the NHMS were: Hezekiah Bissell, the Hon. Roger Newberry, the Hon. Jonathan Treadwell, and the Hon. Jeremiah Wadsworth. Abel Flint, Nathan Perkins, Nehemiah Prudden, and Nathan Strong were the clerical Trustees. Flint, Newberry, Perkins, Strong, and Treadwell all later served as officers of the CMS.

32. CGA, *The Constitution of the Missionary Society of Connecticut; With an Address from the Board of Trustees, to the People of the State, and a Narrative on the Subject of Missions* (Hartford, Conn., 1800). The original six clerical Trustees were: Dr. Benjamin Trumbull, Dr. Jonathan Edwards, Jr., Levi Hart, Nathan Strong, Charles Backus, and Cyprian Strong. Conforti, *Samuel Hopkins and the New Divinity Movement,* pp. 227–32, identifies all six as New Divinity. Treadwell, while not a minister, served as a deacon in the Farmington Congregational Church (a "pure" church) and was well versed in theology. His correspondence shows that he relished theological disputation, and suggests that he embraced an Edwardsean perspective. See, for example, his series of exchanges with the Rev. Nathaniel Niles of West Fairlee, in which he upholds the doctrine of Disinterested Benevolence: Nathaniel Niles to Jonathan Treadwell, 7 January, 17 February, 3 May, and 11 September, 1804, Box 1, Folder 2, Jonathan Treadwell Papers, Connecticut State Library, Hartford, Conn.

33. CGA, *The Constitution of the Missionary Society of Connecticut,* p. 1.

34. On Bacon's mission see Keller, *Second Great Awakening in Connecticut,* pp. 79–81; and James R. Rohrer, "The White Christ and the Red Jesus: Two Early Protestant Missions and the Ojibwa Response," paper presented at the Ohio Valley History Conference, Eastern Kentucky University, October 28, 1988.

35. *The Scourge of Aristocracy and Repository of Important Political Truths,* 1 November 1798, pp. 129–30.

36. Thorning, *Religious Liberty in Transition,* p. 47; Jack Ericson, *Missionary Society of Connecticut Papers, 1759–1948: A Guide to the Microfilm Edition* (Glen Rock, N.J., 1976), pp. 4–5. Hereafter cited as *A Guide to the Microfilm Edition.*

37. Benjamin Trumbull to Jonathan Treadwell, 17 February 1801, Benjamin Trumbull Papers, Connecticut Historical Society, Hartford, Conn.

38. For an excellent discussion of the concept of respectability and its central place in nineteenth-century moral reform, see Robert Hampel, *Temperance and Prohibition in Massachusetts, 1813–1852* (Ann Arbor, Mich., 1982), Chapter 3.

39. CMS, *An Address to the People of the State of Connecticut* (Hartford, Conn., 1801), pp. 13–14; Daniel Noble to Thomas Robbins, 15 May 1798, and Jos. Woodbridge to Thomas Robbins, 31 October 1798, Robbins Papers.

40. CMS, *A Summary of Christian Doctrine and Practice: Designed Especially for the Use of People in the New Settlements* (Hartford, Conn., 1804), pp. 52–55.

41. Williston, "Diaries," Part I, p. 189; Increase N. Tarbox, ed., *Diary of*

Thomas Robbins, D. D., 2 vols. (Boston, 1886) 1:247–48 (hereafter cited as *Robbins Diary*); Giles Cowles, Sermon #841, 4 July 1810, Box 4, Folder 11, Giles Cowles Papers.

42. Nathaniel Robbins to Thomas Robbins, 23 December 1800, Robbins Papers.

43. Recordbook, Trustees of the Missionary Society of Connecticut, vol. 1 (1798–1802), CMS Papers; Ammi Robbins to Thomas Robbins, 4 January 1802; and Thomas Robbins, Mss. Sermon on Proverbs 8:15–16, 28 December 1800, Robbins Papers.

44. See the Minutes of the June 1801 Trustees meeting in Recordbook, vol. 1, CMS Papers. See also CMS, *An Act to Incorporate the Trustees of the Missionary Society of Connecticut: An Address from Said Trustees to the Ministers and People of the State; With a Narrative on the Subject of Missions, and a Statement of the Funds of the Society, for the Year 1802* (Hartford, Conn., 1803).

45. David Higgins to Nathan Strong, 25 November 1801, CMS Papers.

46. The CEM circulated throughout New England and was carried West by the missionaries. It also enjoyed a small circulation in the southern states, probably among Presbyterians primarily. Evidence of a southern readership can be found in *The Georgia Analytical Repository* 1 (1802): 14, and the letter of the Rev. George Baxter of Lexington, Virginia, to Nathan Strong, 11 January 1804, CMS Papers. Quotation is in Calvin Chapin to Jonathan Edwards, Jr., 18 September 1800, Calvin Chapin Letters, Beinecke Library, Yale University.

47. The CMS Papers include dozens of letters from anonymous donors dated from this period. The letter of "Chenaniah" to Nathan Strong, 9 May 1802, is typical. "Chenaniah" cites the "truly animating" and "well authenticated . . . happy revivals of religion in many parts of the new countries" as the motive for contributing $100 to the missionary society. On the female benevolent societies of the era see Nancy F. Cott, *The Bonds of Womanhood: "Woman's Sphere" in New England, 1780–1835* (New Haven, Conn., 1977), pp. 126–59. The Giles Cowles Papers contain the records of the Female Association of Bristol, Connecticut, which was created by awakened women during the 1799 revival, as well as letters highlighting the operations of the Society. Such organizations played an important role in financing domestic missions. See, for example, Female Association in Litchfield to the Trustees, 16 April 1804; and "A Female Friend to Missions" to the Trustees, 26 April 1803, CMS Papers.

48. When Timothy Dwight published a revision of Watt's Psalm Book, for example, he designated twenty dollars of every one thousand in sales to the CMS. Benjamin Trumbull assigned all the profits from the sale of his *Discourses on the Divine Inspiration of Scripture* to the missionary society. See the minutes of the May 1799 and June 1801 meetings of the Board of Trustees in the Recordbook, vol. I, CMS Papers.

49. Ericson, *A Guide to the Microfilm Edition,* p. 4.

50. Asahel Hooker to Abel Flint, 7 July 1803, CMS Papers; Abel Flint to Thomas Robbins, 25 July 1803, Robbins Papers. Some people considered the highly subjective method of evaluating potential missionaries offensive. When

Strong made confidential inquiries concerning Abiel Jones, a candidate recommended by his friend Asa Burton, Jones discovered the investigation and fired off a heated letter to the Hartford clergyman. "When you have obtained what you suppose to be my true character," Jones demanded, "I would thank you to send it to me . . . and give me an opportunity to see how it looks." The irate candidate acknowledged that he was "inclined to be plain hearted, whether I deal in divinity or medicine, & it sometimes disgusts." He also confessed that he was "more apt to think afterwards than before hand, & of course don't think it best often to take back the truth for the sake of pleasing." See Jones to Strong, 15 May 1804, CMS Papers. Ironically, Jones's letter confirmed that he lacked discretion, the quality Strong regarded as most essential in missionaries, and guaranteed that the CMS reject his candidacy.

51. *Robbins Diary,* 1:211, 270.

52. Calvin Chapin to Abel Flint, 1 October 1806, CMS Papers.

53. Trustees to Joseph Badger, David Bacon, and Thomas Robbins, 22 January 1806, CMS Papers.

54. Samuel Mills to Nathan Strong, 11 January 1802; Ephraim Judson to Nathan Strong, 11 December 1800; George Burder to Nathan Strong, August 1803, CMS Papers.

55. Stout, *New England Soul,* pp. 23–31, 259–311, discusses the role of political preaching in colonial New England. Gordon is quoted on p. 284.

56. Scott, *From Office To Profession,* pp. 18–35, discusses the growing division between New England's orthodox clergy and Federalist politicians during the early nineteenth century. By the 1810s most of the clergy were thoroughly disillusioned by the increasing reliance of Federalist party leaders upon "electioneering," while party leaders were finding their association with the clergy a political liability. This fact became obvious to Connecticut's clergy in 1811, when then acting–Governor Jonathan Treadwell made a bid for the governorship of the state. Treadwell staunchly supported the standing order, and was well known for his Calvinistic convictions and his connection with the CMS. Federalist leaders, desiring a candidate who could not be linked to "ecclesiastical tyranny," rejected Treadwell in favor of Roger Griswold, a liberal who did not profess religion. Scott concludes that during the 1810s New England Congregational ministers turned away from politics and toward a more voluntaristic conception of social order. The CMS clearly suggests, however, that Connecticut New Lights were already beginning to embrace voluntarism more than a decade earlier.

57. Ruth Bloch, *Visionary Republic,* p. 214. In Chapter 9 Bloch notes that during the mid–1790s Congregationalists turned away from the highly political "revolutionary millennialism" which characterized the 1770s and which briefly flourished after the commencement of the French Revolution. By the late 1790s, "Federalist clergymen typically invested their millennial hopes in the promotion of true Christianity in America by evangelical rather than political means." See p. 214. The apolitical stance of the CMS clearly supports Bloch's thesis.

CHAPTER FIVE

1. Mills's account of the revival is in Bennet Tyler, ed., *New England Revivals, As They Existed at the Close of the Eighteenth and the Beginning of the Nineteenth Centuries* (Boston, 1846), pp. 55–62; John S. Mills to Thomas Robbins, October 1799, Robbins Papers.

2. Richard D. Birdsall, "The Second Great Awakening and the New England Social Order," *Church History* 39 (1970): 352–55.

3. On the western revival see Ahlstrom, *A Religious History of the American People*, 1:521–28; John B. Boles, *The Great Revival, 1787–1805: The Origins of the Southern Evangelical Mind* (Lexington, Ky., 1972), especially pp. 36–89; Catherine C. Cleveland, *Great Revival in the West, 1797–1805* (Chicago, 1916); Paul Conkin, *Cane Ridge: America's Pentecost* (Madison, Wis., 1990); Charles A. Johnson, *Frontier Camp Meeting: Religion's Harvest Time* (Dallas, 1955); Donald M. Mathews, *Religion in the Old South* (Chicago, 1977); Walter B. Posey, *Frontier Mission: A History of Religion West of the Southern Appalachians to 1861* (Lexington, Ky., 1966); William Warren Sweet, *Revivalism in America* (Nashville, Tenn., 1944), pp. 122–25; and Bernard A. Weisberger, *They Gathered at the River: The Story of the Great Revivalists and Their Impact Upon Religion in America* (Chicago, 1966), pp. 20–49. Leigh Eric Schmidt, *Holy Fairs: Scottish Communions and American Revivals in the Early Modern Period* (Princeton, 1989), is a brilliant study of the Presbyterian sacramental occasion in Scotland and America, and the central significance of this institution in the development of revivalism in the United States. While acknowledging the unique intensity of the camp meetings during the "Great Revival," Schmidt stresses the continuity of the camp meetings with traditional Scots-Irish piety. See especially pp. 59–68.

4. *Western Missionary Magazine* 2 (1804): 460–62.

5. Nancy F. Cott, "Young Women in the Second Great Awakening in New England," *Feminist Studies* 3 (1975): 14–29, finds that young New England women turned to revivalism in order to cope with their social and political isolation and lack of economic opportunity. Paul E. Johnson, *A Shopkeeper's Millennium: Society and Revivals in Rochester, New York, 1815–1837* (New York, 1978), argues that revivals were a bourgeois phenomenon associated with the development of a capitalist market economy. Donald Mathews, "The Second Great Awakening as an Organizing Hypothesis," suggests that revivalism sprang from the social strains produced by economic and demographic changes in post–revolutionary America. Roth, in *The Democratic Dilemma*, concludes that migration and increasing social stratification destroyed Vermont's early covenanted communities, causing young men to turn to religion in an effort to forge stable social networks. Mary Ryan, in *Cradle of the Middle Class: The Family in Oneida County, New York, 1790–1865* (New York, 1981), relates revivalism to the breakup of the intergenerational patriarchal family caused by migration from town to farm. Richard D. Shiels, "The Scope of the Second Great Awakening: Andover, Massachusetts as a Case Study," *Journal of the Early Republic* 5

(1985): 223–46, finds that revival converts in that community defied categorization.

6. Sweet, *Revivalism in America,* p. 128. Accounts of the Awakening in New England include Berk, *Calvinism versus Democracy*; Conforti, *Samuel Hopkins and the New Divinity Movement*; Keller, *The Second Great Awakening in Connecticut*; David M. Ludlum, *Social Ferment in Vermont, 1791–1850* (New York, 1939); and Mead, *Nathaniel William Taylor.* For treatments of the western revivals see the works cited in note 3 above.

7. McLoughlin, *Revivals, Awakenings, and Reform,* pp. 108–12; Marsden, *The Evangelical Mind,* p. 13; Hatch, in Noll, ed., *Christianity in America,* p. 174.

8. J. M. Bumsted and John E. Van de Wetering, *What Must I Do to be Saved? The Great Awakening in Colonial America* (Hinsdale, Ill., 1976), pp. 83–84; Gaustad, *The Great Awakening in New England,* pp. 45–47.

9. For the classic case against enthusiasm see Charles Chauncy, *Enthusiasm Described and Cautioned Against. A Sermon Preach'd . . . the Lord's Day After Commencement . . .* (Boston, 1742), anthologized in Alan Heimert and Perry Miller, eds., *The Great Awakening* (Indianapolis and New York, 1967), pp. 228–56.

10. Ibid., especially pp. 244–56.

11. For the *Harvard Testimony* see ibid., pp. 340–53.

12. Ibid., pp. 263–90, includes excerpts of Edwards's essay. Quotations are on pp. 281–82.

13. Ibid., p. 282.

14. Perkins, *Narrative of a Tour,* p. 26; Williston, "Diaries," Part II, p. 240.

15. Vinson Synan, *The Holiness-Pentecostal Movement in the United States* (Grand Rapids, Mich., 1971), pp. 13–26.

16. Wesley M. Gehwehr, *The Great Awakening in Virginia, 1740–1790* (Durham, N.C., 1930), p. 153.

17. Committee of Middletown to Abel Flint, 5 November 1799; Elias Buel to Nathan Strong, 1 April 1811, CMS Papers; Williston, "Diaries," Part IX, p. 383.

18. *Extracts of Letters Containing Some Accounts of the Work of God Since the Year 1800. Written by Preachers & Members of the Methodist Episcopal Church to their Bishops* (n.p., 1805), pp. 8–10. Shiels suggestively explores the possible relationship between the Methodist and Orthodox revivals in his paper, "The Methodist Circuit Rider in the Second Great Awakening."

19. Tyler, ed., *New England Revivals,* pp. 185, 193.

20. Ibid., pp. 184, 194, 197, 211.

21. Jonathan Miller to Nathan Strong, 29 May 1800; Amasa Porter to Abel Flint, 17 July 1800, CMS Papers; Thomas Robbins, unpublished "Funeral Sermon of Rev. Dr. Flint, Hartford," 10 March 1825, sermon box #2, Robbins Papers. A letter from Ammi to Thomas Robbins suggests that the original Norfolk revival narrative may have been lengthier than the account published in the CEM. See Ammi Robbins to Thomas Robbins, 28 October 1800, Robbins Papers.

22. Jonathan Miller to Nathan Strong, 29 May 1800, CMS Papers.

23. Ammi Robbins to Thomas Robbins, 4 January 1802, Robbins Papers.

24. Laura Hadley Moselsy, ed., *The Diaries of Julia Cowles* (New Haven, Conn., 1931), p. 54; Journal of Robert Hanna, Mss 3838, Folder 2, Western Reserve Historical Society, Cleveland, Ohio.

25. "Berean" to Editors, 24 April 1801, CMS Papers. Another letter, from a Vermont "enemy to enthusiasm or puritanism," describes Congregational missionaries as "a set of sour, morose beings, who have secluded themselves from the enjoyments & commerce of society, in some cloistered cell of hermetical obscurity." Their doctrines and practices, the anticlerical Vermonter informed Strong, amounted to "superstition & enthusiasm." See "Anti–Mitros" to Nathan Strong, 20 April 1801, CMS Papers.

26. Ammi Robbins to Thomas Robbins, 1 June, 11 June, 14 July 1799, Robbins Papers.

27. Sally Cowles to Clara Cowles, 12 May, 11 June, 1799; Sally Cowles to Fanny Albro, 4 July 1799, Giles Cowles Papers, Kent State University, Kent, Ohio.

28. Sally Cowles to Clara Cowles, 2 February 1800, Giles Cowles Papers.

29. Hatch, in Noll. ed., *Christianity in America*, p. 174.

30. Publius Booge to Thomas Robbins, 20 April 1799, Robbins Papers; Levi Hart to Nathan Strong, 25 March 1799, CMS Papers.

31. Manuscript Annual Report of the Trustees to the Connecticut General Association, 1800, CMS Papers.

32. Fifteen of the twenty Connecticut revival narratives published in the CEM were written by pastors in Litchfield or Hartford counties. Several of these men also served at least briefly as missionaries. See Shiels, "The Connecticut Clergy in the Second Great Awakening," pp. 55–57.

33. Manuscript Annual Report of the Trustees to the Connecticut General Association, 1800, CMS Papers. The Trustees reported that it was "extremely difficult" to secure acceptable missionaries, a situation that continued to plague the Society until the war of 1812. During these years the Society at times had to turn to Presbyterian ministers in the West to meet their needs. In 1807, for example, Calvin Chapin wrote to Presbyterian William Wick of Youngstown, Ohio, about the insufficient supply of Connecticut missionaries for the Western Reserve. "Furnish us with suitable men," Chapin asserted, "and we will pay them as we do our missionaries from this quarter." During the next several years most CMS missionaries in the Reserve were Pennsylvania Presbyterians. After 1812 this situation rapidly changed, and orthodox college students began to present themselves to the CMS for missionary service. Many of these were Williams College graduates; others came from Andover Seminary. After the war the CMS received more applications for commissions than it could fill. On the changing supply of Congregational missionaries see William S. Kennedy, *The Plan of Union: or A History of the Presbyterian and Congregational Churches of the Western Reserve* (Hudson, Ohio, 1856), pp. 14–81. Chapin's letter to Wick is excerpted on p. 15.

34. Sprague, *Annals* 2:423–24.

35. Ibid., pp. 422–23.

36. Ibid., p. 423. Bushnell embraced Hopkinsian theology. His mentor, the Reverend Ephraim Judson of Sheffield, Massachusetts, was a student of Joseph Bellamy and a New Divinity teacher. See Conforti, *Samuel Hopkins and the New Divinity Movement,* p. 230.

37. Sprague, *Annals* 2:425.

38. Abel Flint to Jedediah Bushnell, 31 May 1799, CMS Papers.

39. Seth Williston to Benjamin Trumbull, 25 November 1799, Trumbull Papers (Yale); Benjamin Trumbull to Abel Flint, 2 January 1800, CMS Papers.

40. Heman Comstock to Nathan Strong, 4 March 1801; Committee of Otego Society to Nathan Strong, 11 April 1801, CMS Papers.

41. Elijah Dee and Benjamin Holmes to Trustees, 4 October 1801; "Sundry Inhabitants of Fairfield" to Abel Flint, 25 November 1801, CMS Papers.

42. Sprague, *Annals* 2:426, 429.

43. Ibid., pp. 426–27, 429.

44. Ibid., pp. 426–29.

45. Ibid., p. 429.

46. Ibid., p. 423. Missiologists have long recognized that crosscultural evangelism is most effectively promoted by "bridge figures" who, in the words of John Webster Grant, are "able to operate as insiders with respect to both the message and the host culture." Such persons are generally reared with a foot in both cultures, and creatively combine within themselves the compatible elements of both value systems. As a result, bridges have "an unusual ability to make their message speak to the circumstances of those to whom it is addressed." See John W. Grant, *Moon of Wintertime: Missionaries and the Indians of Canada in Encounter since 1534* (Toronto, 1984), p. 260. Congregational missionaries in the new settlements in at least some respects confronted an alien culture that was moving rapidly away from the corporate values that orthodoxy cherished. It is reasonable to hypothesize that the most effective Congregational evangelists, therefore, would be men like Bushnell, who combined a deep commitment to traditional orthodox values with a genuinely egalitarian temperament.

47. Sprague, *Annals* 2:424–25. In 1800 Bushnell asked Strong to send him a shipment of New Divinity books for distribution in New York: "Doctor Trumbull's sermons upon divine Revelation," "Rev. Nathan Strong's sermons," and "the Rev. Charles Backus' sermons upon regeneration." These works, he noted, could be read by the settlers on Sabbath mornings when they could not hear orthodox preaching. Bushnell to Strong, 29 September 1800, CMS Papers.

48. Andrews to Flint, 19 August 1800, CMS Papers; Sprague, *Annals* 2:428–29.

49. Sprague, Annals 2:428.

50. A great majority of the Scots–Irish Presbyterians in Pennsylvania were Jeffersonians. Several hundred Pennsylvania families, most of them from Washington County, early settled in the Reserve, prompting one Federalist proprietor to complain bitterly that there was "too much of the Democracy of Pennsylva-

nia" in the area. See Mary Lou Conlin, *Simon Perkins of the Western Reserve* (Cleveland, 1968), pp. 57–59. Moreover, many of the Connecticut settlers who migrated to Ohio were dissenters or Jeffersonian Congregationalists, and Badger and Robbins often found their motives being publicly assailed. For example, at an 1801 Independence Day celebration in Hudson, Ohio, the local Jeffersonian leader Benjamin Tappan delivered an oration condemning the Connecticut clergy and the CMS for "having done all in their power to introduce a monarchical government." See Journal of Joseph Badger, 1801, CMS Papers.

51. Joseph Badger to Samuel Huntington, 5 March 1803, vertical file, Western Reserve Historical Society, Cleveland, Ohio; Thomas Robbins to Parents, 29 November 1803, Robbins Papers.

52. On Robbins's background see the introduction to his *Diary*, written by Increase Tarbox, pp. iii–iv; McLachlan, *Princetonians*, pp. 315–17; and Sprague, *Annals* 1:367–70. On Badger's history see Henry Day, ed., *A Memoir of Rev. Joseph Badger; Containing an Autobiography and Selections from His Private Journals and Correspondence* (Hudson, Ohio, 1851); and *Robbins Diary* 1:216.

53. Journal of Reverend Joseph Badger, 1803–1804, Manassah Cutler Papers, Western Reserve Historical Society, Cleveland, Ohio; Calvin Chapin to Flint, 1 October 1806, CMS Papers; and Day, *Memoir of Rev. Joseph Badger*.

54. Badger to Strong, 8 January 1801, CMS Papers.

55. Schmidt, *Holy Fairs,* p. 61.

56. Badger to Flint, 19 July 1803, CMS Papers.

57. Ibid.; Thomas Robbins to Parents, 29 November 1803, Robbins Papers.

58. Schmidt, *Holy Fairs,* pp. 65, 145–53; Journal of Joseph Badger, 1801, CMS Papers; Badger to Flint, 19 November 1802, CMS Papers. Elisha Macurdy, in whose congregation an "extraordinary work" commenced in 1802, was popularly known as the preacher "who knocked the people down." According to Schmidt, his evangelistic prowess rivaled that of the famous James McGready. See *Holy Fairs,* p. 61.

59. Badger to Flint, 19 July 1803, CMS Papers.

60. Ibid.

61. Thomas Robbins to Parents, 29 November 1803, Robbins Papers.

62. Ibid.

63. Ibid.

64. Ibid.

65. Ibid.

66. Sally Robbins to Thomas Robbins, 21 January 1804, Robbins Papers.

67. Ammi Robbins to Thomas Robbins, 12 January 1804, Robbins Papers. It is noteworthy that Hooker, Porter, Starr, and Ammi Robbins were among the twenty pastors who wrote revival narratives for the CEM. Rather than denounce the camp meeting as enthusiastic, they found it "peculiarly satisfying." See Ammi Robbins to Thomas Robbins, 26 March 1804, Robbins Papers. Still, caution was in order. In May Thomas's brother James sent a warning to write only "what you are willing many should hear," for "great inquiry is made about your letters, &

most of them are read to many." James Robbins to Thomas Robbins, 23 May 1804, Robbins Papers.

68. "The doctrines of total depravity, of Regeneration, election, sovereignty, and their kindred doctrines," Badger noted, "are insisted on by the ministers with great plainness. It is under the preaching of these doctrines, God has been pleased to carry on his work in . . . hopefully converting many hundred souls in these parts." See Badger to Nathan Strong, 8 January 1801, CMS Papers. Badger was impressed that two of the ministers at Cross Creek, James Hughes and George Scott, were Princeton graduates. Perhaps significantly, they are the only two he acknowledged to be "excellent preachers." See Badger to Flint, 19 July 1803, CMS Papers.

69. Schmidt, *Holy Fairs,* pp. 108–12.

70. Ibid., p. 112. On the centrality of the pure church ideal to post–revolutionary Edwardseans see Walsh, "The Pure Church in Eighteenth Century Connecticut," pp. 216–38.

71. Badger to Flint, 19 July 1803; Thomas Robbins to Parents, 29 November 1803, CMS Papers.

72. Schmidt, *Holy Fairs,* p. 96.

73. Badger to Flint, 19 March 1802, CMS Papers.

74. *Robbins Diary* 1:238.

75. Ibid.

76. Ibid., p. 239.

77. Thomas Robbins to Parents, 29 November 1803, CMS Papers.

78. *Robbins Diary* 1:219; Journal of Reverend Joseph Badger, 1804, Manassah Cutler Papers.

79. *Robbins Diary* 1:221.

CHAPTER SIX

1. Hatch, *Democratization of American Christianity,* pp. 30–34.

2. Roderick Nash, *Wilderness and the American Mind,* 3rd ed. (New Haven, Conn., 1982), pp. 1, 29–30.

3. Ibid., p. 34. On typology and the Puritan sense of mission see Bercovitch, *American Jeremiad,* especially Chapter 4.

4. Nash, *Wilderness and the American Mind,* pp. 13–17.

5. Ibid., pp. 34–39.

6. Ibid., p. 29.

7. The relationship between Methodism and Romanticism needs further research. According to Nash, frontier settlers generally were *less* likely to embrace romantic attitudes toward nature than eastern city dwellers. "Enthusiasm for wilderness," he states, began "among writers, artists, scientists, vacationers, gentlemen—people, in short, who did not face wilderness from the pioneer's perspective" (p. 15). Yet pioneer Methodist circuit riders often exhibited a

pronounced primitivism, and were far more likely than orthodox missionaries to perceive nature as sublime. On the emergence of Romantic primitivism in republican America, see Henry Nash Smith, *Virgin Land: The American West as Symbol and Myth* (Cambridge, Mass., 1978), pp. 51–70.

8. Clark, *Journal of Francis Asbury* 2:25, 241.

9. Strickland, *Autobiography of Cartwright,* p. 81.

10. Giles Cowles, undated missionary sermon, Giles Cowles Papers.

11. Ammi Robbins to Thomas Robbins, 26 March 1804, Robbins Papers; Perkins, *Narrative of a Tour,* pp. 27, 31.

12. CGA, *A Narrative of the Missions to the New Settlements. . . .* (New Haven, Conn., 1794), p. 16; CGA, *A Continuation of the Narrative of the Missions . . . .* (New Haven, Conn., 1797), p. 8.

13. Cowles, undated sermon, Giles Cowles Papers.

14. Ibid.; Cyprian Strong, *A Sermon, Preached at Hartford before the Board of Trustees, of the Missionary Society in Connecticut; at the Ordination of the Rev. Jedediah Bushnell, as a Missionary to the New Settlements; January 15th, A.D. 1800* (Hartford, Conn., 1800), pp. 18–19.

15. Ammi Robbins to Thomas Robbins, 2 July 1793; Sally Robbins to Thomas Robbins, 20 August 1793, Robbins Papers; *Robbins Diary* 1:203.

16. Joseph Conforti, "David Brainerd and the Nineteenth Century Missionary Movement," *Journal of the Early Republic* 5 (1985): 309–29.

17. Ibid. See also Elsbree, *Rise of the Missionary Spirit,* p. 17, for details on Brainerd's career.

18. Conforti suggests that Brainerd's journal became the model for nineteenth century missionary journals in general. Brainerd certainly became the yardstick against which many orthodox evangelists were measured. In 1802, for example, an orthodox settler in Ohio praised missionary Ezekiel Chapman as "a young Mr. Brainerd for piety." E[liphalet] Austin to Samuel J. Mills, 20 November 1802, CMS Papers.

19. John Love to Committee on Missions, 23 February 1798, Trumbull Papers; Theodore Davenport Bacon, *Leonard Bacon, a Statesman in the Church* (New Haven, Conn., 1931), p. 4; Seth Williston, "Diaries," Part I, p. 190.

20. Samuel P. Robbins to Thomas Robbins, 1 February 1803, Robbins Papers; Williston, "Diaries," Part VIII, p. 36.

21. Day, *Memoir of Joseph Badger*; Calvin Chapin to Abel Flint, 1 October 1806, CMS Papers.

22. Williston, "Diaries," Part I, p. 192.

23. Strickland, *Autobiography of Finley,* pp. 330–36.

24. Strickland, *Autobiography of Cartwright,* p. 358.

25. Ibid.

26. Joshua Leonard to Nathan Strong, 5 October 1800, CMS Papers.

27. David Higgins to Benjamin Trumbull, 19 February 1795, CMS Papers.

28. Ibid.

29. Perkins, *Narrative of a Tour,* pp. 19, 20, 34.

CHAPTER SEVEN

1. Wiebe, *The Opening of American Society,* pp. 159–60; Marty, *Pilgrims in Their Own Land,* p. 169; Hatch, *Democratization of American Christianity,* pp. 17–46. Jon Butler, *Awash In A Sea of Faith: Christianizing the American People* (Cambridge, Mass., 1990), pp. 225–56, describes post–revolutionary America as a "spiritual hothouse" that produced new religious movements "astonishing in their variety, numbers, and vitality."

2. Finke and Stark, "How the Upstart Sects Won America," p. 42.

3. Ibid., pp. 33–40.

4. Ibid., p. 41.

5. Bilhartz, *Urban Religion and the Second Great Awakening,* p. 86.

6. Ibid., p. 92.

7. In addition to the works by Hatch already cited, see his article, "Sola Scriptura and Novus Ordo Seclorum," in Nathan Hatch and Mark Noll, eds., *The Bible in America: Essays in Cultural History* (New York, 1982), pp. 59–78.

8. Scott, *From Office to Profession,* pp. 53–54; Perkins, *Narrative of a Tour,* pp. 16–17. Badger apparently came to Day's attention sometime during the Revolution, when he was stationed in New Preston, Connecticut, where Day was the Congregational minister. Day tutored Badger, fitted him for college, and helped him secure admission to Yale. See *Robbins Diary* 1:216, n. 1.

9. Scott, *From Office to Profession,* p. 60.

10. Ibid., pp. 55–56.

11. Conforti, *Samuel Hopkins and the New Divinity Movement,* pp. 9–13.

12. Harrison, *Princetonians,* pp. 97–101.

13. Perkins, *Narrative of a Tour,* pp. 16, 25.

14. See Ericson, ed., *A Guide to the Microfilm Edition,* pp. 27–40, for a listing of all CMS employees and the dates and places of their service. Yale graduates were identified in Dexter, *Biographical Sketches of the Graduates of Yale College.* The CMS hired several Presbyterian ministers during this period; some of these men may have attended Princeton.

15. Kennedy, *Plan of Union,* pp. 82–93, gives the known educational backgrounds of every CMS missionary in the Connecticut Reserve.

16. Finke and Stark, "How the Upstart Sects Won America," pp. 36–37.

17. Ibid., p. 39. Scott, *From Office to Profession,* p. 113, gives a lower estimate of Congregational salaries.

18. See Board of Trustees, Recordbook, vol. I, CMS Papers.

19. David Higgins to Nathan Strong, 24 July 1801, CMS Papers.

20. For an example of orthodox spending habits, see *Robbins Diary* 1:215, 225–26. Methodists and other sectarian preachers often wore shabby clothes. Shiels, "The Methodist Circuit Rider in the Second Great Awakening in New England," suggests that their appearance may have startled refined audiences, but powerfully appealed to common folk.

21. Scott, *From Office to Profession,* pp. 112–32. Scott identifies the 1830s and 1840s as the nadir of the New England clergy, but the pastoral crisis was

already apparent to many ministers in the first two decades of the nineteenth century. On p. 113, Scott suggests that between 1800 and 1810 roughly 40 percent of orthodox Connecticut churches saw a turnover in the pastorate, an astounding rate by eighteenth century standards.

22. Ibid., pp. 70–74. My analysis of the conflict differs from Scott, who suggests that the clergy themselves were principally to blame for the crisis. Many of them, he asserts, wanted to achieve prestigious positions with new seminaries or religious organizations, or hoped to move to more lucrative parishes by making a name for themselves as authors or organizers. Local congregations resented these outside interests and sought to curb their pastors. Certainly this interpretation fits some young ministers, like Lyman Beecher, who devoted themselves largely to organizational tasks. But the problem had other sources. Many ministers clearly wanted to retain their charges, and wished to continue in their traditional pastoral roles, but felt forced to separate from their people by intransigent lay leaders and penurious congregations.

23. Cowles, Sermon on Nehemiah 13:10–12, 1810, Box 6, Folder 3, Giles Cowles Papers.

24. Committee of Austinburgh Society to Trustees, 4 January 1810, CMS Papers.

25. Cowles, Sermon on Nehemiah 13:10–12, Giles Cowles Papers; Joseph Badger to Trustees, n.d., container 1, Folder 3, Joseph Badger Papers, Western Reserve Historical Society, Cleveland, Ohio. Hereafter cited as Badger Papers.

26. Asahel Hooker to Nathan Strong, 3 January 1805, CMS Papers.

27. David Higgins to Nathan Strong, 24 July 1801; William Lyman to Abel Flint, 30 December 1803, CMS Papers.

28. David Bacon to Abel Flint, 11 February 1803, CMS Papers.

29. Joseph Badger to Trustees, n.d., Badger Papers.

30. Sarah Coe to Sally Cowles, 20 September 1827, Giles Cowles Papers.

31. Committee of Worthington, Ohio, to Trustees, 15 August 1807; John Keep to Abel Flint, 18 September 1807; Luther Leland to Trustees, 5 January 1813, CMS Papers.

32. Hatch, "Sola Scriptura and Novus Ordo Seclorum," pp. 66–71.

33. Finke and Stark, "How the Upstart Sects Won America," p. 35–36.

34. Strickland, *Autobiography of Cartwright,* pp. 370–71.

35. Finke and Stark, "How the Upstart Sects Won America," p. 38.

36. Perkins, *Narrative of a Tour,* p. 25.

37. James Andrews to Thomas Robbins, 4 October 1799, Robbins Papers.

38. Moses Welch to Benjamin Trumbull, 5 October 1810, Benjamin Trumbull Papers.

39. Sundry Inhabitants of Wilkesbarre to Trustees, 18 June 1804, CMS Papers.

40. Nathan Strong, *A Sermon Delivered at the Ordination of the Rev. Ichabod Lord Skinner* (Hartford, Conn., 1794), pp. 6–7.

41. "A Charge given me by my beloved Father at my ordination at Norfolk, July 20th 1803," Robbins Papers.

42. Finke and Stark, "How the Upstart Sects Won America," p. 38.

43. Williston, "Diaries," Part VI, p. 234; Randolph Stone to Benjamin Trumbull, 10 June 1819, Benjamin Trumbull Papers; Journal of Robert Hanna, 1811–1816, Ms. 3838, Folder 2, Western Reserve Historical Society, Cleveland, Ohio.

44. Ammi Robbins, "Concio ad Clerum," 5 September 1800, Robbins Papers.

45. See, for example, his sermon on Mark 8:37, "The Worth of the Soul," 17 November 1794, Robbins Papers.

46. Ammi Robbins to Thomas Robbins, 15 March 1806, Robbins Papers.

47. Sally Robbins to Thomas Robbins, 21 January 1804, Robbins Papers.

48. Williston, "Diaries," Part I, p. 207.

49. G. H. Tower to Thomas Robbins, 28 December 1804, Robbins Papers.

50. Giles Cowles to Abel Flint, 13 February 1812, CMS Papers.

51. Williston, "Diaries," Part VIII, p. 29.

52. Ibid., Part I, p. 205.

53. Ibid., Part I, pp. 199–202.

54. *Piscataqua Evangelical Magazine* 1 (1805) 1–3; David Higgins to Benjamin Trumbull, 19 February 1795; Joseph Badger to Abel Flint, 19 March 1803, CMS Papers; Randolph Stone Diary, Western Reserve Historical Society, Cleveland, Ohio.

55. Sundry Inhabitants of Black River to Nathan Strong, 9 December 1799, CMS Papers.

56. Joel Bennedict, Journal of a mission . . . commencing December 1811, CMS Papers.

57. Randolph Stone to Benjamin Trumbull, 10 June 1819, Benjamin Trumbull Papers.

58. Calvin Chapin to Abel Flint, 1 October 1806, CMS Papers.

59. Presbytery of Geneva to Abel Flint, 28 June 1810, CMS Papers.

60. Journal of Simeon Parmele, 18 May 1814, CMS Papers.

61. Joseph Badger to Abel Flint, 19 March 1803, CMS Papers.

62. Joel Bennedict, Journal from September 1812 to September 1813; Abner Benedict, Journal of 1813, CMS Papers.

63. See, for example, Jedediah Ward to Abel Flint, 17 June 1813; Oliver Hill to Abel Flint, 5 July 1813; Oliver Hill to Abel Flint, 18 December 1813, CMS Papers.

64. *A Religious Magazine* 1 (1811) 59–60.

65. Joseph Avery, Journal of a Mission, 24 December 1810; Abner Benedict, Journal of 1813; Joel Bennedict, Journal from September 1812 to September 1813; Oliver Hill, Journal Commencing 3 March 1813, CMS Papers.

66. Randolph Stone to John Seward, n.d., Folder 2, John Seward Papers, Western Reserve Historical Society, Cleveland, Ohio.

67. David Harrower, A Journal of a Tour Commencing 26 March 1813, CMS Papers.

68. Joel Bennedict, Journal from September 1812 to September 1813; Joel Bennedict to Abel Flint, 22 August 1814, CMS Papers.

CHAPTER EIGHT

1. Finke and Stark, "How the Upstart Sects Won America," p. 31. Roger Finke and Rodney Stark, *The Churching of America, 1776–1990: Winners and Losers In Our Religious Economy* (New Brunswick, N.J., 1992), p. 55, assert that by the mid-nineteenth century the Congregationalists "can only be described as a minor body."

2. Many modern writers have argued that strict admission standards are necessary if churches are to conserve their "social strength" and experience growth. See Dean Kelley, *Why Conservative Churches Are Growing* (New York, 1977) pp. 119–32. Congregational evangelists maintained higher admissions standards, I would argue, than their sectarian competitors.

3. Joel Bennedict, Journal from September 1812 to September 1813, CMS Papers.

4. Joel Bennedict, Journal of a Mission . . . Commencing December 1811, CMS Papers.

5. Abel Flint to Thomas Robbins, 25 July 1803, CMS Papers.

6. Thomas Robbins, Sermon on Baptism, 26 January 1799, Robbins Papers; *Robbins Diary* 1:205; "A Charge Given me by my beloved Father at my ordination at Norfolk, July 20th 1803," Robbins Papers.

7. Joel Bennedict, for example, refused to organize a group of orthodox settlers in Preston, New York, into a church, despite their desire to be united. "My doubts arose from the smallness of the people," he explained, "Their division into sectaries, & the few who would compose the church should it be organized, I suppposed to be no more than 7 or 8 persons." Joel Bennedict, Journal Commencing Feb 6th 1814, CMS Papers.

8. CGA, *An Address to the Congregational Ministers and Churches of the State, on the Importance of United Endeavors to Revive Gospel Discipline* (Litchfield, Conn., 1808), p. 8.

9. Finke and Stark, *The Churching of America,* p. 86.

10. Kennedy, *Plan of Union,* contains the standard confession of faith and discipline adopted by almost every early Congregational church in the Connecticut Western Reserve. These were drawn up by the CMS missionaries according to pure church principles. See also the manuscript records of the Congregational churches in Canfield, Tallmadge, and Hudson, Ohio, Western Reserve Historical Society, Cleveland, Ohio.

11. Nathan Strong, *A Sermon, Preached on the State Fast, April 6th, 1798* (Hartford, Conn., 1798), pp. 19–20.

12. Ibid., p. 15.

13. Stout, *New England Soul,* p. 316.

14. See Hatch, *Democratization of American Christianity,* and Shiels, "The Methodist Circuit Rider in the Second Great Awakening," on the egalitarianism of the Methodist message. Hatch, "The Christian Movement and the Demand for a Theology of the People," p. 551, points out that Methodist leaders like Asbury opposed republican government within the church, a fact which led to

the O'Kelly schism. Nonetheless, Methodist preachers and lay people typically possessed strong democratic tendencies, and *locally* Methodism was as democratic as the Baptists, Christians, and other more radical sects.

15. Kelley, *Why Conservative Churches Are Growing,* pp. 56–77.

16. Finke and Stark, *The Churching of America,* pp. 245–50.

17. Finke and Stark acknowledge in *The Churching of America,* pp. 55–56, that despite the "extraordinary shift in their fortunes, Congregationalist leaders during this era expressed surprisingly little concern" about the situation. Perhaps, the two sociologists correctly surmise, Congregational clergy "didn't think in terms of rates." Unfortunately, the authors do not probe deeper into the reasons for orthodox equanimity.

18. See, for example, Nathan Strong, *A Sermon, Preached on the State Thanksgiving, Nov. 29, 1798* (Hartford, Conn., 1798); and *On the Universal Spread of the Gospel, A Sermon, Delivered January 4th. . . .* (Hartford, Conn., 1801). Shiels, "The Connecticut Clergy in the Second Great Awakening," provides an excellent discussion of the Edwardsean view of history.

19. Nathan Strong, *A Sermon, at the Ordination of the Rev. Thomas Robbins* (Hartford, Conn., 1803), pp. 15–17.

Bibliography

PRIMARY SOURCES

Manuscript Collections

American History Research Center, Kent State University, Kent, Ohio
    Cowles Family Papers
    Giles Hooker Cowles Papers
Beinecke Library, Yale University, New Haven, Connecticut
    Calvin Chapin Papers
    Jeremiah Day Papers
    Benjamin Trumbull Papers
Congregational House, Hartford, Connecticut
    Connecticut Missionary Society Papers
    Records of the Fairfield West Association
    Records of the New Haven East Consociation
    Records of the New London Association
    Records of the North Hartford Association
    Records of the South Hartford Association
    Records of the Windham Association
Connecticut Historical Society, Hartford, Connecticut
    Huntington Family Papers
    Andrew Kingsbury Papers
    Robbins Family Papers
    Benjamin Trumbull Papers
Connecticut State Library, Hartford, Connecticut
    Ichabod Skinner Papers
    Jonathan Treadwell Papers
Hartford Seminary Library, Hartford, Connecticut
    Asahel Nettleton Papers

Ohio Historical Society Library, Columbus, Ohio
  Records, First Religious Society of Marietta, Ohio
  Thomas Thomas Journal
Western Reserve Historical Society, Cleveland, Ohio
  Joseph Badger Letters
  Manassah Cutler Papers
  Robert Hanna Papers
  John Seward Papers
  Randolph Stone Papers
  Records, Canfield Congregational Church
  Records, Tallmadge Congregational Church
  Records, Hudson Congregational Church

Newspapers

American Mercury (Hartford, Conn.), 1784–1820
A Religious Magazine (Portland, Maine), 1811
Connecticut Courant (Hartford, Conn.), 1764–
Connecticut Evangelical Magazine (Hartford, Conn.), 1800–1807
Connecticut Evangelical Magazine & Religious Intelligencer (Hartford, Conn.), 1808–1815
Connecticut Gazette (New London, Conn.), 1793–
The Religious Monitor (Danbury, Conn.), 1798
The Theological Magazine (New York), 1795–1798
The Scourge of Aristocracy (Fairhaven, Vt.), 1798
The Weekly Recorder (Chillicothe, Ohio), 1814–1820
The Western Missionary Magazine (Pittsburgh), 1803–1805

Published Reports

Connecticut General Association. *A Narrative of the Missions to the New Settlements, According to the Appointment of the General Association of the State of Connecticut; Together With An Account of the Receipts and Expenditures of the Money Contributed by the People of Connecticut in May 1793, for the Support of the Missionaries, According to an Act of the General Assembly of the State.* New Haven, Conn., 1794.
———. *A Continuation of the Narrative to the New Settlements* . . . . New Haven, Conn., 1795.
———. *A Continuation of the Narrative to the New Settlements* . . . . New Haven, Conn., 1797.
Missionary Society of Connecticut. *The Constitution of the Missionary Society*

of Connecticut: With an Address from the Board of Trustees, to the People of the State, and a Narrative on the Subject of Missions. To Which is Subjoined a Statement on the Funds of the Society. Hartford, Conn., 1800.

————. *A Second Address from the Trustees of the Missionary Society of Connecticut, to the People of the State, and a Narrative on the Subject of Missions. To Which is Subjoined a Statement of the Funds of the Society, to the End of the Year 1800.* Hartford, Conn., 1801. (Successive Narratives continued to be published by the Society with slightly varying titles annually until 1830.)

————. *Communications from the London Missionary Society, to the Missionary Society of Connecticut.* Hartford, Conn., 1803.

Published Sermons and Addresses

Backus, Charles. *The Benevolent Spirit of Christianity Illustrated; in a Sermon Delivered at the Ordination of the Rev. Thomas Snell to the Pastoral Care of the Second Church in Brookfield, Massachusetts.* Worcester, Mass., 1798.

————. *The Principal Causes of the Opposition to Christianity Considered; in a Sermon Delivered at the Ordination of the Rev. Zephaniah Swift Moore.* Worcester, Mass., 1798.

Beecher, Lyman. *The Design, Rights, and Duties of Local Churches. A Sermon Delivered at the Installation of Rev. Elias Cornelius.* Andover, Mass., 1819.

Berkshire County Association and the Northern Associated Presbytery in New York. *A Plan for the More Effectual Religious Instruction of Children and Youth, With an Address to Ministers and Parents on the Subject.* Goshen, Conn., 1801.

Chapin, Calvin. *A Sermon, Delivered at the Ordination of the Rev. Samuel Whittelsey, in New Preston, Dec. 20th, 1807 and at the Ordination of Rev. Hosea Beckley in Dummerston, Vt. March 2nd, 1808.* Hartford, Conn., 1808.

Connecticut General Association. *An Address to the Inhabitants of the New Settlements in the Northern and Western Parts of the United States.* New Haven, Conn., 1795.

————. *An Address of the General Association of Connecticut, to the District Associations on the Subject of a Missionary Society; Together With Summaries and Extracts From Late European Publications on Missions to the Heathen.* Norwich, Conn., 1797.

Dwight, Timothy. *An Address to the Emigrants From Connecticut and From New England Generally, in the New Settlements in the United States.* Hartford, Conn., 1817.

Edwards, Jonathan. *The Works of President Edwards.* 10 vols. Edited by Sereno Dwight. New York, 1829–30.

Missionary Society of Connecticut. *An Address From the Trustees of the Missionary Society of Connecticut, to the Inhabitants of the New Settlements, in the Northern and Western Parts of the United States.* Hartford, Conn., 1803.

———. *A Summary of Christian Doctrine and Practice: Designed Especially For the Use of the People in the New Settlements of the United States of America.* Hartford, Conn., 1804.

Robbins, Thomas. *A Sermon Delivered at the Ordination of the Rev. Samuel P. Robbins, to the Pastoral Care of the First Church and Society in Marietta, State of Ohio.* Marietta, Ohio, 1806.

———. *Ecclesiastical Government. A Sermon, Preached at Winchester, Mass. October 18th, 1820, at the Installation of the Rev. Eber L. Clark.* Worcester, Mass., 1820.

Strong, Cyprian. *A Sermon, Preached at Hartford, Before the Board of Trustees of the Missionary Society in Connecticut. At the Ordination of the Rev. Jedediah Bushnell, as a Missionary to the New Settlements; January 15th, A.D. 1800.* Hartford, Conn., 1800.

Strong, Nathan. *A Sermon, At the Ordination of the Rev. Thomas Robbins, Appointed a Missionary to the County of Trumbull, in the State of Ohio; Delivered at Norfolk, June 19th, 1803.* Hartford, Conn., 1803.

———. *A Sermon, Preached January 3rd, 1804, At the Funeral of the Rev. Charles Backus, D. D. Pastor of the Church in Somers, Who Departed This Life December 30th, 1803.* Hartford, Conn., 1804.

———. *A Sermon, Preached on the State Fast, April 9th, 1798.* Hartford, Conn., 1798.

———. *On The Universal Spread of the Gospel, A Sermon, Delivered January 4th, the First Sabbath in the Nineteenth Century of the Christian Era.* Hartford, Conn., 1801.

———. *Political Instruction From the Prophecies of God's Word. A Sermon, Preached on the State Thanksgiving, Nov. 29, 1798.* Hartford, Conn., 1798.

Trumbull, Benjamin. *Twelve Discourses on the Divine Origins of Scriptures.* Hartford, Conn., 1799.

Published Memoirs, Journals and Letters

Asbury, Francis. *The Journal and Letters of Francis Asbury.* 3 vols. Edited by Elmer C. Clark. Nashville, Tenn., 1958.

Badger, Joseph. *A Memoir of Rev. Joseph Badger; Containing an Autobiography and Selections from His Private Journals and Correspondence.* Edited by Henry Day. Hudson, Ohio, 1851.

Beecher, Lyman. *The Autobiography of Lyman Beecher.* 2 vols. Edited by Barbara M. Cross. Cambridge, Mass., 1961.

Cartwright, Peter. *Autobiography of Peter Cartwright, the Backwoods Preacher.* Edited by W. P. Strickland. New York, 1856.

Cowles, Julia. *The Diaries of Julia Cowles*. Edited by Laura Hadley Moselsy. New Haven, Conn., 1931.

Finley, James B. *Autobiography of Rev. James B. Finley; or, Pioneer Life in the West*. Edited by W. P. Strickland. Cincinnati, 1853.

Griffin, Edward Dorr. "The Memoir of Edward Dorr Griffin," in *Sermons by the Late Edward Dorr Griffin, D. D., to Which is Prefixed a Memoir of His Life*. 2 vols. Edited by William Buell Sprague. New York, 1839.

Perkins, Nathan. *A Narrative of a Tour Through the State of Vermont from April 27 to June 12, 1789*. Woodstock, Vt., 1930.

Robbins, Thomas. *Diary of Thomas Robbins, D. D.* 2 vols. Edited by Increase N. Tarbox. Boston, 1886.

Stiles, Ezra. *The Literary Diary of Ezra Stiles*. 3 vols. Edited by Franklin B. Dexter. New York, 1901.

Tyler, Bennet, ed. *New England Revivals, As They Existed at the Close of the Eighteenth and the Beginning of the Nineteenth Centuries*. Boston, 1856.

Williston, Seth. "The Diaries of the Rev. Seth Williston." Edited by the Rev. John Q. Adams. *Journal of the Presbyterian Historical Society* 7–9 (December 1913–March 1917).

SECONDARY SOURCES

Ahlstrom, Sydney. *A Religious History of the American People*. 2 vols. New York, 1975.

Andrews, John A. III. *Rebuilding the Christian Commonwealth: New England Congregationalists and Foreign Missions, 1800–1830*. Lexington, Ky., 1976.

Appleby, Joyce. *Capitalism and a New Social Order: The Republican Vision of the 1790s*. New York, 1984.

Atkins, Gaius Glenn, and Frederick L. Fagley. *History of American Congregationalism*. Boston, 1942.

Bacon, Leonard, et al., eds. *Contributions to the Ecclesiastical History of Connecticut*. 2 vols. New Haven, Conn., 1861.

———. "David Bacon." *Congregational Quarterly* 43 (October 1876): 562–91.

Bacon, Theodore Davenport. *Leonard Bacon, a Statesman in the Church*. New Haven, Conn., 1931.

Banner, Lois. "The Protestant Crusade: Religious Missions, Benevolence, and Reform in the United States, 1790–1840." Ph.D. diss., Columbia University, 1970.

———. "Religious Benevolence as Social Control: A Critique of an Interpretation." *Journal of American History* 60 (1973): 23–42.

Barclay, Wade Crawford. *Early American Methodism, 1769–1844*. 3 vols. New York, 1949.

Beasley, James R. "Emerging Republicanism and the Standing Order: The Appropriation Act Controversy in Connecticut, 1793 to 1795." *William & Mary Quarterly* 29 (1972): 587–610.

Beaver, R. Pierce. "The Concert of Prayer for Missions." *Ecumenical Review* 10 (1957–58): 816–20.

———. "Missionary Motivation Through Three Centuries." In *Reinterpretation of American Church History,* edited by Jerald C. Brauer. Chicago, 1968.

Bercovitch, Sacvan. *The American Jeremiad.* Madison, Wis., 1978.

Berk, Stephen. *Calvinism versus Democracy: Timothy Dwight and the Origins of American Evangelical Orthodoxy.* Hamden, Conn., 1974.

Berkhofer, Robert F., Jr. *Salvation and the Savage: An Analysis of Protestant Missions and American Indian Response, 1787–1862.* Lexington, Ky., 1965.

Bilhartz, Terry D. *Urban Religion and the Second Great Awakening: Church and Society in Early National Baltimore.* Rutherford, N.J., 1986.

Billington, Ray Allen, and Martin Ridge. *Westward Expansion: A History of the American Frontier.* New York, 1982.

Birdsall, Richard D. "The Second Great Awakening and the New England Social Order." *Church History* 39 (1970): 345–64.

Bloch, Ruth. *Visionary Republic: Millennial Themes in American Thought, 1756–1800.* Cambridge, Mass., 1985.

Bodo, John R. *The Protestant Clergy and Public Issues, 1812–1848.* Princeton, 1954.

Boles, John B. *The Great Revival, 1787–1805: The Origins of the Southern Evangelical Mind.* Lexington, Ky., 1972.

Bowden, Henry Warner. *American Indians and Christian Missions: Studies in Cultural Conflict.* Chicago, 1981.

Boylan, Anne. *Sunday School: The Formation of an American Institution, 1790–1880.* New Haven, Conn., 1988.

Breitenbach, William. "The Consistent Calvinism of the New Divinity Movement." *William & Mary Quarterly* 41 (1984): 241–64.

Briceland, Alan V. "The Philadelphia *Aurora,* the New England Illuminati, and the Election of 1800." *The Pennsylvania Magazine of History and Biography* 100 (1976): 4–36.

Brunson, Alfred. "History of Methodism on the Connecticut Western Reserve, Ohio." *The Methodist Magazine and Quarterly Review* 14 (1832): 255–74.

Bumsted, J. M., and John E. Van de Watering. *What Must I Do To Be Saved? The Great Awakening in Colonial America.* Hinsdale, Ill., 1976.

Bushman, Richard. *From Puritan to Yankee: Character and Social Order in Connecticut, 1690–1765.* New York, 1967.

———. *Joseph Smith and the Beginnings of Mormonism.* Urbana, Ill., 1984.

Butler, Jon. *Awash in a Sea of Faith: Christianizing the American People.* Cambridge, Mass., 1990.

Carwardine, Richard. "The Second Great Awakening in the Urban Centers: An Examination of Methodism and the 'New Measures'." *Journal of American History* 59 (1972): 327–40.

————. *Transatlantic Revivalism: Popular Evangelicalism in Britain and America, 1790–1865.* Westport, Conn., 1978.

Cayton, Andrew R. L. *The Frontier Republic: Ideology and Politics in the Ohio Country, 1780 to 1825.* Kent, Ohio, 1986.

Cleveland, Catherine C. *Great Revival in the West, 1797–1805.* Chicago, 1916.

Comstock, John. *The Congregational Churches in Vermont and Their Ministry, 1762–1942.* St. Johnsbury, Vt., 1942.

Conforti, Joseph. "Samuel Hopkins and the New Divinity: Theology, Ethics, and Social Reform in Eighteenth Century New England." *William & Mary Quarterly* 34 (1977): 572–89.

————. *Samuel Hopkins and the New Divinity Movement: Calvinism, the Congregational Ministry, and Reform in New England Between the Great Awakenings.* Grand Rapids, Mich., 1981.

————. "David Brainerd and the Nineteenth Century Missionary Movement." *Journal of the Early Republic* 5 (1985): 309–29.

Conkin, Paul. *Cane Ridge: America's Pentecost.* Madison, Wis., 1990.

Conlin, Mary Lou. *Simon Perkins of the Western Reserve.* Cleveland, 1968.

Cott, Nancy F. *The Bonds of Womanhood.* New Haven, Conn., 1977.

Crissey, Theron. *History of Norfolk.* Everett, Mass., 1900.

Cross, Whitney R. *The Burned-Over District: The Social and Intellectual History of Enthusiastic Religion in Western New York, 1800–1850.* Ithaca, N.Y., 1950.

Cuningham, Charles. *Timothy Dwight, 1752–1817.* New York, 1942.

Davidson, James West. *The Logic of Millennial Thought: Eighteenth-Century New England.* New Haven, Conn., 1977.

Deblasio, Donna Marie. "Her Own Society: The Life and Times of Betsy Mix Cowles." Ph.D. diss., Kent State University, 1980.

Dexter, Franklin B. *Biographical Sketches of the Graduates of Yale College.* 6 vols. New York, 1885–1912.

Elsbree, Oliver W. *The Rise of the Missionary Spirit in America, 1790–1815.* Williamsport, Pa., 1928.

Elwood, Douglas. *The Philosophical Theology of Jonathan Edwards.* New York, 1960.

Ericson, Jack. *Missionary Society of Connecticut Papers, 1759–1948: A Guide to the Microfilm Edition.* Glen Rock, N.J., 1976.

Fawcett, Archibald. *The Cambuslang Revival: The Scottish Evangelical Revival of the Eighteenth Century.* London, 1971.

Finke, Roger, and Rodney Stark. "How the Upstart Sects Won America: 1776–1850." *Journal for the Scientific Study of Religion* 28 (1989): 27–44.

————. *The Churching of America, 1776–1990: Winners and Losers in Our Religious Economy.* New Brunswick, N.J., 1992.

Fischer, David Hackett. *The Revolution of American Conservatism: The Federalist Party in the Era of Jeffersonian Democracy.* New York, 1965.

Fitzmier, John R. "The Godly Federalism of Timothy Dwight, 1752–1817: Soci-

ety, Doctrine, and Religion in the Life of New England's 'Moral Legislator'."
Ph.D. diss., Princeton University, 1986.

Foster, Charles I. *An Errand of Mercy: The Evangelical United Front, 1790–1837.* Chapel Hill, N.C., 1960.

Foster, Frank H. *A Genetic History of New England Theology.* Chicago, 1907.

Fox, Dixon R. *Yankees and Yorkers.* New York, 1940.

Gaustad, Edwin Scott. *Historical Atlas of Religion in America.* New York, 1962.

———. *The Great Awakening in New England.* Chicago, 1968.

Gehwehr, Wesley. *The Great Awakening in Virginia, 1740–1790.* Durham, N.C., 1930.

Goen, Charles C. "Jonathan Edwards: A New Departure in Eschatology." *Church History* 38 (1959): 25–40.

———. *Revivalism and Separatism in New England, 1740–1800.* New Haven, Conn., 1962.

Goodykoontz, Colin B. *Home Missions on the American Frontier.* Caldwell, Idaho, 1939.

Griffin, Clifford S. *Their Brothers' Keepers: Moral Stewardship in the United States, 1800–1865.* New Brunswick, N.J., 1960.

Gross, Robert. *The Minutemen and Their World.* New York, 1976.

Guelzo, Allen C. *Edwards on the Will: A Century of American Theological Debate.* Middletown, Conn., 1989.

Hall, David D. *The Faithful Shepherd: A History of the New England Ministry in the Seventeenth Century.* Chapel Hill, N.C., 1972.

———. *Worlds of Wonder, Days of Judgment: Popular Religious Belief in Early New England.* New York, 1989.

Hamilton, Samuel. "History of Methodism in Washington County, Ohio." *The Methodist Magazine and Quarterly Review* 12 (1830): 404–11.

Hammond, John L. "Revivals, Consensus, and American Political Culture." *Journal of the American Academy of Religion* 46 (1978): 293–312.

Hampel, Robert. *Temperance and Prohibition in Massachusetts, 1813–1852.* Ann Arbor, Mich., 1982.

Handy, Robert T. *A History of the Churches in the United States and Canada.* Oxford, 1976.

Harrison, Richard A. *Princetonians, 1769–1775: A Biographical Dictionary.* Princeton, 1980.

Hatch, Nathan O. "The Christian Movement and the Demand for a Theology of the People." *Journal of American History* 67 (1980): 545–66.

———. "Christianity and Democracy: From the Revolution to the Civil War." In *Christianity In America: A Handbook,* edited by Mark Noll, et. al. Grand Rapids, Mich., 1983.

———. *The Democratization of American Christianity* New Haven, Conn., 1989.

Hatcher, Harlan. *The Western Reserve: The Story of New Connecticut in Ohio.* New York, 1949.

Heimert, Alan, and Perry Miller. *The Great Awakening*. New York, 1967.

Holbrook, Clyde A. *The Ethics of Jonathan Edwards: Aesthetics and Morality*. Ann Arbor, Mich., 1973.

Hood, Fred J. *Reformed America: The Middle and Southern States, 1783–1837*. University, Ala., 1980.

Hotchkin, James H. *A History of the Purchase and Settlement of Western New York, and of the Rise, Progress and Present State of the Presbyterian Church in That Section*. New York, 1848.

Hudson, Winthrop. *Religion in America: An Historical Account of the Development of American Religious Life*. New York, 1965.

Jameson, J. Franklin. *The American Revolution Considered as a Social Movement*. Princeton, 1926.

Jennings, Francis. *The Invasion of America: Indians, Colonialism, and the Cant of Conquest*. New York, 1976.

Johnson, Charles A. *Frontier Camp Meeting: Religion's Harvest Time*. Dallas, 1955.

Johnson, Curtis D. *Islands of Holiness: Rural Religion in Upstate New York, 1790–1860*. Ithaca, N.Y., 1989.

———. *Redeeming America: Evangelicals and the Road to Civil War*. Chicago, 1993.

Johnson, Paul. *A Shopkeeper's Millennium: Society and Revivals in Rochester, New York, 1815–1837*. New York, 1978.

Keller, Charles Roy. *The Second Great Awakening in Connecticut*. New Haven, Conn., 1942.

Kelley, Dean M. *Why Conservative Churches Are Growing*. New York, 1977.

Kennedy, William S. *The Plan of Union: or a History of the Presbyterian and Congregational Churches of the Western Reserve*. Hudson, Ohio, 1856.

Kirsch, George B. "Clerical Dismissals in Colonial and Revolutionary New Hampshire." *Church History* 49 (1980): 160–77.

Kuklick, Bruce. *Churchmen and Philosophers: From Jonathan Edwards to John Dewey*. New Haven, Conn., 1983.

Littell, F. H. *From State Church to Pluralism: Protestant Interpretation of Religion in American History*. New York, 1962.

Ludlum, David M. *Social Ferment in Vermont, 1791–1850*. New York, 1939.

Marini, Stephen A. *Radical Sects of Revolutionary New England*. New York, 1982.

Marsden, George M. *The Evangelical Mind and the New School Presbyterian Experience*. New Haven, Conn., 1970.

Marty, Martin. *Righteous Empire: The Protestant Experience in America*. New York, 1970.

———. *Pilgrims in Their Own Land: 500 Years of Religion in America*. New York, 1985.

Mathews, Donald M. "The Second Great Awakening as an Organizing Process, 1780–1830: An Hypothesis." *American Quarterly* 21 (1969): 23–43.

————. Religion in the Old South. Chicago, 1977.

Mathews, Lois Kimball. The Expansion of New England: The Spread of New England Settlements and Institutions to the Mississippi River, 1620–1865. Boston, 1909.

May, Henry F. The Enlightenment in America. New York, 1976.

McLachlan, James. Princetonians, 1748–1768: A Biographical Dictionary. Princeton, 1976.

McLoughlin, William G. New England Dissent, 1630–1833: The Baptists and the Separation of Church and State. 2 vols. Cambridge, Mass., 1971.

————. Revivals, Awakenings, and Reform: An Essay on Religion and Social Change in America, 1607–1977. Chicago, 1978.

Mead, Sidney E. Nathaniel William Taylor, 1786–1858: A Connecticut Liberal. Chicago, 1942.

————. "The Rise of the Evangelical Conception of the Ministry in America (1607–1850)." In The Ministry in Historical Perspectives, edited by H. Richard Niebuhr and Daniel D. Williams. New York, 1956.

Miller, Perry. Errand Into the Wilderness. New York, 1964.

————. Life of the Mind in America: From the Revolution to the Civil War. New York, 1965.

Miller, Russell E. The Larger Hope: The First Century of the Universalist Church in America, 1770–1870. Boston, 1979.

Miyakawa, T. Scott. Protestants and Pioneers. Chicago, 1964.

Moore, R. Laurence. Religious Outsiders and the Making of Americans. New York, 1986.

Moorehead, James H. "Between Progress and the Apocalypse: A Reassessment of Millennialism in American Religious Thought, 1800–1880." Journal of American History 71 (1984): 524–42.

Morgan, Edmund S. The Gentle Puritan: A Life of Ezra Stiles, 1727–1795. New Haven, Conn., 1962.

Nash, Roderick. Wilderness and the American Mind. 3d ed. New Haven, Conn., 1982.

Neill, Stephen. Christian Missions. Grand Rapids, Mich., 1964.

Nichols, R. H. "The Plan of Union in New York." Church History 5 (1936): 29–51.

Nichols, Robert Hastings. Presbyterianism in New York State. Philadelphia, 1963.

Niebuhr, H. Richard. The Social Sources of Denominationalism. New York, 1957.

Noll, Mark. "God at the Center: Jonathan Edwards on True Virtue," Christian Century 110 (September 8–15, 1993): 854–58.

Noricks, Ronald H. "To Turn Them From Darkness: The Missionary Society of Connecticut on the Early Frontier, 1798–1814." Ph.D. diss., University of California, Riverside, 1975.

————. "'Jealousies & Contentions': The Plan of Union and the Western Reserve, 1801–37," Journal of Presbyterian History 60 (1982): 130–43.

O'Brien, Susan. "A Transatlantic Community of Saints: The Great Awakening and the First Evangelical Network, 1735–1755." *American Historical Review* 91 (1986): 811–32.

Olmstead. Clifton. *Religion in America: Past and Present.* Englewood Cliffs, N.J., 1961.

Orr, J. Edwin. *The Eager Feet: Evangelical Awakenings, 1790–1830.* Chicago, 1975.

Parker, Edwin Pond. *History of the Second Church of Christ in Hartford.* Hartford, Conn., 1892.

Patton, William W. *The Last Century of Congregationalism; or the Influence on Church and State of the Faith and Polity of the Pilgrim Fathers.* Washington, D.C., 1878.

Payne, Ernest A. *Prayer Call of 1784.* London, 1941.

Pearson, Samuel C. "From Church to Denomination: American Congregationalism in the Nineteenth Century." *Church History* 38 (1969): 67–85.

Posey, Walter B. *Frontier Mission: A History of Religion West of the Southern Appalachians to 1861.* Lexington, Ky., 1966.

Potash, Paul Jeffrey. "Welfare of the Regions Beyond." *Vermont History* 46 (1978): 109–28.

Purcell, Richard. *Connecticut in Transition, 1775–1818.* Washington, D.C., 1918.

Rohrbough, Malcolm. *The Trans–Appalachian Frontier: People, Societies, and Institutions, 1775–1850.* New York, 1978.

Roth, Randolph A. *The Democratic Dilemma: Religion, Reform, and Social Order in the Connecticut River Valley of Vermont, 1791–1850.* Cambridge, Mass., 1987.

Ryan, Mary. *Cradle of the Middle Class: The Family in Oneida County, New York, 1790–1865.* New York, 1981.

Sandeen, Ernest. *The Roots of Fundamentalism: British and American Millenarianism, 1800–1930.* Chicago, 1970.

Schmidt, Leigh Eric. *Holy Fairs: Scottish Communions and American Revivals in the Early Modern Period.* Princeton, 1989.

Scott, Donald M. *From Office to Profession: The New England Ministry, 1750–1850.* Philadelphia, 1978.

Shiels, Richard. "The Connecticut Clergy in the Second Great Awakening." Ph.D. diss., Boston University, 1976.

———. "The Second Great Awakening in Connecticut: Critique of the Traditional Interpretation." *Church History* 49 (1980): 401–32.

———. "The Scope of the Second Great Awakening: Andover, Massachusetts, as a Case Study." *Journal of the Early Republic* 5 (1985): 223–46.

———. "The Methodist Circuit Rider in the Second Great Awakening in New England." Paper presented at Asbury College, June 10, 1988.

Smith, Elwyn A. "The Forming of a Modern American Denomination." *Church History* 21 (1962): 74–99.

———. Religious Liberty in the United States: The Development of Church–State Thought Since the Revolutionary Era. Philadelphia, 1972.

Smith, Joseph. Old Redstone; or Historical Sketches of Western Presbyterianism, its Early Ministers and its First Records. Philadelphia, 1854.

Smith, Timothy L. Revivalism and Social Reform: American Protestantism on the Eve of the Civil War. Baltimore, 1980.

Sprague, William B. Annals of the American Pulpit; or Commemorative Notices of Distinguished American Clergymen of Various Denominations. 6 vols. New York, 1859.

Stilwell, Lewis D. Migration From Vermont (1776–1860). Montpelier, Vt., 1937.

Stout, Harry S. The New England Soul: Preaching and Religious Culture in Colonial New England. New York, 1986.

Strout, Cushing. The New Heavens and the New Earth: Political Religion in America. New York, 1974.

Sweet, William Warren. Religion on the American Frontier. vol. 2, The Presbyterians. Chicago, 1936. Vol. 3, The Congregationalists. Chicago, 1939.

———. Revivalism In America. New York, 1944.

Synan, Vinson. The Holiness–Pentecostal Movement in the United States. Grand Rapids, Mich., 1971.

Thorning, J. F. Religious Liberty In Transition. New York, 1931.

Tucker, Ruth A. From Jerusalem to Irian Jaya: A Biographical History of Christian Missions. Grand Rapids, Mich., 1983.

Tuveson, Ernest. Redeemer Nation: The Idea of America's Millennial Role. Chicago, 1968.

Van den Berg, Johannes. Constrained By Jesus' Love: An Inquiry Into the Motives of the Missionary Awakening in Great Britain in the Period Between 1698 and 1815. Kampen, Netherlands, 1956.

Vaughan, Alden T., and Francis Bremner, eds. Puritan New England: Essays on Religion, Society, and Culture. New York, 1977.

Walker, George Leon. History of First Church in Hartford, 1633–1883. Hartford, Conn., 1884.

Walker, Williston. A History of the Congregational Churches in the United States. New York, 1894.

Walsh, James. "The Pure Church in Eighteenth Century Connecticut." Ph.D. diss., Columbia University, 1967.

Watts, Michael R. The Dissenters: From the Reformation to the French Revolution. Oxford, 1978.

Weisberger, Bernard A. They Gathered at the River: The Story of the Great Revivalists and Their Impact Upon Religion in America. Chicago, 1966.

Westerkamp, Marilyn J. Triumph of the Laity: Scots-Irish Piety and the Great Awakening, 1625–1760. New York, 1988.

Wiebe, Robert. The Opening of American Society: From the Adoption of the Constitution to the Eve of Disunion. New York, 1984.

Wood, Gordon S. *The Creation of the American Republic, 1776–1787.* Chapel Hill, N.C., 1969.

————. "The Democratization of Mind in the American Revolution." In *Leadership in the American Revolution.* Washington, D.C., 1974.

Youngs, J. William T., Jr. *God's Messengers: Religious Leadership in Colonial New England, 1700–1750.* Baltimore, 1976.

INDEX

Africa, 53, 55

Allegheny mountains, 74

American Revolution, 9–10, 17, 89, 91; and religious reorientation, 3–4, 154n.10; and egalitarian impulse, 6–7, 35, 64, 68, 117; as influence upon missions, 21–24; conservatism of, 22

Amherst College, 119

Andover Seminary, 170n.33

Andrews, Josiah B., 89

Anglican church, 4, 9, 17

Antiauthoritarianism, 3, 32, 35, 115. *See also* Anticlericalism; Egalitarian Impulse

Anticlericalism: and opposition to Appropriation Act, 33–35; and criticism of Congregational missions, 37, 40, 58, 62; in new settlements, 42, 49–51, 67, 125, 170n.25; and populist religious sects, 103; and attacks upon Congregational clergy, 121; among Congregational laity, 123

Appropriation Act, 33, 41

Arminianism: in new settlements, 11, 135, 138, 140; Congregational hostility toward, 43; and western revivals, 73

Asbury, Francis, 36, 51, 106, 178n.14

Avery, John, 158n.20

Awakening, definition of, 57, 164n.16

Backus, Azel, 38

Backus, Charles, 20, 53, 165n.32, 171n.47

Bacon, David, 62, 109–10, 121, 125

Badger, Joseph, 84, 90–92, 96, 118, 172n.50; and political controversy, 67; elitism of, 90; attitude toward falling, 93–94; impression of sacramental occasion, 97; and Western Reserve camp meetings, 98–100; as innovator, 101; notoriety of, 110–11; education of, 119, 175n.8; salary

of, 122; financial woes of, 124–26; views on missionary vocation, 137–38; opinion of Presbyterian revivalists, 173n.68

Banner, Lois, 16

Baptist Missionary Society, 55, 60

Baptists, 25, 47, 115, 126, 130; growth of, 4, 14, 36; competitive advantage of, 5–6, 118, 148; impact of Great Awakening upon, 17; and missionary collection, 32–33; Congregationalist views of, 48, 129; Congregationalist competition with, 49, 138, 140–41, 144–45; attitude toward Congregational clergy, 81; populism of, 116, 128, 149; salary of preachers, 121

Beasley, James, 33

Beaver, R. Pierce, 15

Beecher, Lyman, 8, 118, 155n.12, 176n.22

Beer, Jonathan, 121

Bellamy, Joseph, 20, 38, 42, 163n.14, 170–71n.36

Benedict, Abner, 14, 124, 138

Benevolence, 19

Benevolent Associations, 84

Bennedict, Joel, 135, 138, 140–41, 146, 178n.7

Berkshire Missionary Society, 143

Berkshire Mountains, 21, 25

Bilhartz, Terry, 48, 116–17

Bissell, Hezekiah, 164n.31

Bloch, Ruth, 167n.57

"Bodily Exercises": in Great Revival, 72; in Great Awakening, 74–75; Jonathan Edwards on, 76–77; associated with enthusiasm, 78–79; at Presbyterian sacramental seasons, 92–96; in Western Reserve, 100–101

Bostwick, Shadrack, 79

Bowdoin College, 119

Brace, Jonathan, 63
Brainerd, David, 61, 109, 110–11, 174n.18
Bray, Thomas Wells, 36
Bunyan, John, 105
Burder, George, 68
"Burned-over" District, 4
Burton, Asa, 167n.50
Bushnell, Jedediah, 84, 120; biographical
  sketch of, 85–91; as innovator, 101; ordi-
  nation of, 108; resignation from CMS, 124;
  theological orientation of, 171n.36; as
  bridge figure, 171n.46; and book distribu-
  tion, 171n.47

Calvin, John, 81
Calvinism: revolt against, 6–7, 36, 48, 117,
  137, 154n.10; antidemocratic tendencies
  of, 8, 73; and definition of Congregational orthodoxy, 12–13; and missionary
  motivation, 15; and millennialism, 18;
  and civil government, 65; and attitude
  toward education, 81–82; and CMS missionaries, 89–90, 134, 138, 146; and
  Western camp meetings, 97–98; openness
  of settlers to, 90, 141, 144; and revival-
  ism, 162n.5
Camp meetings: during Great Revival, 72;
  historical assessments of, 73, 98, 168n.3;
  and CMS missionaries, 74, 92–96, 99, 132;
  response to in Western Reserve, 100
Candidates, ministerial, 11, 27–28, 84,
  158n.20; insufficiency of, 37, 39; at Cross
  Creek, 93
Cane Ridge, 72, 92
Carey, William, 55
Cartwright, Peter, 5, 8, 106, 112–13, 127–28
Catskill Turnpike, 31
Champion, Judah, 96
Chapin, Calvin, 67, 91, 110, 136, 170n.33
Chapman, Ezekial, 137, 174n.18
Chauncy, Charles, 20
Christian Movement, 7, 127, 179n.14
Churches: as covenanted communities, 16,
  147; gathering of, 44, 46–47, 146. *See
  also* Covenant Theology; Pure Church
  Ideal
Clergy. *See* Ministers
Coe, Alvan, 121, 126
Committee on missions: members of, 36;
  duties of, 37; and problems confronting
  leaders, 37–42; and millennialism, 53;
  succeeded by CMS, 60
Compartmentalization, 69
Competition, religious, 3–4, 145, 152; pros-
  elytism in new settlements, 10, 49, 115–
  16, 118, 134–35; as missionary motivation, 17; as missionary responsibility,
  137–38; and revivals, 139–41
Conforti, Joseph, 21, 109, 120, 165n.32,
  174n.18

Congregationalism: decline of, 4; explanations for declension of, 5–8, 143–51,
  154n.9; traditionalism of, 9–10; definition
  of, 13; as frontier phenomenon, 14. *See
  also* Calvinism; Churches; Competition,
  religious; Ministerial associations; Ministers; Missions
Connecticut: claim to Wyoming Valley, 10;
  disestablishment of, 12; emigration from,
  31–32; Council of Assistants, 33, 41;
  General Assembly, 32–33, 37, 40–41; political developments in, 32–34, 67,
  167n.56; populism in, 36; revivals in, 71–
  72, 84, 96. *See also* Appropriation Act;
  Connecticut Academy of Arts and Sciences; Connecticut Missionary Society
  (CMS); Migration to new settlements
Connecticut Academy of Arts and Sciences,
  120
Connecticut Evangelical Magazine: found-
  ing of, 65, 79–80; nonpolitical stance of,
  68; and revival narratives, 71, 79–83,
  169n.21, 172n.67; criticism of, 113; circulation of, 138, 166n.46
Connecticut Gazette, 32
Connecticut Missionary Society (CMS), 11–
  12, 21, 143; organization of, 62, 115; and
  politics, 63–69; as link between New England and West, 73–74; impact of revivals
  upon, 83–84, 170n.33; wages paid by,
  122–23
Connecticut River Valley, 24
Connecticut Western Reserve, 50, 79, 131,
  133; religious competition in, 4, 81, 134–
  35, 136; and Appropriation Act, 33; political controversy in, 67, 90, 99; and
  Congregational missions, 74, 91, 110–11,
  121, 124–25, 170n.33, 178n.10; and revivals, 98–101. *See also* Ohio
Continental Army, 91
Cott, Nancy F., 168n.5
Covenant Theology: and Congregationalist
  identity, 9–10, 148, 151; and Congregationalist ecclesiology, 16, 147, 152; and
  Revolutionary movement, 22; as motive
  for mission, 22, 101, 143; and organization of churches, 46–47; and settlement
  of frontier, 105. *See also* Pure Church
  Ideal
Cowles, Clara, 83
Cowles, Giles, 14, 82, 123–24, 131, 133;
  and antiparty sentiments, 65; and revival
  narratives, 79–80; as preacher, 81; views
  on missionary vocation, 107–8
Cowles, Sally White, 82–84, 126
Cross Creek, 92, 94

Dana, James, 36, 43, 60, 61
Darrow, Zadock, 32, 33
Dartmouth College, 119, 121

Davenport, John, Jr., 63
Davies, Samuel, 132
Day, Jeremiah, 37, 96, 119, 160n.28,
    175n.8; views on sectarian gains, 48–49;
    mission in Vermont, 158n.20
Deists, 80, 81, 140
Delaware River, 48
Democratization: of post-revolutionary soci-
    ety, 4, 6, 134; and Congregationalist
    clergy, 7–8, 64, 68, 143; and sectarian
    success, 149. *See also* Antiauthoritaria-
    nism; Anticlericalism; Egalitarian Impulse
Disinterested benevolence, 20, 109, 165n.32
Dismission, 35, 39–40, 123, 124, 176n21
Duane, William, 50
Dutch Reformed Church, 48, 140
Dwight, Timothy, 8, 50, 60–61, 68, 118,
    166n.48

Earl of Shaftesbury, 19
Edwardsean Clergy, 13, 109; spreading in-
    fluence of, 21; theological views of, 20–
    21, 81–82, 151–52, 163n.15; and Com-
    mittee on Missions, 42–43; and CMS, 51,
    61–62; and millennialism, 55; attitude
    toward Methodists, 78; and Presbyterian
    sacramental occasions, 97; and preaching,
    130; and Congregationalist declension,
    145–52. See also Ministers; Missionaries;
    New Divinity
Edwards, Jonathan, 20, 74, 81, 132; es-
    chatological thinking of, 18–19; and *Dis-
    sertation on the Nature of True Virtue,*
    19; and *Some Thoughts Concerning the
    Present Revival of Religion in New En-
    gland,* 18, 76–77; and United Concert for
    Prayer, 54–55; and *History of the Work
    of Redemption,* 58; and religious enthusi-
    asm, 75–77; and David Brainerd, 109
Edwards, Jonathan Jr.: and Committee on
    Missions, 32, 36, 38–41, 49; theological
    orientation of, 43; anticlerical attacks
    upon, 50; and birth of CMS, 62, 165n.32
Egalitarian Impulse: and religious voluntar-
    ism, 3; and populist religion, 6–7, 36,
    103, 117, 127
Election of 1800, 65
Eliot, John, 20, 61, 106
Ells, Samuel, 43–45, 48, 160n.28
Emerson, William, 22
Emmons, Nathaniel, 20, 132
England, 53–54, 57–58
Enthusiasm: definition of, 75; association
    with Methodism, 74, 77–79; Edwardsean
    views on, 76–77; and Second Awakening,
    80–81; and western camp meetings, 91–
    92, 94–97, 100
Episcopal Church, 25, 33, 55, 117, 126. *See
    also* Ogden, John C.
Ericson, Jack, 63

Eschatology, 18, 58, 62, 151, 163n.15
Evangelist, office of, 59–60, 86, 130, 143,
    151
Extemporaneous preaching, 5, 116, 129–33

Fast days, 54, 130
Federalists: as factor in Congregationalist
    decline, 6, 144; and relationship to Con-
    gregational clergy, 62–64; split with Con-
    gregational clergy, 167n.56, 167n.57
Female benevolent societes, 66, 166n.47
Field, John, 133
Finke, Roger, 116, 118–19, 121–22, 128,
    130, 141, 144, 148–51, 154n.9, 179n.17
Finley, James B., 5, 111–13
First Great Awakening, 12, 59, 78, 81; as
    spur to mission, 17–18, 21; and power
    of laity, 35; transatlantic dimension of,
    54; and controversy over enthusiasm,
    74–77, 79; and evangelical preaching,
    130
Flavel, John, 132
Flint, Abel: and CMS, 62–63, 66, 69, 145;
    and NHMS, 62, 165n.31; and CEM, 80–81
Freethinkers, 115, 148
Freewill Baptists, 6–7, 25, 115, 139–40
Frontier: as challenge to Congregationalism,
    5, 8, 10–12; and egalitarian impulse, 42,
    69, 90–91, 103; and religious adherence,
    49; and Congregational missionaries, 103–
    14, 135, 143, 147. *See also* Migration to
    new settlements; Missionaries; Wilderness

Gasper River, 72, 92
Genesee Country, 43, 48, 72
Georgia, 72, 92, 106
Gordon, William, 68
Grant, John Webster, 171n.46
Great Genesee Road, 32
Great Revival, 85, 92, 98, 168n.3
Green Mountains, 25, 90
Greensburgh Academy, 121
Griffin, Edward Dorr, 72
Griswold, Roger, 167n.56
Gross, Robert, 22

Half-way covenant, 146
Hamilton College, 119, 121
Hampshire Missionary Society, 143
Hanna, Robert, 131
Harrower, David, 140–41
Hart, Levi, 60, 62, 83, 165n.32
Harvard College, 76, 116, 119, 120
Hatch, Nathan O., 6, 7, 42, 48, 73, 83, 103,
    117, 127–29, 134, 144, 149
Hawley, Gideon, 158n.20
Higgins, David, 160n.28; as Vermont mis-
    sionary, 45–46, 49, 65, 113–14; com-
    plaints about CMS policy, 122, 125
Hinsdale, Theodore, 37

Hooker, Asahel, 49–50, 96, 160n.28, 172n.67
Hopkins, Samuel, 19–20, 21, 50, 163n.14
Hudson River, 5, 10, 109, 131
Hughes, James, 97, 173n.68
Huntington, Dan, 96
Huntington, David 45, 160n.28

Individualism, 127, 134, 149
Infidels, 81
Itinerancy, 17, 23, 60, 144

Jacobinism, 64, 68
Jameson, J. Franklin, 154n.10
Jefferson College, 121
Jeffersonians, 40, 65, 68; and opposition to Congregational establishment, 13, 50–51; and attacks upon CMS, 62–63, 67, 172n.50; in Western Reserve, 90, 99, 171–72n.50; and populist religion, 103, 149
Jefferson, Thomas, 65
Johnson, Edward, 104
Johnson, Paul E., 168n.5
Jones, Abiel, 167n.50
Judd, Benjamin, 66
Judd, William, 34
Judson, Ephraim, 86, 171n.36

Keller, Charles Roy, 155n.12
Kelley, Dean, 150, 178n.2
Kentucky, 72, 80
Kinne, Aaron, 43–45, 48, 160n.28

Laity: power of, 34–35; insurgency of 35–36, 38, 123, 176n.22
Land proprietors, 11, 90
Land speculators, 31
Leonard, Joshua, 113–14
Liberal education: significance of, 118–20
Life of Brainerd, 109–10
Litchfield County (Connecticut): and Congregational missions, 42–43, 84, 160n.28
Little, Robert, 56
Localism, 35
London Missionary Society, 55–56, 60–62, 72, 109
Love, John, 61, 109
Lutherans, 140
Lyman, William, 39, 43, 125
Lyon, James, 63

Macurdy, Elisha, 93, 172n.58
Maine, 106
Marsden, George, 73
Marty, Martin, 3, 5, 115
Massachusetts, 15–17, 75, 103; and New Divinity movement, 20–22; migration from, 25, 31–32
Massachusetts Missonary Society, 143

Mather, Cotton, 20
Mathews, Donald M., 6, 17, 154n.9, 168n.5
Mayhew, Jonathan, 20
McGready, James, 172n.58
McLoughlin, William, 8, 58, 73
Mead, Sidney, 34
Merrill, Thomas, 85, 89
Merwin, Noah, 38
Methodists, 9, 12, 14, 28, 164n.23; growth of, 4, 48, 144–45; attitude toward Congregational clergy, 5, 81, 111–13, 120; organizational structure of, 6, 44, 154n.9; egalitarianism of, 7–8, 51, 178n.14; influence of Great Awakening upon, 17; in new settlements, 25, 44, 47–49, 115, 131, 135, 136,140; in Connecticut, 36, 38, 74, 78–79, 82–83, 96, 169n.18; associated with enthusiasm, 77–78, 81, 97; and Romanticism, 106, 173n.7; contrasted with Congregationalists, 116–18, 147–48, 175n.20; wages of, 121–22; as targets of Congregational evangelism, 138–41; antitraditionalism of, 149
Middlebury College, 119, 121
Migration to new settlements: as challenge to Congregationalism, 9–11, 47, 103, 123; as spur to missions, 17, 22–29, 115; economic incentive for, 31–32
Millennialism: influence of Jonathan Edwards upon, 18, 54; and Edwardsean clergy, 20, 150, 163n.15; and Congregational missions, 21, 57–58, 62, 115, 143, 167n.57; and revivals, 53, 83, 163n.15; and prayer concert, 55
Miller, Jonathan, 79, 80
Miller, Perry, 18
Miller, Samuel J., 60, 160n.28
Mills, Joseph, 124
Mills, Samuel J., 71
Ministerial associations, 17, 23–24, 119
Ministers: adaptation to republican culture, 10, 114, 117–18; in new settlements, 11, 126, 128, 136, 144; as evangelists, 15; ordination of, 17; bond with laity, 26–27; courtly tendencies of, 35; submission to laity, 38–39; as political advisors, 68–69; standard portrayal of, 116; salary of, 122–24
Ministry: as dignified office, 42, 114; declining status of, 119, 123
Missionaries: objectives of, 28–29; chronic shortage of, 40, 145, 170n.33; pastoral duties of, 43–47; as specialized office, 59–60, 84, 143; political views of, 65–67; and opposition to enthusiasm, 77; as innovators, 100–101; adjustment to republican culture, 103–4, 113–14; self-understanding of, 107–19; social status of, 118–20; education of, 119–20, 127; wages of, 122–23, 124–26; and preaching, 128–34; and

religious confrontation, 134–41; and pure church ideal, 145–48

Missionary narratives, 111, 113

Missionary wives, 125–26

Missions, British, 15, 55–56

Missions: motivation for, 17–22, 29, 98; and state support for, 32, 34, 41; opposition to, 32–33; and public opinion, 41; transatlantic dimension of, 54–58

Mississippi River, 10

Mohawk River, 43

Mohawk Turnpike, 31

Mohawk Valley, 32, 44, 47, 108

Morse, Jedediah, 68, 118

Napoleon, 68

Nash, Roderick, 104–5, 173n.7

Native Americans: as objects of conversion, 15–17, 20, 60–62; at New Stockbridge, 44–45; and David Brainerd, 109; and the Bacon mission, 125

Newberry, Roger, 63, 165n.31

New Divinity, 13; theological views of, 20–21; appeal of, 21–22; and Committee on Missions, 42–43; and CMS, 62, 120, 165n.32, 171n.36, 171n.47

New England, 4, 7, 14; religious establishment in, 7, 9; and Second Great Awakening, 8, 57–59, 72–73; emigration from, 10; erosion of communal values in, 21–22, 98; changing political climate of, 35, 41–42

New Hampshire, 24–25, 72

New Hampshire Grants, 24

New Jersey, 109

New London Association, 60

New settlements, 10; religious characteristics of, 11, 24–25, 46–47, 114, 129; ministry needs of, 26–28, 48; rapid growth of, 31, 44; adaptation of ministers in, 113–14, 117–18

New Stockbridge, 44–45

New York, 12, 14, 34, 98, 113; settlement of, 10, 24, 31–32; as mission field, 43–49, 57, 134–35; and Second Great Awakening, 74, 83, 86–87, 89, 140

Niebuhr, H. Richard, 6, 84

Niles, Nathaniel, 165n.32

Noble, Seth, 126

North Hartford Association, 55, 59

North Hartford Missionary Society, 61–63

Northwest Territory, 12, 74

Nott, Samuel, 38

O'Brien, Susan, 54

Occam, John, 44

Ogden, John C., 49–51

Ohio, 14, 65, 85, 94, 126, 131. *See also* Connecticut Western Reserve

Ohio River, 12

O'Kelly schism, 179n.14

"Old Calvinists," 13, 21

Old Lights, 11, 13, 20, 43, 75

Olmstead, Clifton, 5

Orr, J. Edwin, 163n.16

Parmele, Simeon, 137

Party Politics: and missionary movement, 40–41, 50; in new settlements, 90–91, 99, 103; in Connecticut, 167n.56

Pastor's Power, A, 23

Patton, William W., 6

Pennsylvania, 12, 109, 132, 171n.50; and Susquehanna Company land claims, 10; as mission field, 14, 34, 45, 48, 74, 85, 129–30; migration to, 31; and Great Revival, 72–73, 90–96

Perkins, Nathan, 27, 107, 113, 126; and tour of Vermont, 25, 28–29, 77, 158n.20; opinion of Vermont clergy, 114, 128; biographical sketch of, 120; and North Hartford Missionary Society, 165n.31

Phelps, Charles, 34

Philadelphia Aurora, 50

Pilgrim's Progress, 105

Plan of Union, 13

Porter, Ebenezer, 96, 172n.67

Prayer Call of 1784, 55

Preaching: contrasting styles of, 5, 44, 127–29; extemporaneous delivery of missionaries, 129–34

"Presbygationalists," 13

Presbyterians, 4, 6, 17, 60, 117, 166n.46; in the new settlements, 11, 25, 48; and Plan of Union, 13, 170n.33; and British missions, 55; and sacramental occasions, 72, 91–95, 97–99; and Greensburgh Academy, 121; political views of, 171n.50

Princeton College, 97, 120, 173n.68

Prudden, Nehemiah, 165n.31

Public opinion: as influence upon missions, 32, 40–42, 144; and revivals, 80

Pure Church Ideal, 46–47, 97; and Puritans, 16; and New Divinity, 21, 38, 42, 165n.32; and Congregational declension, 145–48, 150; in Western Reserve, 178n.10

Puritans, 6, 13, 19, 81, 149; and covenant theology, 9; and evangelism, 15–17, 20; social values of, 21, 47; and wilderness myth, 104–7

Quakers, 25

Rationalists, 75, 78, 89, 147

Reformation, 16

Respectability: concept of, 63, 165n.38

Revival narratives, 79–83, 155n.12, 169n.21, 172n.67

Revivals, 4, 68; in Second Great Awakening, 7–8, 53, 57; in First Great Awakening,

Revivals (*Cont.*)
 17–18, 54, 74–77; and donations to CMS, 66; in Connecticut, 71–72, 82–83, 162n.5, 163n.15; in the Trans-Appalachian West, 72–74; and enthusiasm controversy, 75–77; impact upon CMS, 83–84; and CMS missionaries, 85–87, 88–101, 139–41, 145; and Presbyterian "Holy Fairs," 92–98, 168n.3
Rhode Island, 25, 75
Robbins, Ammi, 36, 96, 108, 160n.28, 172n.67; and tour of Mohawk Valley, 44; and efforts to organize pure church, 46–47; and prayer concert, 55–56; and election of 1800, 65; and Norfolk revival, 79, 82; and Kentucky revivals, 81; and wilderness myth, 107; preaching style, 131
Robbins, Chandler, 56
Robbins, James, 172n.67
Robbins, Sally, 96, 108, 132
Robbins, Samuel P., 110, 131
Robbins, Thomas, 55, 56, 71, 84, 109; as Vermont missionary, 28; political views of, 64–65, 67, 90–91; and western camp meetings, 93–101; education of, 121; ordination of, 130, 151–52; preaching style, 131–32; and baptism controversy, 147
Robinson, William, 37
Romanticism, 106, 173n.7
Roth, Randolph, 168n.5
Ryan, Mary, 168n5

Sacramental "Holy Fairs," 92–93, 98–99
Sanctification: Wesleyon doctrine of, 77–78, 80
Saybrook Platform, 6, 8, 13, 33
Schmidt, Leigh Eric, 92–93, 97–98, 168n.3
Scotland: evangelical movement in, 53–55
Scott, Donald M. 199, 123, 176n.21, 176n.22
Scott, George, 173n.68
Scourge of Aristocracy, 63
Second Great Awakening, 57; historiography of, 8, 48, 58, 73, 155n.12, 164n.16; in Connecticut, 71–72, 78–83, 162n.5, 163n.15; in Trans-Appalachian West, 72–74
Secularism, 8
Sergeant, John, 44–45
Seward, John, 118, 140
Shays's Rebellion, 103
Shepherd, John, 160n28
Shiels, Richard D., 162n.5, 164n.16, 168n.5, 169n.18, 175n.20
Skeptics, 81
Smith, Cotton Mather, 49, 160.n28
Smith, Elias, 3, 127
Society in Scotland for Propagating Christian Knowledge, 109

South Hartford Association, 60
South Seas, 53, 56
Stark, Rodney, 118–19, 121–22, 128, 130, 141, 144, 148–51, 154n.9, 179n.17
Starr, Peter, 96, 160n.28, 172n.67
Stiles, Ezra, 21, 32, 36, 43, 50
Stone, Randolph, 131, 134–36, 140
Stout, Harry S., 9, 22, 68, 149, 155n.14
Strong, Cyprian, 37, 108, 165n.32
Strong, Joseph, 60
Strong, Nathan, 40, 59, 69, 83, 126, 171n.47; and birth of CMS, 61–62, 165n.32; opposition to political controversy, 63–64, 66; and selection of missionaries, 66, 145, 167n.50; and CEM, 68, 81; remarks on Bushnell, 88–89; on preaching, 130, 132; on keeping covenant, 148; at ordination of Robbins, 151–52; and North Hartford Missionary Society, 165n.31
Susquehanna Company, 10
Susquehanna River, 31, 45, 48
Sweet, William Warren, 5, 73, 143
Swift, Heman, 63
Swift, Zephaniah, 96

Tappan, Benjamin, 172n.50
Tennent, Gilbert, 74
Tennessee, 72
Theological Education, 127
Theological Magazine, The, 59
Thorning, J. F., 6, 63
Tower, G. H., 132–33
Transatlantic evangelical movement, 54–57
Treadwell, Jonathan, 61–63, 165n.31, 167n.56
Trumbull, Benjamin, 26, 66, 86, 114, 126; and Committee on Missions, 36, 39–41; theological orientation of, 43; and John C. Ogden, 50–51; and prayer concert, 56; and birth of CMS, 60–61, 63; and *Discourses on the Divine Inspiration of Scripture,* 166n.48, 171n.47

United Concert for Prayer, 89; origins of, 54; renewal of in 1784, 55; established in America, 55–56, 163n.8; and Second Great Awakening, 57–58, 72, 162n.5
Universalists, 48, 115, 136; egalitarianism of, 7; opposition to Congregationalist missions, 25, 49, 81, 138; as object of Congregationalist evangelism, 140

Vermont, 4, 12, 31, 72, 120; settlement of, 10, 24–25, 43; as mission field, 26–29, 34, 45–46, 84, 158n.20; and populist religion, 49, 129, 134; and opposition to Congregational mission, 50–51, 63, 170n.25; and revivals, 83, 85, 134; and wilderness

myth, 107, 113–14; and Congregational pastors, 114, 126, 128
Virginia, 72, 78
Voluntarism, 3, 12, 144, 167n.56

Wadsworth, Jeremiah, 165n.31
Wales, 54
War of 1812, 84, 170n.33
Washburn, Joseph, 61
Watts, Isaac: Psalm Book, 166n.48
Welch, Moses, 36, 38, 129
Wentworth, Bennington, 24
Wesley, John, 77–78, 112
Western Missionary Magazine, 72
West Fairfield Association, 60
West, Stephen, 56–57, 163n.14
Wheelock, Eleazer, 74
Whiskey Insurrection, 103
Whitefield, George, 59, 74, 76, 133
Why Conservative Churches Are Growing, 150
Wick, William, 170n.33
Wiebe, Robert, 3, 6, 115
Wilderness: Puritan concept of, 104–5; Methodist and Congregationalist views contrasted, 106–7; impact of wilderness myth upon missions, 108–14

Williams College, 60, 85, 119, 121, 170n.33
Williams, Nathan, 32, 36, 39
Williams, Roger, 105
Williston, Noah, 160n.28
Williston, Seth, 14, 118; and awakening in New York, 53, 59, 77; and transatlantic network, 57; and millennial impulse, 58–59; and office of evangelist, 59–60; and North Hartford Missionary Society, 61; political views of, 64; opinion of Methodists, 78; remarks on Bushnell, 85–89; and wilderness myth, 110–11; wages of, 124; and preaching, 130, 132, 133–34
Wines, E. C., 87–89
Winthrop, John, 16
Wood, Gordon S., 6
Wooster, Benjamin, 160n.28
Wyoming Valley, 10

Yale College, 74, 90, 106, 116, 131, 136; and Ezra Stiles, 21, 36, 50; and Timothy Dwight, 50, 60; as object of anticlerical attack, 50–51; and education of ministers, 116, 119–21
Yohogeny camp meeting, 95
Youngs, J. William, Jr., 26, 35